THE
WORLD COOKBOOK
FOR STUDENTS

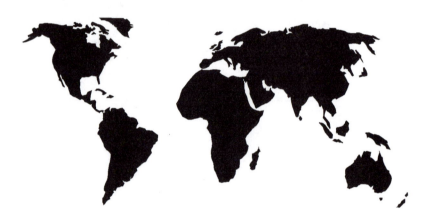

THE
WORLD COOKBOOK
FOR STUDENTS

VOLUME 3
Iraq to Myanmar

JEANNE JACOB

MICHAEL ASHKENAZI

GREENWOOD PRESS
Westport, Connecticut • London

Library of Congress Cataloging-in-Publication Data

Jacob, Jeanne.
    The world cookbook for students / Jeanne Jacob and Michael Ashkenazi.
        p. cm.
    Includes bibliographical references and index.
    ISBN 0–313–33454–4 (set : alk. paper)—ISBN 0–313–33455–2 (vol. 1 : alk. paper)—
ISBN 0–313–33456–0 (vol. 2 : alk. paper)—ISBN 0–313–33457–9 (vol. 3 : alk. paper)—
ISBN 0–313–33458–7 (vol. 4 : alk. paper)—ISBN 0–313–33459–5 (vol. 5 : alk. paper)
    1. Cookery, International.   2. Food habits.   I. Ashkenazi, Michael.   II. Title.
    TX725.A1J23 2007
    641.59—dc22   2006026184

British Library Cataloguing in Publication Data is available.

Library of Congress Catalog Card Number: 2006026184
ISBN-10: 0–313–33454–4 (set)   ISBN-13: 978–0–313–33454–2 (set)
            0–313–33455–2 (vol. 1)   978–0–313–33455–9 (vol. 1)
            0–313–33456–0 (vol. 2)   978–0–313–33456–6 (vol. 2)
            0–313–33457–9 (vol. 3)   978–0–313–33457–3 (vol. 3)
            0–313–33458–7 (vol. 4)   978–0–313–33458–0 (vol. 4)
            0–313–33459–5 (vol. 5)   978–0–313–33459–7 (vol. 5)

First published in 2007

Greenwood Press, 88 Post Road West, Westport, CT 06881
An imprint of Greenwood Publishing Group, Inc.
www.greenwood.com

Printed in the United States of America

The paper used in this book complies with the
Permanent Paper Standard issued by the National
Information Standards Organization (Z39.48–1984).

10 9 8 7 6 5 4 3 2 1

The publisher has done its best to make sure the instructions and/or recipes in this book are correct.
However, users should apply judgment and experience when preparing recipes, especially parents and
teachers working with young people. The publisher accepts no responsibility for the outcome of any
recipe included in this volume.

Illustrations by Jeanne Jacob and Maayan Ashkenazi.

CONTENTS

VOLUME 3

IRAQ

At times divided among local kingdoms, part or center of an empire, Iraq has also been occupied by various foreign powers. Desert makes up most of its territory, and the two great rivers, the Tigris and the Euphrates, create a well-watered wide stretch of arable land. With mild winters and hot summers, various Mediterranean-type crops are grown.

The population comprises Arabs, Persians, and Kurds, with mixtures of smaller ethnic groups such as Assyrians. Muslims (Arab and Kurdish Sunnis and Arab Shi'ites) constitute a majority of the population.

Iraq has one of the most ancient cuisines, recorded since the days of the Sumerian kingdoms, about 5,000 years ago.

Foodstuffs

- Staples are rice and wheat.
- The preferred meats in Iraq are lamb, beef, goat, mutton, and poultry (pork is not eaten). Fish are caught in the Tigris and the Euphrates (though the catch has declined due to overuse of the waters and damming) and in the canals.
- Vegetables include onions and garlic, beans and peas, various greens, eggplants, tomatoes, peppers, carrots, cucumbers.
- Fruit include melons and watermelons, figs, pomegranates, and many varieties of dates, some of them world famous and major exports. Grapes are grown in the north.
- Milk products include soft cheeses, yogurts, and butter.

Typical Dishes

- Popular main courses include skewered chunks of grilled meat; roasted and stuffed lamb; and *kibbe*, which is minced meat with nuts, raisins, and spices.
- *Labaneh*, a soft cheese made by draining natural yogurt, is eaten with olive oil and is also used in cooking.
- Pastries are very sweet and often include dates.
- The most widely consumed drinks in Iraq are black, bitter coffee (essential for hospitality) and sweet, milkless tea.

Styles of Eating

- Three meals a day and plentiful snacks are consumed by all urbanites and many villagers. Most meals are accompanied by flat rounds of bread.
- Families generally prefer to eat the morning and evening meals together. Individual settings are common among townspeople, while villagers tend to share a central dish, eating only with the right hand.
- Breakfast: bread, vegetables, or a salad, olive oil, cheese (usually *labaneh*) pastry washed down with tea or sometimes milk or yogurt.
- Lunch: a variety of salads; grilled meat on a skewer, or fish or chicken; tomatoes and other vegetables; fruit.
- Dinner: similar to lunch, but often more elaborate.

Pomegranate Soup (Shorbat Rumman)

This is an unusual, refreshingly sour, soup for a hot evening.

4 cups water
½ pound lamb (turkey, beef, or chicken) on the bone
¼ cup yellow split peas
½ cup onion, chopped
2 beets, peeled and diced (preferably with tops, chopped fine)
¼ cup rice
½ bunch scallions (green and white parts), sliced
1 TBS sugar
2 TBS lime juice
¼ cup parsley
1 TBS pomegranate concentrate (available from Middle Eastern and South Asian stores and sometimes labeled "pomegranate molasses")
¼ cup cilantro, finely minced
1 cup spinach, finely chopped
1 TBS dried mint, crumbled, mixed with ¼ TBS each cinnamon and freshly ground black pepper for garnish

Bring water, meat, split peas, and onion to a boil in a large pot.
Skim froth if necessary.
Reduce heat, cover, and simmer for an hour or until meat is tender.
Add the beets and rice and cook for 30–40 minutes.
Remove meat. Discard bone and fat. Shred meat and return to the pot with scallions, sugar, half of the lime juice, parsley, and pomegranate concentrate.
Simmer for 15 minutes.
Just before serving, bring to a boil and stir in beet tops (if using) and spinach.
Remove from heat.
Stir in cilantro, more lime juice, if needed, seasonings, and garnish.
Serve hot in bowls.

Plain Rice (Timman)

Plain white rice is the center of all major meals and is served with a variety of meat or vegetable dishes.

1½ cups long-grain rice, washed   2 TBS olive oil
    and drained   plenty of water

Place rice in a large pot with water to cover by 3–4 inches.
Bring to a boil and cook for no more than 5 minutes. It should just be slightly
    soft on the outside.
Remove from heat and drain rice thoroughly in a colander.
Return the pot to the heat. Add oil and stir in rice.
Cover with a well-fitting lid.
Cook on lowest heat for 20 minutes, or until fluffy.
The crisp, slightly burned, layer at the bottom is considered a delicacy.

"Judge's Tongue": Eggplant-Wrapped Meat (Lissan el Quadi)

This is served as a main dish in the evening, or as an element in a feast.
Eggplant is a ubiquitous vegetable, appearing in various guises at every meal.

2 large eggplants   salt
about 1 cup vegetable oil (if frying 3–4 medium tomatoes, sliced
    eggplant, less if oven-roasting)   crosswise, ¼-inch thick

Stuffing

2 pounds ground meat   1 tsp salt
1 medium onion, finely chopped   ¼ tsp black pepper

Sauce

2 TBS vegetable oil   1 cup stock
1 large onion, chopped   ½ cup lemon juice
3 cups fresh or canned chopped   1 tsp salt
    tomato   ½ tsp pepper
1 cup tomato puree or paste   1 tsp turmeric powder

Trim the eggplants. Cut lengthwise into ⅛-inch-thick slices.
Sprinkle with salt and leave on a tray for about 15–20 minutes.
Rinse off the accumulated brown juice and pat eggplants dry with paper towels.
Heat about 2 tablespoons oil in a frying pan and brown the eggplants on both
    sides, a few at a time. Add more oil as needed (the eggplants will absorb a lot
    of oil).
Drain eggplant slices on paper towels. (Low-fat alternative: Place eggplant
    slices on baking sheets and brush with oil. Bake in the oven at 350°F for
    approximately 20–30 minutes until brown but not crisp, turning the
    eggplant halfway.)
Now prepare the stuffing. Mix together the meat, onion, salt, and pepper.
Form into small sausage shapes, about ⅔–1-inch thick and 2 inches long.
Place stuffing at one end of an eggplant slice and roll up. Secure with a
    toothpick.

(continued)

Place rolls in a large baking dish; spread tomato slices and any remaining unstuffed eggplant slices on top.

Next prepare the sauce. Heat oil and sauté the chopped onions until soft.

Stir in chopped tomatoes, tomato puree, stock, lemon juice, salt, pepper, and turmeric.

Cover and simmer for 15 minutes.

Pour sauce over the rolls in the baking dish, cover tightly with aluminum foil, and bake for 1 hour at 350°F.

Serve hot with rice.

Rice and Eggplant Casserole (Chalabis Re'id Magloube)

Eggplants grow well in the desert climate and are considered the poor man's meat. This layered casserole, usually without or with very little meat, would be the main dish for many poor families.

1 cup long-grain rice
2 cups water
2 eggplants, trimmed and sliced crosswise about ½-inch thick
salt as needed
½ cup oil
2 onions, sliced thinly

½ pound lamb (turkey, chicken, or beef) cubed or ground (omit for vegetarian version)
½ cup tomato sauce or paste
1 cup water
1 cinnamon stick
2 cardamoms, whole

Clean, wash, and soak rice in water for 30 minutes. Drain and reserve until needed.

Meanwhile, lightly sprinkle salt on eggplant slices. After 20 minutes, rinse off the brown liquid, and pat dry with paper towels.

Heat half the oil in a heavy saucepan with tight-fitting lid. Sauté eggplants until light brown on both sides.

Remove, drain on paper towels and set aside.

In the same pan, sauté onions until soft (add about 1–2 tablespoons oil if needed). Remove and set aside. (There is no need to wash the pan in between sautéing the different ingredients.)

Add the remaining oil and sauté the meat until it has changed color. Remove and set aside.

Simmer together the tomato sauce, water, salt, cinnamon, and cardamoms for 10 minutes.

Add rice and simmer for 10 more minutes (the rice will not be completely cooked).

Remove and set aside.

Now for final assembly: arrange a layer of eggplants at the bottom of the saucepan. Next lay the onions, then the lamb. Finally pour over all the tomato and rice mixture.

Cover and gently simmer on very low heat for 30 minutes. Let rest for 10 minutes before serving.

To serve: with a knife, cut through the casserole, and make sure each portion has all the layers.

Semolina and Syrup Dessert (Ma'mounia)

This dessert was first recorded in an Arabic cookbook in the ninth century, though it may well be much older.

3 cups water
1 cup sugar
1 tsp lemon juice
$\frac{1}{2}$ cup sweet butter

1 cup semolina
$\frac{1}{2}$ cup cream
1 tsp ground cinnamon

Make the syrup: bring to a boil the water, sugar, and lemon juice. Reduce heat and simmer for about 10 minutes more until slightly thickened.
In another saucepan, melt butter and add semolina. Stir until semolina is lightly fried, then add the syrup. Let mixture simmer for about 3 minutes, stirring constantly.
Remove from heat and let cool for about 20 minutes.
Spoon *ma'mounia* into individual serving bowls, top with cream (unwhipped), and sprinkle with cinnamon.

Cardamom Cookies (Hajji Badah)

Iraqis love sweets and these cookies are eaten as snacks at any time of the day.

2 cups flour
1 tsp ground cardamom
$\frac{1}{4}$ tsp salt
$\frac{1}{4}$ tsp baking powder
$1\frac{1}{3}$ cups sugar

4 large eggs
2 cups ground almonds
$\frac{1}{2}$ TBS rosewater
6 dozen whole skinned
hazelnuts, pistachios, or almonds

Preheat oven to 350°F. Grease several large baking sheets.
Sift together flour, cardamom, salt, and baking powder.
Beat the sugar and eggs until light and creamy. Stir in the flour mixture, then the ground almonds.
With hands moistened with rosewater, form the dough into 1-inch balls. (Add more ground almonds or flour if too soft to shape.)
Place balls on the prepared baking sheets and press to flatten slightly. Press a whole almond into the center of each cookie.
Bake until just lightly golden, for about 10–15 minutes.
Transfer to a wire rack and allow to cool.
Store in an airtight container.

IRELAND (EIRE)

An island in the Atlantic, west of Britain, Ireland is about the size of West Virginia. The climate here is cool and very damp with high annual rainfall. The topography is mainly rolling hills, with a few rugged mountains, and plenty of tarns and lakes.

Ireland was conquered by the English in the fifteenth century and was a part of the British empire until it regained independence (except for six northern counties which elected to remain in Britain) in the twentieth century under the name "Eire."

Irish cooking has many commonalities with that of neighboring Britain: based on meat and potatoes and flavored mildly with a few herbs.

Foodstuffs

- Potatoes, cabbage and other greens, and pork are the basics of Irish food. Potatoes were so important to the Irish diet that a blight in the early mid-nineteenth century caused a massive famine.
- Favored meats are pork and beef.
- Milk products, including notably milk, butter, and cheese.
- Fish (cod, mackerel, skate, herring) and a variety of seafood (shrimp and prawns, oysters, mussels), both farmed and wild.

Typical Dishes

- Boiled or simmered cabbage with some flavoring (bacon, lard, fried onions).
- Cooked potatoes and cabbage.
- Fried or boiled eggs eaten with boiled potatoes.
- Sausages and chips are consumed by most people.
- Fish, notably herring and mackerel, often boiled, and eaten with boiled potatoes.
- Beer, milky tea, and a local brew called *poteen* (pronounced *po-cheen*).

Styles of Eating

- Settings are European standard, though they are often much less formal in the countryside.
- Breakfasts vary from extensive fry-ups of sausages, eggs, and fresh bread to simple slices of bread with jam or lard, washed down by milky tea.

- Lunch can be heavier or lighter, depending partly on the season and partly on the individual. They may include a soup or stew with bread.
- The main meal of the day is in the evening.
- Snacks include chips (French fries) and a variety of sweet cakes and cookies.

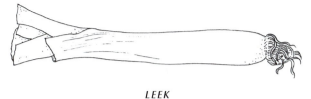

LEEK

Irish Stew

This makes a substantial main dish.

4–5 large potatoes, peeled and cubed
1½ pounds boneless stewing lamb (substitute beef or pork)
2 large onions, cut into eighths
2 fat stalks celery, sliced into 1-inch long pieces

2 turnips, cubed
salt and pepper to taste
1½ cups meat stock
3 sprigs fresh thyme or 1 bay leaf
3 TBS parsley, chopped

Alternately layer the ingredients in a buttered casserole or baking dish with a cover, beginning and ending with potatoes.
Season each layer well with salt and pepper.
Pour in the stock and add thyme or bay leaf. Cover with a piece of buttered foil, then the lid.
Bake in a slow oven, at 300°F for about 2 hours.
Discard thyme or bay leaf, sprinkle with parsley, and serve.

Boiled Smoked Pork and Cabbage

This dish is served very commonly among working-class people for a main meal. The original meat used is a large whole piece of bacon.

2½–3 pounds piece of smoked picnic shoulder, ham shank, or corned beef brisket
1 onion, peeled and studded with 6 whole cloves
1 clove garlic

1 bay leaf
8 peppercorns
water as needed
1 medium-sized cabbage, cut into quarters
butter, salt, and pepper to taste

Place the meat, onion, garlic, bay leaf, and peppercorns in a heavy saucepan.
    Add water just to cover and slowly bring to a boil.
Skim any scum that floats to the surface.

(*continued*)

Cover and simmer for 1½–2 hours or until tender. Remove meat and keep
warm.
Bring the broth in the pan to a boil. Add cabbage and cook for about 15
minutes, or until tender but not mushy.
Remove the cabbage, drain, and season with butter, salt, and pepper.
Slice the meat into serving portions. Serve with cabbage, boiled potatoes,
sharp mustard, or hot (not sweetened) prepared horseradish sauce
(available at specialty shops).

Colcannon

This is a traditional dish for Halloween night. Serve with a meat main dish or
sometimes on its own.

4 cups kale or cabbage, core and
  tough ribs removed, shredded
  (or half kale, half cabbage)
2 cups boiling salted water
2 small leeks, white parts only,
  chopped

½ cup half-and-half or milk
1 pound potatoes, peeled,
  quartered, boiled, and mashed
¼ tsp mace
salt and pepper to taste
4 TBS butter, melted

Boil kale in boiling salted water until tender but not too soft, about
  5–8 minutes.
Drain and set aside.
In a saucepan, simmer leeks in half-and-half for about 10 minutes.
Add potatoes, mace, salt, and pepper, mixing well. Simmer until potatoes are
heated through. Stir in reserved kale and mix thoroughly.
Remove from heat.
To serve: mound the mixture in a warm serving dish or four dishes. Press in
to make a well in the center. Pour in butter and serve at once.

Cod Cobbler

Fish, including cod, are quite often baked or steamed. This would be an
evening dish.

1½ pounds skinless fillets of cod
2 ounces butter
2 ounces flour
1 pint milk (plus extra for
  brushing over scones)

3½ ounces grated cheese
scones (recipe follows; or
  substitute 4 English
  muffins, split in half)

Preheat the oven to 350°F.
Place cod fillets in the bottom of a round or oval oven dish.

Over low heat, melt butter in a heavy saucepan, sprinkle flour over, and mix well until flour is golden.
Slowly add milk, stirring constantly and adding more only when the previous amount has been fully incorporated.
When sauce is fairly liquid, add rest of milk and stir.
Add cheese, stirring as little as possible. Allow cheese to melt.
Pour sauce over fish.
Cover the surface of the fish and sauce with scone dough rounds (or English muffins, crust side down).
Glaze them with a little milk, and sprinkle some more grated cheese over them.
Bake for about 20–25 minutes, or until the scones are golden brown.

Scones

8 ounces flour	2 ounces grated strong cheese
2 tsp baking powder	(mature Cheddar)
pinch salt	1 egg yolk
2 ounces butter	¼ cup milk

Combine flour with baking powder and salt.
Rub butter into flour until mixture resembles coarse meal.
Mix in grated cheese, egg yolk, and enough milk to make a dough.
Knead lightly and briefly.
Roll dough out on floured surface ½-inch thick and cut into small rounds with a cookie cutter.

Potato Pie Dessert

Potatoes are so important in the Irish diet that they are also used for dessert.

¼ pound butter, melted	½ pound boiled potatoes,
1 TBS grated almonds	mashed
1 tsp orange extract	
¾ pound sugar	
6 eggs, separated and beaten separately (yolks until lemon colored, the whites until stiff)	

Line a buttered and floured cake pan with buttered wax paper.
Add almonds, orange extract, sugar, and egg yolks to potatoes. Mix thoroughly. Gently fold in egg whites.
Pour batter into pan. Bake at 375°F for 40–45 minutes until light brown.

ISRAEL

Israel is a small country on the eastern shore of the Mediterranean. The climate is Mediterranean, with mild winters and hot summers, and the country raises a great variety of temperate, desert, and even tropical fruits and vegetables. Agricultural products and technologies are a major export item.

Majority of the population is Jewish, with substantial Muslim and Christian minorities. Much of the Jewish population are immigrants or children of immigrants from all over the world, so the cuisine tends to be eclectic, with strong Middle Eastern, Mediterranean, and European overtones.

Foodstuffs

- Staples are rice, bread, pastas, and potatoes, depending on preference and on personal or parental origin.
- Most temperate and many tropical fruits, vegetables, and herbs are raised for local consumption and export.
- Fruit: common fruit such as citrus, tomatoes, Asian persimmons, avocados, bananas, cherries, apples, plums, pomegranates, grapes, olives; and some exotics such as dragon fruit and lychees.
- Vegetables: tomatoes, cucumbers, peppers, cabbage, lettuce, radish. Both cooked and raw vegetables are a major item of diet.
- Chicken and turkey are the most common meats, due largely to the high prices of other meats. Grilled meat is extremely popular as it is in the rest of the Middle East. Pork is not supposed to be consumed by Jews or Muslims, but in practice nonreligious members of both religions do consume pork.
- Milk products: cheeses, many types copied from European hard-cheese originals, as well as soft white cheeses, yogurts, and sour milk of various types.

Typical Dishes

- Fresh salads and fresh fruit are extremely popular. Probably the favorite meal starter is *hummus* (chickpea paste) flavored with *tahina* (sesame seed sauce) and scooped with a pita (flat or pocket bread).
- Street foods, particularly *falafel* and *shawarma* (Turkish-style grilled meats) in pocket breads are extremely popular snacks.

- All three major religions have special foods for their main holidays. Virtually all Jewish holidays have ritually required foods. Id-al-Fitr for Muslims requires roast meat, as does Easter for Christians. Druze (a secretive offshoot of Shi'a Islam) eat special grain mixes and roasts during Nebi Shueib, their main festival.

Styles of Eating

- Three meals a day and snacks.
- Various styles of eating, due largely to different ethnic origins and current lifestyles. In the cities, European place settings with individuals eating from their own plates using fork, knife, and spoon are almost universal. Nomadic Bedouin Israelis and Ethiopian Israelis help themselves from a shared central dish.
- *Kibbutz* (collective settlement) members serve themselves cafeteria style from a wide variety of salads. Families tend to eat together (except in *kibbutzim*, where people tend to eat with their age-mates). The main meal is often at noon, particularly for those from a European background.

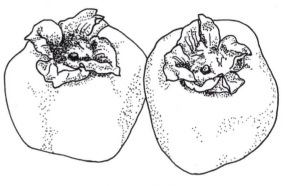

PERSIMMON

- Most meals include a fresh vegetable salad, and olives and pickles are almost always on the table.
- Separation between milk and meat required by Jewish ritual law means that in many Jewish households main meals (whether lunch or dinner) are based on meat, whereas all others are often milk-based, with cheeses and yogurts.
- Breakfast: fresh vegetables, eggs, bread or toast, olives, smoked or canned fish. Coffee or, more rarely, tea. Milk and juices.
- Lunch (for some, the main meal of the day; for others, a lighter meal): a salad and a main dish of meat, chicken, or fish with rice, potatoes, pasta, or bread. Fruit or a cooked dessert. Meals often end with coffee.
- Supper (for some, the main meal of the day; for others, a lighter meal): similar to breakfast, but possibly more elaborate.
- Snacks include both Middle Eastern pastries such as *baklava* (layers of *filo* pastry and nuts drenched in syrup) and *kataif* (cheese-stuffed vermicelli). Western pastries such as cheesecake and doughnuts are consumed with coffee. Fruit may be eaten at any time during the day.
- Coffee and, to a lesser extent, tea; beer and wines; orange juice and soft drinks are the most popular drinks.

Cucumber Salad (Salat Melafefonim)

Most meals in Israel include a salad of some sort, and arguments about how to make the perfect salad are commonplace.

4 small cucumbers (about 5
   inches), washed and sliced thin
1 onion, sliced thin
$\frac{1}{8}$ cup sugar

$\frac{1}{2}$ cup water
1 cup white vinegar
$\frac{1}{2}$ TBS fresh dill

Combine cucumbers and onion.
Boil sugar, water, vinegar, and dill.
Cool.
Pour over salad, stir well, and chill.

Jerusalem-Style Mixed Grill (Meorav Yerushalmi)

This is a specialty of Jewish Jerusalem. It emerged as a street delicacy about 30 years ago.

3 TBS oil
1 medium onion, finely sliced
1 garlic clove, crushed
$\frac{1}{2}$ pound chicken innards: hearts,
   spleen, liver
$\frac{1}{2}$ pound chicken breast cut into
   bite-sized pieces
$\frac{1}{2}$ tsp turmeric powder
$\frac{1}{2}$ tsp cumin powder
$\frac{1}{2}$ tsp coriander powder
salt and black pepper to taste
Finely sliced fresh vegetables
   of your choice (tomatoes,

sweet peppers, cucumbers)
   for garnish
Finely sliced mixed pickles of
   your choice (cucumbers,
   sauerkraut, pickled peppers,
   radishes, carrots) for garnish
1 TBS *tahina* sauce per person
1 good pita bread per person,
   top slit to make a pocket, and
   kept warm

In a heavy skillet, heat oil and stir-fry the onions until translucent.
Add garlic and stir-fry for 30 seconds.
Add innards and cook, stirring constantly, about 5 minutes.
Add all spices and condiments and mix well.
Add breast meat, and cook while stirring until meat is done, for about 5 more
   minutes.
Remove from heat.
Place a helping of meat inside the pita pocket. Add vegetables of choice, and
   pickles. Pour *tahina* sauce on top.
Eat warm.

Chicken with Jerusalem Artichokes (Of Bekharshaf Yerushalmi)

Though "Jerusalem" artichokes have nothing to do with the city (the word is a corruption of the Italian *girassole*, meaning sunflower), these tubers are very popular throughout the country.

½ cup lemon juice
¼ cup olive oil
10 cloves garlic, peeled and halved
1 chicken, cut into serving pieces
½ pound Jerusalem artichokes,
   peeled and sliced into
   bite-sized chunks
10 saffron threads, soaked in 1
   TBS water or, preferably, white
   wine for 5 minutes

water, as needed
salt and pepper to taste
a handful of fresh basil leaves
2 ounces pine nuts, toasted
   lightly

In a large heavy saucepan, mix lemon juice and olive oil.
Add the garlic halves, chicken, Jerusalem artichokes, and saffron.
Add water just to the tops of the chicken, cover, and bring to a boil over
   moderate heat.
Add seasoning and gently simmer for about 1 hour, or until chicken is tender.
Add basil, check seasoning, and remove from heat.
Garnish with pine nuts.
Serve with cooked rice.

Meat Baked in Sesame Sauce (Siniya)

This is a popular dish in most Arab-Israeli towns and villages.

1 pound ground meat (beef,
   turkey, chicken or lamb)
¾ tsp cumin powder
¾ tsp coriander powder
1 tsp chopped fresh mint
1 tsp fresh dill
½ cup parsley

2 TBS pine nuts
salt and pepper to taste
juice of 1 lemon
1 cup tahina (sesame sauce)
2 cloves garlic, crushed
1 cup water

Preheat oven to 350°F.
Mix well the beef, cumin, coriander, mint, dill, parsley, pine nuts, salt, and
   pepper.
Set aside.
In a blender, add ¼ of the lemon juice to the raw tahina and mix well.
The sauce will thicken almost immediately, becoming almost like plaster,
   and its color will darken.
Gradually add more lemon juice, keeping the blender running constantly.
If thicker than the consistency of yogurt when the juice is all done, add water
   while beating. Add garlic.
Place a layer of the meat mixture in individual baking dishes, or shape the
   mixture into 4 large meat patties and place in a casserole or baking dish.
Pour prepared tahina over the meat.

(continued)

Bake until the meat is cooked and the surface is brown (about 30 minutes).
Baste the meat with the tahina sauce several times during baking.
Serve over rice.

"Binder" for Passover (Haroset)

This dish is an important ritual element during the Seder (Passover feast). It represents the mortar that the Hebrew slaves used for building in ancient Egypt. Contemporary Israeli Jewish traditions are mixed, so two of the many versions used in homes across the country are presented here.

Moroccan Haroset

1 cup pitted dates	grated coconut
1 cup walnut or pecan meats	

Mince nuts and dates together in a manual meat grinder using a fine blade.
Form into small balls, about ¾ inch in diameter.
Roll in coconut.
Pile balls on a small serving plate.

European Haroset

1 dessert apple (sweet or tangy)	1 TBS cinnamon
½ cup walnut or pecan meats	¼ cup sweet red wine
½ cup seedless raisins	

Quickly and roughly blend apples and nuts in a food processor
Blend in raisins, cinnamon, and enough wine for a sticky but firm consistency.
Mound on a serving dish or bowl.
Serve *haroset* on its own with *matza* (unleavened bread) or as relish with any savory dish.

Stuffed Eggplant (Hazilim Memula'im)

As in much of the Middle East, eggplants serve to replace meat in times of dearth. This dish may be served as the main dish or as a side dish in a meat meal.

2 medium eggplants	salt and pepper to taste
5 TBS oil	½ tsp cinnamon
1 large onion, finely chopped	chopped mint to taste
3 tomatoes, chopped	juice of 1 lemon
½ cup cooked rice	

Cut eggplant in half lengthwise, leaving stalk intact, if wished. Scoop out
   pulp leaving a shell about $\frac{1}{2}$-inch thick.
Prepare the stuffing: cube pulp roughly.
Heat oil in a heavy skillet. Fry onion until translucent. Add eggplant cubes.
   Cook until soft, about 8–10 minutes.
Remove from heat. Stir in tomatoes, rice, salt, pepper, cinnamon, and mint,
   and mix well.
To assemble: fill the eggplant shells with the stuffing.
Pour 2 TBS oil into a heavy saucepan with tight-fitting lid and place the
   stuffed eggplants.
Cook on the lowest heat possible until the shells are soft, about 30–40
   minutes. Alternatively, place in a greased baking dish with 2 TBS oil,
   cover tightly with foil, and bake in a preheated 325°F oven for about
   45–60 minutes.
Remove from heat and drizzle with lemon juice.
Allow to rest for about 10 minutes and serve.

Fruit Soup (Marak Perot)

This dish is eaten as dessert. It betrays its Eastern European origin but has been
modified in Israel to use local fruit.

1 cup sour red cherries, pitted, halved	1 tsp lemon juice
1 cup firm peaches, peeled, pitted, and sliced	1 cinnamon stick
	4 whole cloves
1 cup plums, peeled, pitted, and cubed small	$\frac{1}{4}$ tsp salt
	$1\frac{1}{2}$ TBS cornstarch mixed in 3 TBS water (optional)
1 cup cooking apples, grated	1 cup sour cream (optional)
1 cup sugar	fresh sweet cherries, pitted, for
6 cups water	garnish

Combine fruit, sugar, water, lemon juice, spices, and salt.
Bring to a boil. Reduce heat, and simmer gently for 20 minutes until fruits
   are tender.
Discard cinnamon and cloves.
Blend mixture roughly in a food processor so that there are plenty of chunky
   bits (alternatively, leave fruits whole).
For a thicker consistency, mix cornstarch and water and stir into the fruit
   soup.
Reheat and cook, stirring until slightly thickened.
Chill thoroughly. Adjust taste with lemon juice or sugar.
Serve in chilled compote glasses with dollops of sour cream topped with a
   cherry.

ITALY

Italy, in southern Europe, was settled by Greeks, Etruscans, Celts, Romans, and Byzantines, and comprised city-states fought over by Spain and France until unification in 1871. A varied climate enables a range of crops to be grown, particularly in the fertile Po River Valley, despite the predominantly mountainous terrain.

The history of cuisine in Italy goes back to the Roman age. Some of the earliest cookbook writers, for example Apicius, came from Rome. A lengthy imperial and colonial history means that Rome, and subsequently Italy, developed a complex and rich cuisine, some of it retained even through the Dark Ages after the fall of the Roman Empire. Italian cuisine has influenced French cuisine early in the latter's development.

Italian cooking is far more varied than the pizza-spaghetti-osso bucco that many tend to think of. The topography has isolated certain regions but has also created distinctive cuisines: Roman, Tuscan, Apulian, Venetian, and many more. In the south (south of Rome, that is), sauces and cooking are more Mediterranean style, with olive oil and tomatoes predominating. In the north, there is greater influence from neighboring French cuisines, and butter and rice are major constituents. In Emiglia-Romana, renowned as the gastronomic center of Italy, dishes are cooked with pork fat (lard), or all three (olive oil, butter, and lard in its major city, Bologna). Other regions are also influenced by neighboring German or Austrian elements. Various pastas, sauces, wines, and specialties based on local produce characterize each region.

Foodstuffs

- Generally speaking, Italian foodstuffs consist of Mediterranean products, and there is a noted preference for only the freshest ingredients to be used.
- Staples include cornmeal (in the south), rice (in the north), and many local forms of wheat pasta in all areas, predominantly flat, ribbon shapes in the north, and tubular ones in the south.
- Favorite meats are beef (particularly veal) and pork. All parts of the animal are used. Much meat goes into the preparation of salted hams (the prosciutto of Parma is world famous) and sausages (*salame* and *luganeghe*) of various sorts and other preserved meats (such as *pancetta* or bacon). Chicken, duck, squab, and other birds are eaten as well.

- Fish and seafood are in great demand. Mediterranean fish such as mullet, grouper, and tuna, and sardines are eaten fresh. Octopus, squid, shrimp, and a variety of shellfish are often eaten as antipasto (starters).
- Fruit include citrus fruit, melons and watermelons, apples, pears and peaches, strawberries and figs. Grapes are also eaten as well as used for preparing the many wines and liqueurs that Italy is famous for. Olives are grown throughout Italy, some for pickling, others for making olive oil.
- Vegetables include tomatoes (fresh and dried), potatoes, lettuce, arugula, and other greens, beans (signature foods in Tuscan cuisine), squashes such as zucchini, artichokes, onions, and garlic.
- Milk products include creams and particularly a great variety of both soft cheeses such as *mozzarella* (from buffalo milk), ricotta, provolone, veined gorgonzola, and *mascarpone*, to hard ones (generically called *grana* from their grainy texture, such as *pecorino* from sheep's milk and Parma's famous parmesan (*parmigiano*).

Typical Dishes

- Pizza, originating from Southern Italy, is the most widespread food in the world. The original pizza *Napolitana* (created to celebrate the visit of the Italian queen to Naples), is a simple dish of baked dough topped with basil, tomatoes, and *mozzarella di buffala* cheese, the colors representing the Italian flag.
- Pasta, dough made from hard durum wheat in various shapes, is a classic dish served as a first course. Different areas have their own preferred shapes, and new shapes such as *radiatori* are created from time to time. Pasta is served as a separate course with various sauces, ranging from plain butter and cream in the north to seafood in the south.
- Rice features in many northern dishes, where *risotto*—rice cooked while stirring in wine and simmering stock a cupful at a time—is a common main dish or first course.
- A variety of soups are prepared regionally, including the famous *zuppa di fagioli* (bean soup) from Tuscany, Rome's egg and cheese soup (*stracciatella*), and Ravenna's fish chowder (*brodetto*).
- Italian bakers make a wide variety of pastries and breads, and most areas have their special breads. Some of these, such as those on the island of Tuscany, are filled with ham or cheeses, while others are plain. Cakes and cookies are made throughout the country, ranging from simple sugared almond cookies in Sicily to elaborate sponge cake, sugar, and coffee creations in Venice, in particular *tiramisu*, its most famous dessert.
- In the northwest, typical dishes are rich in butter and cream or cheese, the products of a flourishing dairy and cattle industry, such as Lombardy's chicken in cream (*penne pollo e crema*) or polenta with butter and cheese (*polenta taragna*); the Piedmont's famed white truffles in a fondue of local Fontina cheese (*fonduta con tartufi bianchi*) or little dumplings layered with Fontina cheese and topped with butter (*gnocchi alla bava*); and Milan's signature dish of risotto with saffron, Parmesan, white wine, and butter (*risotto milanese*), often accompanied by wine-braised veal knuckles (*osso bucco*), another regional specialty. Seafood and fish are the specialties of the Ligurian coast, in particular Genoa's fish stew (*burrida*), as well as an Easter pie of ricotta, eggs, and spinach (*torta pasqualina*).

- Northeast Italy's Emiglia-Romana region is renowned for its rich cuisine (often compared to France's Burgundy) derived from its quality beef and dairy products, vegetables, and wheat. The most world renowned of its dishes is its spaghetti sauce (*ragú bolognese*) that accompanies local pasta *tagliatelle*, meat- or cheese-stuffed *tortellini*, or baked *lasagne*. Quality veal is rolled around a stuffing of liver, local Parma ham, and onions (*involtini alla cacciatora*). Typical Venetian dishes are thinly sliced calf's liver with onions (*fegato alla veneziana*) and salt cod dishes. The Austrian influence is evident in the Trentino region's typical dishes of sauerkraut, apple strudel, goulash, and rye bread.
- Rome, at the center of Italy, integrates the cooking of north and south, but also has its own specialties: whole roast suckling pig (*porchetta*) stuffed with herbs; cannelloni; egg ribbon pasta with butter and cheese (*fettucine al burro*); and deep-fried young artichokes (*carciofi alla giudea*), originally from Rome's Jewish ghetto.
- Besides pizza and pasta from its wheat, Southern Italy's specialties feature seafood from its coast in spaghetti with clams (*vermicelli alla vongole*) and eggplants with Parmesan cheese (*melanzane alla parmigiana*). Sicily's *cuscusu* (fish soup with semolina) dates back to historical Arabic influence, and Sardinia's meat pies (*impanadas*) and bean soup (*fabbada*) reveal a Spanish origin.
- There are a wide variety of drinks. Wine (many regional varieties, including sparkling wine) and mineral water are commonly consumed by all during main meals (children receive highly diluted wine from an early age during family meals). Beer is also popular. Coffee is drunk in great quantities and in various forms by most adults during the day. Tea is sometimes drunk, usually cold during the summer. Aperitifs, flavored with wormwood (vermouth) or citrus (*limoncello*), and distilled grape must to drink after dinner (*grappa*), are also popular.

Styles of Eating

- Three meals a day and many short stops for tiny cups of coffee are the norm throughout Italy.
- Families generally eat together, or at least on weekends. Street foods are popular as well.
- Breakfast: fresh bread or rolls, butter, and large cups of milky coffee.
- Mid-morning: *panini*, or pastries of some kind, together with a cup or two of espresso or some other coffee.
- A classic Italian meal consists of an *antipasto*, small plates of fresh or preserved fish or meat or vegetables, often tangy, to stimulate appetite; a *pasta* with some light sauce or soup (*minestra*, possibly a *minestrone* with noodles); one or two main dishes (*piatti*) of meat, poultry, or fish; and a cooked vegetable or salad of various fresh vegetables. This is washed down by wine and mineral water. Most meals end with a simple dessert of ice cream or sherbet, or, more commonly, cheese and fruit, then a cup of coffee. This may be eaten at lunch but also likely in the evening.
- Afternoon: a pastry and coffee.
- Evening meal: usually a lighter, simpler meal than lunch.
- Large and small cafes serve various styles of coffee and many kinds of pastry during all hours of the day and in the evening.

Marinated Zucchini (Concia)

This is a popular antipasto created in the ancient Jewish community of Rome to whet the appetite.

4 medium zucchini
¼ cup olive oil
2 cloves garlic, minced

1 sprig basil, shredded
salt and pepper to taste
1 TBS wine vinegar

Trim the ends of the zucchini.
Cut each in half crosswise, then thinly slice the halves lengthwise.
Dry the slices on paper towel overnight or for several hours.
Heat oil in a heavy skillet until hazy.
Fry slices a few at a time in a single layer until golden. Drain.
Arrange in layers in a deep glass container, seasoning each layer with small amounts of garlic, basil, salt, pepper, and a sprinkle of vinegar.
Cover container and store in the refrigerator for 2–3 hours.
Serve as antipasto.

Tuscan Bean Soup (Zuppa Fagioli a la Toscana)

Tuscany is famous for its bean dishes, spinach, and the many bay hedges that adorn the countryside and cities and whose leaves flavor its food.

2 pounds white kidney beans
(or 3 cans cooked kidney beans, drained)
4 ounces very lean bacon, diced fine
¼ cup olive oil
½ cup red onion, chopped fine
½ cup celery, chopped fine

1 tsp fresh sage
1 tsp salt
1 tsp white pepper
4 cups chicken stock
1½ cups penne pasta
1 TBS parsley, finely minced
freshly grated Romano or Parmegiano cheese

Pour boiling water over dried beans and allow to soak overnight. Omit if using canned beans. Drain before cooking.
Heat oil and sauté bacon until soft.
Add onion and celery and sauté, stirring, for about 5 minutes.
Add sage, salt, and pepper.
Add chicken stock, cover and bring to a boil.
Add beans, cover and simmer until beans are soft (if using canned beans, simmer for 30 minutes).
Boil a large pot of fresh water, lightly salted. Add pasta, stir once. Bring water to rolling boil again.
Boil uncovered until noodles are *al dente* (chewy but cooked throughout).

(continued)

Drain and add to soup. Remove from heat.
Stir in minced parsley.
Serve immediately with grated cheese for sprinkling.

Fettuccine with Butter and Cream (Fettuccine al Burro)

This is a pasta recipe from northern Italy.

1 pound fresh fettuccine noodles	salt and white pepper to taste
$\frac{1}{4}$ cup butter	$\frac{1}{4}$ cup freshly grated Parmesan
1 cup cream	cheese

Boil a large pot of fresh water, lightly salted. Add noodles. Stir once. Bring
  water to rolling boil again. Boil uncovered until noodles are *al dente*
  (chewy but cooked throughout).
In the meantime, melt butter in a large skillet until it foams. Add cream.
  Simmer over medium heat for 2 minutes until slightly thickened.
Season.
Remove noodles from water and drain well. Add noodles to cream.
Add $\frac{1}{4}$ cup Parmesan cheese.
Toss noodles and sauce quickly over medium heat until sauce coats noodles.
Serve immediately with additional Parmesan cheese.

Basic Corn Mush (Polenta)

Polenta is the staple of southern Italy.

5 cups water	$1\frac{1}{2}$ cups cornmeal
1 tsp salt	

Bring water to a boil in a large, heavy pot. Add salt and reduce heat.
Add cornmeal to water very slowly, streaming from ladle or your hand. Stir
  quickly with a wooden spoon while adding cornmeal.
If necessary, stop adding cornmeal from time to time and beat mixture
  vigorously.
Cook, stirring constantly, for 20–30 minutes.
Polenta is done when it comes away cleanly from the sides of the pot.
Pour onto a large platter.
Wet your hands and smooth out about 2 inches thick.
Cool until it solidifies.
Cut into slices, put in each plate, and pour over sauce of your choice or eat
  with a meat dish.

Seasoned Cutlets (Piccata)

This is often served as a main dish.

1 cup flour
salt and white pepper to taste
4 cutlets (turkey or chicken breast,
    boneless lean veal, or pork)

6 TBS butter
juice of 1 lemon, sieved
3 TBS parsley, minced fine

Season flour with salt and pepper, and dredge cutlets with the mixture.
Heat butter in a large, heavy frying pan.
Gently cook the cutlets without crowding, turning over once, until done.
    Drain on paper towels and keep warm while the rest are cooking.
Add 1 tablespoon butter and lemon juice to the hot pan.
Increase heat to reduce the liquid, stirring constantly. Correct the seasoning.
Pour butter and lemon sauce over the cutlets.
Serve garnished with parsley.

Deviled Chicken (Pollo alla Diavola)

This is served as a main dish.

1 (2 pounds) whole chicken,
    quartered (or 4 chicken
    quarters)
½ cup olive oil
2 TBS hot pepper sauce of your
    choice or 1 tsp dried chili
    pepper flakes

juice of 2 lemons
1 TBS black pepper
1 tsp salt

Place chicken cut side down in roasting pan.
Mix remaining ingredients in a large bowl. Pour over chicken and and
    marinate for 2 hours.
Grill on a medium hot charcoal barbecue (or under a grill), skin side to heat,
    for 25 minutes.
Turn and cook for another 20 minutes until the juices run clear.
Baste continuously with remaining marinade.

Coffee Ice Cream (Gelato di Caffe)

The form of ice cream we eat today was invented in Italy, and Italian ice
creams have a worldwide reputation.

⅓ cup sugar

4 TBS instant coffee powder

2 egg yolks

1 cup whipping cream,

½ cup milk, at room temperature
chilled

a pinch of salt

Beat sugar and egg yolks together until lemon yellow and very thick.
Slowly add milk, beating gently.
Stir in salt. Transfer the mixture to the top of a double boiler over, not in, boiling water. Stir continuously for 10 minutes until custard is thick enough to coat the spoon.
Remove top of double boiler and set in a large bowl of ice water.
Keep stirring for 2 minutes to avoid lumps.
Transfer to a bowl and add coffee, stirring well.
Cover and set in refrigerator to chill thoroughly.
Whip cream into soft peaks and stir into coffee custard.
Place bowl in freezer (or ice cream maker). Whisk custard every 5 minutes to break up ice. Serve when it reaches right consistency (or use ice cream machine according to directions).

Iced Tea (Té con Granita)

A very popular drink during summer in southern Italy.

2 good tea bags

juice of 1 lemon

1 cup boiling water

4 drops vanilla extract

sugar to taste
(optional)

3 cups cold water

4 TBS lemon or orange sherbet,
or 2 popsicles, crushed in bowl

Steep tea bags in freshly boiled water to make a strong tea (remove before tea becomes bitter and tannin floats to surface).
Add sugar and stir to dissolve.
Mix hot tea into cold water (*not* the reverse).
Add lemon juice and vanilla, if desired. Refrigerate for at least 30 minutes.
To serve, place equivalent amounts of sherbet/popsicle in 4 glasses.
Pour in tea and serve.

JAMAICA

Jamaica, the third largest Caribbean island, was first settled by Spain, then colonized by Britain in 1655. It eventually gained independence in 1962, though still remains within the British Commonwealth. Sugar has traditionally been Jamaica's major crop, with African, East Indian, and Chinese laborers brought in to the plantations. Jamaica's hot and humid climate in the coastal plains is ideal for bananas and other tropical crops, the temperate interior mountains are ideal for coffee, and the coasts yield fish and seafood. Jamaican food is spicy and reflects its mixed culture with African, Caribbean, East Indian, British, and Chinese influences.

Foodstuffs

- Staples: rice, cornmeal, beans, cassava, plantain.
- Vegetables: yam, *callaloo* (leaves of *Amaranthus viridis*, also known as Chinese spinach or Indian kale, and different from *callaloo* in the eastern Caribbean, which refers to leaves of taro tubers), pumpkin, sweet potatoes, okra, cabbage, sweet and hot peppers, christophene (called *cho-cho*), avocado, breadfruit.
- Fruit: citrus, mango, pineapple, guava, star apple, jackfruit (related to breadfruit but larger and aromatic), June or Spanish plum, naseberry (a small, brown, heart-shaped fruit tasting like cinnamon), unusual "Tinkin Toe" (also called "Stinking Toe"), an oblong-shaped fruit with very sweet flesh.
- Goat, chicken, preserved meats (salt pork, corned beef), fish, shrimp, conch, crab, lobster.
- Seasonings: allspice, Scotch bonnet hot peppers, curry spices (from the East Indian legacy), thyme, nutmeg, mace, jerk (a spice and herb blend; see recipe below), fresh ginger, star anise (from the Chinese influence).

Typical Dishes

- Ackee and salt fish is the national dish, usually eaten at breakfast. Ackee, the fruit of a West African tree, is poisonous until ripe. Its yellow flesh has a nutty, delicate flavor like avocado, and is used as a vegetable (see box "Poisonous Foods"). Salt fish is usually salted cod.
- Escovitch fish: fried fish marinated in vinegar, spices, and vegetables.
- Jerked chicken or pork, curried chicken, souse (pickled pig's trotters), cowfoot soup.

POISONOUS FOODS

A number of foods that humans eat are poisonous in their natural state and require careful handling or processing to be made edible. The three most prominent poisonous foods are *akee*, cassava, and *fugu*. *Akee* is the fruit of a tree (*Blighia sapida*) originating in Africa and now common in the Caribbean. The aril (fleshy pulp around the seeds) is edible when the fruit is ripe and has split naturally. Unripe and overripe fruit are both poisonous, as is all the fruit except the aril.

Cassava, a bush originating in tropical South America produces cyanogenic glucosides in the edible tubers, which, in some species, needs to be removed before the richly nutritious root can be consumed.

Fugu, one of several species of the puffer fish (*Tetraodontidae* sp.) are eaten in Japan and some other Pacific islands. An algae resident in the fish's tissues, and particularly concentrated in the liver, produces tetrodotoxin, one of the deadliest poisons. Nontheless, the flesh of the *fugu* is esteemed as a delicacy. Only specially experienced and licensed cooks are allowed to prepare and serve *fugu* in Japan.

How these various poisonous foods came to be eaten is something of a puzzle. The answer may lie partly in the variation in poison concentrate in specific specimens (which means that some people who ate these foods survived to tell how good the foods tasted) and partly in the inherent human desire for exotic and interesting things to eat.

- Curried goat (called "curry goat"), mannish water (goat soup), for special occasions such as Sunday dinner, birthdays, and anniversaries.
- Rice and peas (usually kidney beans or, less often, gungo peas).
- Pan-fried breads: bakes (actually fried), *bammies* (made of grated cassava), johnnycakes, coconut bake, hot pepper bread (sweet and spicy).
- Snacks: fresh tropical fruits, roasted corn on the cob, pan-fried breads, meat pies (patties).
- Sweets: tropical fruit ice creams (mango, soursop).
- Drinks: sky juice (shaved ice with flavored syrup), suck suck (cold, fresh coconut juice, called "jelly" coconut because of the soft interior meat), exotic fruit juices (tamarind, soursop, strawberry, and cucumber), ginger beer, limeade, local bottled soft drinks (carbonated grapefruit). Blue Mountain coffee, the world's most expensive coffee, is grown here and widely drunk. Rum and beer are also locally brewed.

Styles of Eating

- Three meals a day and snacks.
- Breakfast is substantial, with fresh fruits, bully beef, and johnnycakes (spicy corned beef hash and fried biscuits); cornmeal porridge with fried or boiled plantains. On weekends, goat's liver fried with onions, served with bammies or boiled dumplings and yam. Coffee, hot malted milk drinks (Milo, Horlicks), or chocolate to drink.
- Lunch is similar to dinner but lighter: fried chicken or grilled fish with baked sweet potato or yam, boiled breadfruit or dumplings.

ACKEE

- Dinner is the heaviest meal and consists of three courses: jerked, curried, or stewed chicken or shrimp, stewed pork or peas, served with rice and peas, or pan-fried breads or baked sweet potato; salad (potato salad or fancy coleslaw with pineapple and coconut); dessert of fresh fruits or ice cream. Sunday meals are extra special, featuring drinks such as sorrel (in season), carrot, or beet juice.
- Take-out meals ("buy and bring home") at dinner once a week, usually Friday: jerked chicken, pork, or sausage; fried chicken; pizza; fried fish and festival (sweet cornmeal fritters); roast fish and yam.

Festival

These deep-fried cornmeal fritters, often sold at street stalls, are usually eaten with fried fish or jerked meats as snacks.

1 cup flour	½ cup salted butter
1 cup yellow cornmeal	¼ tsp almond extract
1 tsp baking powder	½ tsp vanilla extract
½ tsp cinnamon	⅔–1 cup whole milk
a pinch of salt	vegetable oil for deep-frying
1 TBS sugar	

In a mixing bowl, combine flour, cornmeal, baking powder, cinnamon, salt, and sugar.

Rub the butter well into the flour mixture.

Add flavorings and just enough milk to flour the mixture to make a stiff dough.

Knead lightly and divide into twelve portions.

Form into small, flattened cigars.

In a deep skillet or heavy-bottomed saucepan, heat enough vegetable oil for deep-frying to 350°F.

Fry just a few festivals at a time until golden brown. Drain on paper towels to absorb excess oil. Serve hot.

Corned Beef Scotch Eggs

This Jamaican version of a Scottish favorite originates, no doubt, from the managers of traditional sugar plantations, many of whom were from Scotland. The use of corned beef, salt pork, and salted cod was from historical necessity, because before refrigeration, it was difficult to keep fresh food from spoiling. As well, beef and cod are not local Jamaican ingredients; being imported from the United States and northern Europe. Even with modern refrigeration and transportation, however, these preserved items remain popular, as their flavor and texture now form an essential element of traditional Jamaican taste.

Serve this dish with coleslaw (the Jamaican version features pineapple slices and shredded fresh coconut) or a tossed vegetable salad with pan-fried bread as a light dish for lunch or as a snack.

12 ounces corned beef
3 stalks spring onions, chopped
  fine
3 stalks fresh thyme or parsley,
  chopped fine
$\frac{1}{2}$ tsp black pepper

1 beaten egg
4 hard-boiled eggs, shelled
1 cup bread crumbs
flour for dusting
oil to deep-fat fry (or bake in
  oven)

Mix the corned beef well with herbs, black pepper, and beaten egg.
Divide into four portions.
Dust your hands with flour and place one portion of the corned beef mixture
  on your palm to make a patty.
Place 1 hard-boiled egg in the center of the patty, and stretch the patty to
  cover the egg completely.
Dip in bread crumbs, lay on a plate, and chill until ready to fry.
In a deep skillet, heat enough oil for deep-frying to 350°F.
Fry the Scotch eggs until golden brown.
Cut across the middle of each Scotch egg and serve at once.

Jamaica Ginger and Apple Drink

Apples are not locally grown in Jamaica, so this is one imaginative way of
making apple juice at home. Another popular homemade drink in Jamaica that
features ginger is ginger beer, which, contrary to its name, is not a true beer.

10 cups water
1 cup granulated sugar
6 apples, washed, cored, and
  diced

1 cup grated fresh ginger

In a large stainless steel pan, bring water and sugar to a boil.
Add apples and simmer for about 15 minutes, or until the apples are tender.
Add ginger.
Set aside to cool.
Strain through a fine sieve or a cheesecloth.

Jerk Burger

Jerk seasoning, said to have been introduced by the Maroons (who were
escaped black slaves) to preserve their food, has become very popular not only in
Jamaica and the Caribbean but also worldwide. The Jamaican method of jerking
is to slowly grill the well-marinated meat (chicken, pork, sometimes fish or sausages) over coals from allspice wood, covering the entire grill with metal sheets,
which at the same time keeps the smoke in, imparts a smoky flavor to the meat,
and preserves its moisture. This variation teams up with a U.S. import—the

burger—which has become a popular snack. Serve this with festivals and potato salad (another familiar food, but which may have sweet potatoes together with regular potatoes in the Jamaican version).

2 TBS butter	½ tsp freshly ground black pepper
1 onion, finely chopped	jerk seasoning
3 garlic cloves, minced	parsley
1 cup fresh mushrooms, chopped	young spinach leaves or lettuce
1½ pounds ground beef	leaves
½ pound ground fatty pork	mustard
1 tsp salt	8 red onion rings

Melt butter in a skillet over medium heat and sauté onion and garlic until soft, for about 3 minutes.

Stir in mushrooms, quickly frying until mushrooms have absorbed the butter, for about 3 minutes.

Place the mushroom mixture in a large bowl, using a rubber scraper to get all the pan juices.

Add meat, jerk seasoning, parsley, salt, and pepper. Cover and let stand in the refrigerator for at least 1 hour or overnight.

Shape the burgers into four large or eight medium patties.

Grill or fry in a skillet over medium-high heat for 7–8 minutes on each side, or until done.

Serve on toasted crusty rolls with mustard, spinach or lettuce leaves, and red onion rings.

Jerk Seasoning

Jerk seasoning has many variations, but the traditional elements are allspice, thyme, hot pepper (preferably Jamaican Scotch bonnet), green onion, ginger, cinnamon, and black pepper. The freshness of the ingredients is key.

3 TBS oil	½ tsp ground cinnamon
3 stalks green onions	½ tsp ground nutmeg
3 stalks fresh thyme (leaves only)	1 tsp fresh ginger, grated
1 Scotch bonnet or other hot	1 tsp brown sugar
pepper (optional)	2 TBS malt or cane vinegar
½ tsp allspice berries or ground	
allspice	

In a blender or food processor, put the oil, then add the rest of the ingredients. Process to a puree.

Coffee Ice Cream

Rich ice cream flavored with Jamaica's fruits such as soursop or coconut is the most popular dessert. If you can get Blue Mountain coffee, that would make the perfect Jamaican flavor for this cream. If not, any strong and freshly brewed coffee will make just as good a result.

6 egg yolks	2 cups double cream
1 cup sugar	1 TBS vanilla
1 cup strong, freshly brewed coffee	1 TBS instant coffee

In a bowl, mix egg yolks and sugar till thick.

In a saucepan, mix coffee and cream and heat gently until bubbles form around the edge of the pan. Remove from heat and set aside.

Spoon, little by little, about a quarter of the coffee-cream mixture into the yolks, mixing well.

Pour the entire yolk and coffee mixture into the saucepan, to make a rich coffee custard, which is the basis of the ice cream.

Cook the custard at low heat, stirring continuously with a wooden spoon until thick enough to coat the back of a spoon, for about 15 minutes.

Take care not to overcook the custard as it will curdle.

Remove from heat. Stir in vanilla and instant coffee. Set aside to cool. When the custard is completely cold, chill in the refrigerator for 3 hours or overnight.

Pour into an ice cream maker following manufacturer's instructions.

If you do not have an ice cream maker, freeze the mixture in a covered container for $2\frac{1}{2}$ hours or until the edges have started to freeze.

With an electric hand mixer, beat the frozen custard for about 5 minutes.

Return to the freezer and keep for another 2–3 hours. Beat again. Then let freeze completely.

JAPAN

A mountainous island chain in East Asia, Japan is a constitutional monarchy and a major economic power. The four major islands and the thousands of smaller ones are largely volcanic, and there is limited agricultural area in the river valleys. The climate ranges from subarctic (long winters with plenty of snow) in Hokkaido to tropical in the Ryukyu Islands to the south.

Japan's agro technology enables high yields of cereals, fruit, vegetables, and livestock. Its fishing fleets range worldwide to supply the country's high demand for fresh fish and seafood, which are often consumed raw. Increased meat, poultry, and dairy consumption is satisfied by imports, mainly from the United States, Australia, and New Zealand.

The population is predominantly Japanese, with minorities of Koreans, Chinese, and other Asians. Historically, Japan has been influenced by Korea and China, and since the past century by Europe and the United States. Many Japanese dishes are adaptations to local foods and recipes that originated from those places.

Japanese cuisine is sophisticated, emphasizing the freshness of ingredients and their artistic presentation. It is also highly inventive and adaptive, and many foreign foods are part of daily Japanese fare. Its prosperous urban population enjoy eating out at the wide range of eating venues that provide food fitting all budgets and tastes, from traditional Japanese, Chinese, Italian, and other ethnic cuisines, and east-west fusion to major international cuisines. Regional food varies and, though influenced by city trends, continues to maintain traditions (see box "East Asian Table Settings").

Foodstuffs

- The staple is rice, though younger people sometimes substitute bread.
- Buckwheat and wheat noodles, bean noodles; Western-style bread.
- Fish and seafood of all kinds, including jellyfish, sea cucumber, and sea squirt.
- Chicken, pork, and beef, much of it imported. For many, bean curd (*tofu*) substitutes for meat, as it has traditionally.
- Vegetables include seaweed of many kinds, which are cultivated in bays along the coast, giant radish (*daikon*), bamboo shoots, Chinese cabbage, spinach, eggplant, cultivated mushrooms, dried gourds, wild fungi, wild mountain vegetables (ferns), cucumbers, tomatoes.

- Fruit: Asian pear, apple, peach, melon, watermelon, loquat, grapes (Japanese cultivars—small-berried and giant-berried varieties), tangerines.
- Drinks: tea (both native green varieties and semi-smoked oolong from China), coffee, fruit juices, health drinks, fermented milk drinks, yogurt drinks.
- Seasonings: fermented soybean paste (*miso*), soy sauce, dried seaweed and dried bonito for cooking stock, trefoil (*mitsuba*), red and green *shiso* (*Perilla*), *sansho* (*Zanthozylum*).

Typical Dishes

- Fish and seafood dishes: *sashimi* (raw fish); *sushi* (vinegared rice and raw fish); salt-grilled fish; *tempura* (batter-coated fried seafood and vegetables).
- Soups and stews: *miso* soup; meat or poultry and vegetables.
- Table-cooked dishes: meat and vegetables simmered or grilled (Korean style) on a tabletop cooker.
- Rice dishes: curry and rice (*kare raisu*); rice and meat bowl (*donburi*); seafood or poultry rice soup (*zosui*); Chinese-style fried rice.
- Noodle dishes: fried noodles (*yakisoba*); Chinese-style soup noodles (*ramen*).
- Pickles: eggplant or gourd preserved in *miso* (soybean paste) or rice wine lees or soy sauce.
- Sweets: traditional Japanese rice cakes made with glutinous rice, Western-type cakes (especially cheese and chocolate), green tea–flavored cake (fusion of Japanese flavor and Western baking technique).

EAST ASIAN TABLE SETTINGS

Traditional table settings in East Asia are dependent on chopsticks, invented in China. The use of chopsticks is common in all Chinese-influenced societies as well (Japan, Korea, and to a lesser extent Vietnam and Thailand). Confucius claimed that the use of chopsticks inhibited men from fighting during meals, which seems to indicate that early Chinese ate with their belt knives and possibly spoons.

East Asian table settings consist of a pair of chopsticks, a bowl for the staple (normally rice today), bowls or dishes for other foods, and possibly a spoon. The precise use of these utensils varies from culture to culture and depends on the materials used. Chinese chopsticks tend to be long and cylindrical, of bamboo, ivory, wood, or, more recently, plastic. Japanese chopsticks tend to be of wood or bamboo and are shorter, with a taper toward the point. Korea, wood-poor, traditionally makes metal chopsticks. Bowls in China are traditionally ceramic; in Japan, a mix of lacquered wood and ceramics; and in Korea, metal.

Perhaps as a consequence, dining arrangements differ as well. In China, each place setting includes chopsticks, a ceramic spoon, a rice bowl and a dish for condiments/side dishes. The side dishes are placed in the center of the table for diners to help themselves (and, hopefully, not to let them take more than their fair share). Soup is drunk from a bowl with a spoon. Rice is eaten from the raised bowl with the aid of chopsticks. In Japan, each diner is provided with chopsticks, a soup bowl, and individual plates with side dishes. Soup is drunk directly from the bowl. In Korea, diners may have all food in front of them or there may be a central plate of side dishes for all to share. Diners eat with chopsticks in one hand and a spoon in the other. Hot metal bowls and plates are not moved from the table.

Styles of Eating

- Three main meals and snacks daily.
- Breakfast: Western style, with toast, cooked egg, butter, coffee, fruit juice. Japanese style, with rice, seaweed, raw egg, fermented beans (*natto*), grilled fish, *miso* soup, green tea.
- Lunch: rice and meat bowl (*donburi*); curry rice (a mild, thick curry sauce with very little meat served over rice, eaten with Japanese-style pickles); Western-style pasta (spaghetti with seafood or meat sauce; *doria*, a casserole of rice and meat or seafood with cream sauce, topped with grilled cheese); traditional lunchbox-type meal (*obento*) of rice, pickles, and small servings of fish or meat and vegetables; fresh fruit for dessert.
- Dinner: usually rice, *miso* soup, pickles, and two to three side dishes of raw or grilled fish, stewed or fried meat dish, and steamed vegetable dish. Fresh fruit for dessert. Rarely sweet cake.
- Snacks: raw fruit or salty pickles with tea, sweet pastries with coffee, rice cakes, rice ball soup, pizza, spaghetti, noodles.

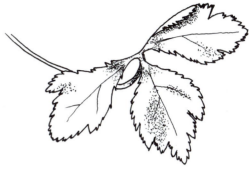

MITSUBA

Rice Omelet (Omuraisu)

This dish, frequently made at home, is a favorite of children of all ages and a standard dish at small eateries and family restaurants for a light meal at anytime. This is usually served with a clear consommé-type soup strewn with chopped spring onions.

1 cup cooked rice per person	8 TBS oil
8 eggs, well beaten, lightly seasoned	salt to taste
	tomato ketchup

Heat 1 tablespoon oil in a frying pan.

Stir-fry rice for about 2 minutes, until all rice grains have separated and rice has been coated with oil.

Add 1 tablespoon ketchup, and cook stirring well until all rice is coated. Season with salt if necessary.

Remove from pan and mold into a long almond shape on a warmed plate.

Heat an additional 2 tablespoons oil in the pan until smoking.

Pour in 1 quarter of the eggs, tilting the pan to ensure maximum spread. Cook over medium heat until bottom is cooked. Turn omelet over (with practice, you can do this by gently tapping on the frying pan handle while it is tilted toward you).

When cooked, slide onto rice (if you have used the tapping method, you will have a thick omelet "sausage"; slit this gently lengthwise, about $\frac{1}{2}$ inch the thickness through, and unfold the omelet to cover the rice mound).

(continued)

Garnish with a generous dollop of ketchup.
Repeat for the remaining rice and egg.
Serve hot.

Beef and Rice Bowl
(Gyūdon, *also* Gyūniku Donburi)

This is a very easy everyday dish, commonly offered in roadside diners and family restaurants and also made at home for a quick meal. While beef is not a traditional Japanese food ingredient (because of the Buddhist injunction against taking the lives of animals for food), for several decades now, beef and pork have become commonplace, and meat consumption has risen dramatically. This dish is eaten at midday or in the evening, accompanied by pickled vegetables and *miso* soup.

The thinner the meat, the faster it cooks, so if you cannot request a butcher to cut it thinly, buy a solid chunk of meat, freeze it for about 1 hour, and slice it against the grain, using a good, sharp knife.

4 servings hot, freshly cooked plain white rice, preferably short grain
3 TBS oil
1 onion, thinly sliced
1 pound thinly sliced strips of beef (round or London broil) or boneless pork, $3 \times 1 \times \frac{1}{8}$ inches

2–3 TBS Japanese-style soy sauce
2 TBS sugar, or to taste
$\frac{1}{2}$ cup beef stock or hot water
1 block firm tofu (optional), cut into 16 cubes
1 leek, white part only, thinly sliced diagonally

Warm four large, deep soup bowls by filling them up to two-thirds with very hot water. Let stand while you prepare the meat.
Heat a wok over medium heat.
Add oil; stir in onions and fry until softened, for about 2–3 minutes.
Increase heat to medium-hot.
Add beef, briskly stirring so that all pieces are seared; fry for about 1–2 minutes.
Stir in soy sauce, sugar, and stock; fry for about half a minute, mixing the sauce well with the meat.
Stir in tofu and leek. Let cook for about 1 minute or until thoroughly heated through. Turn off heat.
Quickly discard hot water and wipe the bowls dry.
Place roughly $1\frac{1}{4}$ cups hot rice into each bowl.
Distribute meat equally among the bowls, with an eye to neatness and appearance: make sure the meat, onions, and tofu are side by side (not obscured by another item) on the surface of the bowls.
Serve at once.

Cabbage Pickle (Kyabetsu no Tsukemono)

When rice is served in the home, pickles and *miso* soup are usually served with it. These three items in themselves constitute a complete meal and used to be all that most families ate in less prosperous times.

There are many types of pickles: each locality has its own specialty, and each family will make its own variation. While the remembered taste of mom's apple pie is what makes Americans yearn for home, in Japan it is the taste of home-made pickles.

There are long-term and quick pickles. The long-term ones are, as their name implies, intended to last for months, if not a year. The quick ones are ready in 2–3 hours or overnight. Most rural households used to make their own pickles, vital where winters are long and snow covers the ground until spring. Nowadays, very few bother to make their own for year-round use, but quick pickles are still being made.

1 small head Chinese cabbage, as fresh as possible, about 1 pound	water salt ice-cold water

Remove the leaves from cabbage, keeping them whole.
Fill a large pot two-thirds full with water. Add 1 tsp salt and bring to boil.
Add cabbage and blanch for 1 minute.
Transfer blanched cabbage to a large bowl half-filled with ice-cold water. Leave cabbage to chill.
Meanwhile, prepare pickling brine in the proportion of 1 cup water to 1 tsp salt. (Prepare about 16 cups initially; you may need to prepare more, depending on the size of the cabbage and the bowl. The cabbage must be completely submerged in the brine.)
Boil the pickling brine and let cool.
Drain the cabbage and place in layers in a large bowl.
Pour cooled brine over.
Place a clean plate above, and top with a heavy can to weigh the cabbage down so that all are completely covered by the brine. Cover all with foil or plastic wrap.
Set aside for 2–3 hours.
Drain leaves; stack 3–5 leaves on top of one another.
Cut into neat bite-size squares, leaving the stacks intact. Repeat until all the leaves have been cut, keeping the squares as uniform as possible.
For each diner, make up two stacks of pickled cabbage, each roughly 1½ inches in height.
In four small, shallow bowls (preferably with a dark glaze), lay the stacks on their side so that the layers face up.
Pass around some soy sauce for each diner to drizzle just a few drops over the pickles, if desired.

Savory Custard Soup (Chawan Mushi)

This is an unusual soup: although on top it looks like a solid custard, it is not sweet, and at the bottom, there is plenty of hot stock. This is usually served for an evening meal, especially in the winter. The ingredients given here are the most commonly used in Japan, but depending on the season or locale, other items can be substituted. Instead of shrimp, a small piece of fish fillet may be substituted, in which case omit the chicken breast. Or, instead of ginkgo nuts, use button mushrooms. Trefoil is a delicately aromatic herb; if not available, substitute three matchstick-size strips of lemon or lime rind, without the white, bitter part.

½ cup chicken breast, diced
1 tsp Japanese-style soy sauce
1 tsp sake or *mirin* (sweet cooking wine) (optional)
4 small raw shrimp, briefly blanched in hot water until they turn pink (about 30 seconds)
12 fresh ginkgo nuts, shelled and peeled (or substitute broad bean kernels, peeled, or 24 green peas)
12 stalks trefoil (or substitute watercress or flat-leaf parsley, chopped)

2½ cups *dashi* or good chicken stock, degreased
½ tsp salt
1 TBS soy sauce
1 TBS *mirin* or sake (or 1 tsp sugar)
4 eggs, lightly beaten until just mixed
4 ceramic cups (teacups are fine, even better if they have no handles)
foil or plastic wrap, 4 sheets large enough to cover cups

Marinate chicken in soy sauce and sake or *mirin* for 15–20 minutes. Drain and discard marinade.
Into the cups, place chicken, shrimp, and ginkgo nuts or substitutes.
To prepare custard, in a bowl, mix thoroughly *dashi* or stock with salt, soy sauce, and *mirin* or sugar.
Slowly add eggs, mixing well without raising bubbles.
Strain egg mixture carefully into cups, leaving a ½-inch clear space to the top.
Top with chopped greens; cover tightly with foil or plastic wrap.
Set cups in a steamer; steam over medium heat for 20 minutes.
Alternatively, arrange a grid inside a wok. Set cups on grid.
Pour hot water in wok well below the level of the grid and cups.
Cover wok and let water come to a gentle boil. Steam as directed above.
Serve at once.

Pearl Onions in Walnut Miso *Salad Dressing* (Kotamanegi no Kurumi Miso Ae)

This dressing comes from Yuzawa, Akita, in northern Japan. The original dish is made with tiny wild onions. This is served in individual small bowls as an accompaniment to meat or fish for an evening meal. Each serving is spooned into the middle of the bowl and left as a mound; the top of the salad should not be level.

3 cups small white onions
2 cups walnuts
2 TBS sugar, or to taste
2 TBS sake, or water

¼ cup *miso*
1 walnut half per diner, or a small
  watercress sprig, for garnish

Parboil the onions for 2–3 minutes. Depending on size, you may need to
  leave them longer. Take one, peel and taste; they should be cooked
  through but not mushy.
Quickly dip into cold water and drain thoroughly.
Peel the onions: the skins should slip off easily.
In a blender or food processor, blend the nuts with sugar until ground very
  fine.
Transfer nut mixture to a medium-sized bowl.
Mix in sake or water and *miso*; blend well to a thick paste. Check seasoning.
  Add more sugar to balance the saltiness of the *miso*, if desired.
Keep dressing and onions refrigerated until ready to serve.
One hour or preferably less before serving, blend dressing with peeled on-
  ions. (If mixed any earlier, moisture from the onions will seep through
  and spoil the appearance of the dish.)
Mound the salad in individual bowls; place the garnish just below the
  summit of the mound.

Grilled Skewered Chicken (Yakitori)

This is a very popular dish, often sold at outdoor kiosks during festivals, but
also offered in restaurants specializing in grilled skewered meats and vegetables.
Cook this for an outdoor barbecue, or, alternatively, cook under the grill indoors.
This method of grilling the ingredients separately at first, before threading them
through the skewers for the final grilling, ensures that every item is done
just right. Take care not to overcook the chicken; it should retain its moisture.
Serve as an appetizer with drinks, or as a side dish with rice, vegetables, and *miso*
soup.

2 pounds chicken thighs,
  deboned, skin left on, sliced
  into 2-inch cubes
4 TBS soy sauce
4 TBS *mirin* (sweet rice liquor,
  available from Japanese stores),
  or 2 TBS sugar and 2 TBS water
2 leeks, white part only, sliced
  into 2-inch lengths

12 small green bell peppers, left
  whole, including stalk, or 2
  large green bell peppers, cored,
  seeded, and cut into 1-inch
  cubes
1 tsp sugar
bamboo skewers, soaked in water
  1 hour before using
oil for greasing grill

Marinate chicken in soy sauce and *mirin* or sugar for 1 hour, turning several
  times to marinate evenly.

(continued)

Drain chicken; transfer to a bowl. Put marinade in a small pan, add sugar (if you are using *mirin*; omit if sugar has been used already) and boil till reduced by about half. Set aside.

Brush a grilling grid with oil; allow to heat up.

Place the leeks on the grid and grill at low medium heat until done, for about 3–5 minutes, turning them to cook evenly.

Next grill the peppers for about 1–3 minutes; these do not need to be turned.

Grill the chicken last of all, for about 3–4 minutes, turning them to cook evenly.

When the ingredients have cooled down a bit, thread them alternately on skewers: green pepper first, then chicken, then leek. Allow 2–3 skewers per person.

Brush the skewered items with the cooked marinade.

Grill for 1–3 minutes, or until heated through. Do not be alarmed if the chicken and vegetables get a few seared bits: to the contrary, these add to the flavor.

Brush with marinade again.

Serve hot.

Fruit Ice (Kōri)

This very popular summer treat is eaten throughout Japan. Shops selling it generally advertise with a blue, white, and red sign marked with the ideograph for "ice." Flavors depend on the customer's choice, as do the garnishes. Any kind of flavored fruit syrup is fine.

4 or more heaping cups shaved ice (if you do not have an ice shaver—available from most Oriental stores—crush ice cubes in a blender to a slush)

8 TBS or more flavored syrup (strawberry, raspberry, or melon)

Garnishes: A choice of canned orange or tangerine sections, apple slices, halved strawberries, blueberries, watermelon wedges about 2 inches long, melon balls, sweet red beans (*adzuki*, sold in small cans at Oriental groceries), or soft jelly bean candies.

Place four glass bowls in refrigerator for at least 1 hour before preparation.

Fill with shaved ice to make a mound.

Pour 2 tablespoons of your syrup of choice over the mound.

Garnish with fruit of your choice.

Serve with a dessert spoon.

Cheesecake (Chīzu Kēki)

Cheese is not part of traditional Japanese food culture, but, in modern times, cheesecake has become a part of everyday eating: most coffee shops will have it on the menu, and almost all bakeries and sweet shops up and down the country carry it. It is eaten as a snack or dessert, and is drunk with either Japanese green tea, Western tea, or freshly brewed coffee.

Cheesecake comes in several variations. "Rare" (*rea*) is the usual term for a refrigerated gelatin cheesecake. Another variation is flavored with green tea powder (the kind used for the traditional tea ceremony). The recipe given here is for a baked Japanese-style cheesecake.

1 cup cream cheese
2 ounces butter
½ cup whipping cream
¼ cup cake flour mixed with 1 TBS
  cornstarch
6 eggs, separated

¼ tsp salt
1 TBS lemon juice
1 tsp lemon rind, grated
¼ tsp cream of tartar
⅔ cup granulated sugar

Line the bottom and sides of an 8-inch cake pan with wax paper, to extend
  1½ inches above the pan. Lightly butter wax paper.
Melt cream cheese, butter, and cream in a double boiler over hot water.
Remove and quickly cool the mixture by placing in an iced basin, stirring
  well.
Mix in thoroughly flour, egg yolks, salt, lemon juice, and grated lemon rind.
Using an electric mixer, gently beat egg whites and cream of tartar.
Gradually add sugar and beat to soft peaks.
Fold in one-third of the whisked egg white into cream cheese mixture.
Fold in remaining egg white thoroughly, but do not overmix.
Pour into prepared cake pan.
Place pan inside a bain-marie or a baking tray.
Pour boiling water half way up the tray.
Bake in preheated 300°F oven for 1½ hours, or until set and golden brown.
Leave in the oven with door ajar for an hour until cake cools.
Remove from oven and unmold cake.
Refrigerate, covered.
Serve cold with Japanese or English tea.

JORDAN

The Kingdom of Jordan lies on the eastern bank of the Jordan River. The climate is desert hot with mild winters. The northwestern plateau and the Jordan Valley beneath it are very fertile, enabling the cultivation of vegetables, fruit, and wheat.

The population is largely Arab Muslim, divided between Bedouin and those of settled descent. The cuisine reflects this division, with nomadic and agricultural Middle Eastern dishes featuring on most meals.

Foodstuffs

- Flat breads (*khubes saj*), baked on a stone or an inverted iron bowl, are the staple for many. Oven-baked breads (*khubes tabun*). Whole-meal flat breads (*shrak*), soft or crisp, which are as thin as paper. Rice and noodles are common in urban areas.
- Meat, particularly mutton and chicken, is eaten as often as possible.
- Milk products include fresh and soured milk, both from cows and sheep. Milk is made into butter, thickened yogurt and dried yogurt (*labaneh* and *jameed*), and soft cheeses.
- Vegetables: tomatoes, cucumbers, peppers, onions, beans, sesame, eggplants. Many country people collect wild greens to add to the food.
- Fruit: apples, citrus, grapes, figs, pomegranates.
- Spices used include cumin, garlic, pepper, coriander, turmeric, ghee, and *sumac*, dried ground purple berries with a tangy lemon flavor.

Typical Dishes

- Rice dishes are common; particularly the nomad's *mansaf* (common dish), which is served to guests.
- Eggs, olives, white goat's cheese, *labane* (strained yogurt), and olive oil are the foods most commonly eaten at all times, by rich and poor alike, usually with tomatoes and cucumbers.
- *Fassouliah* (beans) of various sorts eaten as a mash, garnished with olive oil and scooped with flat breads.
- Many meals are composed of a single dish of meat and rice, with vegetables, which is shared by everyone.

- *Ma'alak*: lamb heart, lungs, liver, and innards, chopped and fried in garlic, often eaten on Friday mornings by many families for breakfast.
- *Musakhan*: wraps of chicken and onions cooked with sour, purple *sumac* spice.

Styles of Eating

- Three meals a day and snacks are eaten by most people, though Bedouin traditionally eat only twice a day (and only once on long journeys).
- In traditional homes, diners share common dishes of rice, meat, and flat bread, eating only with the three middle fingers of the right hand.
- Meals are often preceded by soup, drunk from glasses.
- Breakfast: freshly baked bread dipped in olive oil or yogurt; fresh-cut tomatoes, cucumbers, or onions. Washed down with sweet tea.
- Lunch: often skipped by Bedouin. Bean mash, a salad, boiled egg, and flat breads are common, washed down by sweet tea. It can be taken as a major meal in the form of a *mansaf* (a rice and lamb dish) if guests arrive.

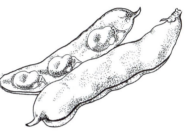

FAVA BEAN

- Evening meal: for urban people, the main meal of the day, though for many, a lighter meal. As main meal it will contain meat, if available, and rice and vegetables, sometimes cooked together.
- Fruit may be consumed at any time during the day.
- Coffee, tea, and juices are consumed, as are a variety of local and international sweet sodas. Coffee service can be elaborate in towns and countryside alike.

Fried Tomatoes
(Bandoora Maqliya Ma' thoom)

This is served as an appetizer in many urban homes.

4 cloves garlic
salt and pepper to taste
½ small hot pepper, cored, seeded, and shredded

2 TBS fresh parsley, chopped
2 TBS oil
2 large, firm tomatoes, thickly sliced

Crush garlic with pepper, salt, and hot pepper.

Stir mixture into parsley and set aside.

Heat oil in a frying pan over medium heat. Add the tomato slices and cook for about a minute on one side. Turn over and sprinkle slices with the garlic mixture.

Continue to cook for another minute, moving tomatoes gently with a spatula to keep them from sticking.

Turn slices again and cook until they are done but not disintegrating.

Slide the tomato slices onto a plate and serve immediately.

Country-Style Beans (Fassouliah al Balad)

This may be eaten as a main or only dish for lunch. It is also served as an appetizer in urban homes, particularly in the countryside. It is a Jordanian version of the Egyptian *ful medames*.

1 cup dried small fava beans, rinsed	3 medium onions, diced
8 cups water	5 cloves garlic, crushed
1 can cooked chickpeas, with liquid	¼ cup cilantro, finely chopped
2 medium potatoes, peeled and diced	1 can chopped tomatoes
¼ cup olive oil	1 tsp oregano
	salt and pepper to taste
	cayenne pepper to taste

Bring the fava beans and water to a boil in a large pot. Cover and cook over medium heat for an hour and a half.

Add potatoes and cook for a further 25 minutes.

Meanwhile, heat oil in a frying pan and sauté onions until golden.

Add garlic and cilantro and stir-fry for 2 minutes.

Add the contents of the frying pan with the remaining ingredients to the fava beans and bring to a boil.

Simmer over medium heat for 30 minutes.

Serve hot.

Note: If you use large fava beans you may need to soak them for 24 hours. Peel before cooking by squeezing between your fingers.

Meat and Rice Dish (Mansaf)

A typical Bedouin (nomad) dish, this is prepared for weddings and other celebrations such as welcoming a guest.

8 TBS ghee (clarified butter)	salt and pepper to taste
½ cup pine nuts	3 cups long-grain rice
½ cup flaked almonds	1 pound *jameed* (dried yogurt, or substitute 2 containers plain yogurt)
2 large onions, cut into thick slices	
1 tsp turmeric	
½ tsp allspice	2 TBS cornflour dissolved in 4 TBS water
½ tsp cinnamon	
2 pounds cubed stewing lamb	3–4 pieces of large, soft Middle Eastern flat bread (or 8 pita)
water as needed	

If you have no *jameed* (sometimes available from Middle Eastern shops), prepare the yogurt curd a day before by placing yogurt into a fine kitchen sieve or cheesecloth and allowing whey to drain. Reserve the whey and sieved curd separately.

Heat 2 tablespoons ghee in a frying pan and quickly fry pine nuts and almonds until golden. Remove and set aside.

Add 2 tablespoons ghee to frying pan, and sauté onions until softened, about 5–7 minutes. Add turmeric, allspice, and cinnamon, and fry for 1–2 minutes, stirring constantly. Set aside.

In a covered saucepan, simmer lamb with water just to cover for about 30 minutes; season with salt and pepper, add the spiced onion mixture, and continue to simmer until very tender, about 45–60 minutes more.

Meanwhile prepare the rice. Heat 1 tablespoon clarified butter in a heavy pot with a tight-fitting lid.

Stir in the rice and add 6 cups water. Bring to a boil, cover, and cook on very low heat until rice is done, about 15–20 minutes. Stir in 2 tablespoons ghee and let the rice rest undisurbed, covered, for about 15–20 minutes.

When the meat is done, transfer it to a covered oven-proof container and mix well with *jameed* or drained yogurt. Keep warm in a low oven until assembly.

To the broth in the saucepan, add the whey and cornstarch mixture and allow to thicken over medium heat, stirring constantly. Set aside.

To assemble (work quickly so that lamb is hot when it gets to the table): in a large, deep serving dish (a large enamel basin is often used), place a layer of the flat breads so they protrude above the dish rim and entirely cover the bottom.

Moisten the bread with some of the broth and whey mixture. (Place the rest in bowl or gravy boat for passing at the table.)

Place a pyramid of rice on the bread.

Arrange the meat on the rice. Decorate with pine nuts and almonds.

Mix remaining 1 tablespoon ghee with remaining whey and sprinkle over the rice.

Eat warm, not hot, with all diners helping themselves from the dish. Diners use only the right hand to make a small ball of rice and meat to pop into the mouth; the fingers must not touch the lips (takes some practice).

Meat and Eggplant Platter (Makhlubbi)

This is a popular dish for a main meal, usually served with pita bread, thick yogurt, and sliced cucumbers drizzled with olive oil and lemon juice.

1 medium eggplant, sliced ⅛-inch thick	¼ tsp ground allspice
	¼ tsp ground nutmeg
4 TBS olive oil	¼ tsp ground cinnamon
2 medium carrots, peeled and sliced into ⅛-inch disks	salt to taste
	½ tsp black pepper
1 pound lamb, cubed	water as needed
⅓ cup finely chopped onion	2 cups long-grain rice
2 cloves garlic, minced	¼ tsp turmeric

(continued)

| 2 fresh, firm tomatoes, cut in wedges | 4–5 sprigs of parsley |
| 2 lemons, cut in wedges | ¼ cup toasted almonds |

Salt eggplant and allow to drain for 30 minutes. Rinse, drain then pat dry.

In a large, heavy saucepan heat 2 tablespoons olive oil. Fry eggplant until golden. Remove and set aside. Fry carrots lightly in same pan. Remove and add to eggplant.

Add the remaining oil to the saucepan. Brown meat quickly, then add the onion and garlic and stir-fry for 2–3 minutes.

Stir in spices, salt, pepper, and 2 cups water.

Bring to a boil. Reduce heat and gently simmer, covered, until meat is tender (30–45 minutes).

Boil 3 cups water in a separate pot. Remove from heat. Add rice and turmeric. Stir once.

Cover and soak for 10 minutes. Drain and set rice aside.

Drain the meat, reserving the broth.

In a heavy saucepan with tight-fitting lid, place the meat in one layer.

Layer the fried vegetables over the meat.

Top with the soaked rice, carefully leveling it.

Add enough water to the reserved meat broth to make 4 cups. Slowly pour over the rice (do not stir).

Place the saucepan over medium heat, bring to a boil, and then reduce heat to gently simmer, covered, until all the liquid is absorbed (about 15 minutes).

Remove from heat and let stand, covered, for 15–20 minutes.

Invert the saucepan (you may need help from another person with this) on a large serving platter, at least 2–3 inches larger in diameter than the saucepan.

Let stand for 10 minutes to let the contents slowly descend.

Carefully remove the pan so that rice mound retains its shape.

Sprinkle with toasted almonds.

Garnish with tomato and lemon wedges and parsley.

Coffee (Qahwa)

This coffee is consumed all over the Middle East and is nowhere more important than among the nomads. The sound of the mortar and pestle means a guest has arrived (see also Eritrea for the box "Coffee Ritual").

| 2 TBS unroasted Arabica-type coffee beans | 4 cardamom pods |
| 3 cups water | 1–4 threads saffron (optional) |

Toast the coffee beans rapidly in an iron wok until they brown slightly and you can smell a strong coffee odor. Be careful not to burn.

Using a brass mortar and pestle, pound the beans thoroughly into as fine a powder as you can manage.

Boil water in a pot.

Add coffee and bring to a boil over low heat.

Remove from heat as the coffee foams up.

Allow to settle for a minute.

Add cardamom to the pot (and saffron if desired).

Boil again once and serve.

Pour carefully into small coffee cups, trying to avoid the sediment.

Allow a minute or two before drinking for the sediment to settle in the cup.

Do not stir.

KAZAKHSTAN

Kazakhstan, the ninth largest country in the world, spans three time zones, from the Caspian Sea to China. Once part of the Russian empire (from the eighteenth century), then the USSR, Kazakhstan became independent in 1991. The name Kazakh derives from Turkish and means "free or free-roaming," referring to the nomadic horseback lifestyle, and is related to the word "cossack." A third of the country is desert and a fifth is mountainous. It has four seasons with very cold winters and hot summers. Wheat, barley, rice, and other grains are widely grown, making Kazakhstan one among the world's largest grain exporters. Livestock is raised for meat and dairy products. Kazakhstan's coastline on the Caspian Sea also provides fish.

The main ethnic groups are Kazakhs and Russians, with minorities of Ukrainians, Uzbeks, Uighur, Germans, and Jews. Roughly half are Muslims and the remainder Christians, mainly Russian Orthodox.

Kazakh cuisine is similar to other nomadic central and northern Asian foods (Mongolian, Uzbek, Uighur) in its reliance on meat, fermented dairy products, and flat breads. It is strongly influenced by Russian, Tatar, central, and northeastern Asian (especially Korean) foods. In common with all nomadic cultures, Kazakhs are very hospitable and generous with food, even to unexpected guests.

Foodstuffs

- Staple is bread; fried bread (*baursak*) and flat bread (*non*, also *nan*).
- Meat: lamb, horse, camel, poultry (chicken, goose, turkey, pheasant, duck), fish (sturgeon, salmon, pike-perch, carp, bream), and fish roe (caviar).
- Preserved meats: horsemeat sausages (*kazy*, *shuzhuk*).
- Dairy products: sour cream, butter, yogurt, cheese from goat's, cow's, or horse's milk, dried or fresh curds, fermented milk drinks from yogurt, horse or camel milk.
- Onion, cabbage, eggplant, carrot, potato, greens, radish, cucumber, tomato, pumpkin, peas. Preserved vegetables: sauerkraut, Korean-style *kimchi* (spicy pickled cabbage).
- Apricots, apples, raspberries, strawberries, peaches, grapes (locally grown or imported from neighboring countries).

- Seasonings: onion, black pepper corns, garlic, bay leaf, dill, parsley, fennel, cilantro; *tuzdyk*—a special herb sauce with cilantro (*kinza*).

Typical Dishes

- *Besbarmak*—diamond-shaped pasta eaten with thin slices of horsemeat, mutton, or camel and vegetables. *Besbarmak* literally means five fingers, because the dish is eaten with the fingers of the right hand following Muslim eating tradition.
- Rice dishes: *plov* (pilaf) made with mutton, yellow turnip, and rice; sweet *plov* made of dried apricots, raisins, and prunes.
- *Naryn*: sliced sausages served with cold noodles for special occasions.
- Soups: fat-rich broth (*sorpa*), soup of internal organs.
- Grilled/roasted meats: brisket or leg of mutton marinated in vinegar, salt, and pepper and roasted over coals; skewered mutton or other meat (*shashlyk*) served with raw onion.
- Noodle dishes: layered pasta with spicy meat and vegetable gravy (*lagman*); noodles with meat and vegetable sauce of black radish, sweet pepper, onions, tomatoes, and cilantro, dill, or parsley (*kespe*).
- Meat pies: pastry stuffed with meat and onion or pumpkin, potato, cabbage, mushrooms or nuts (*samsa*), deep-fried with meat and onion (*chibureki*).
- Savory dumplings (*manty*) steamed and filled with lamb, mutton, horse, fish, or mixed with pumpkin or carrot; fried meat-filled dumplings (*beliashis*).
- Sweet steamed pastry rolls (*zhuta*) filled with pumpkin or carrot and sugar.
- Drinks: *kumys* (fermented mare's milk drink); *airan* (yogurt drink from horse's milk); *shubat* (drink from camel's milk). Salted milky tea is the most common drink.

Styles of Eating

- Three meals a day and snacks.
- Breakfast: millet porridge with sour cream, curd, or other dairy product; salty milk tea; or *nan* with *kumys* (fermented milk drink).
- Lunch: *nan*, *kumys*, curds or cheese, and fruit in summer; salty milk tea, noodles with soup and bits of meat in winter.
- Dinner: grilled meat with bread or *plov*; broth or soup; fruit; sweet.
- Snacks: savory or sweet pies (*samsa*, *chibureki*); fruits or nuts in syrup; fried fritters.
- Feasts: guests (expected or unexpected) are entertained lavishly with several courses, according to nomadic etiquette. First, fermented milk drinks; then salty milk tea accompanied by dairy products, dried and fresh fruit, fruit preserves, sweet fritters, cakes, other sweetmeats. Appetizers follow, usually assorted sausages and dried meats eaten with flat bread and salad. Next come boiled meats, eaten with pasta; the broth served separately. Afterward come grilled marinated meats, eaten with onion-flavored flat bread or fried bread. Sweetmeats and fresh and dried fruits end the feast.

FLAT BREAD

PILAF(S)

A dish of rice, fried quickly in hot oil, then cooked in stock with meat and vegetables, and fruit. The dish may be of Persian or central Asian origin. The word has numerous variants (*pilav*, *plov*, *polow*, *pulao*, and possibly Spanish *paella*) and is common throughout the Persian-influenced world. *Pilaf* is a very old dish and was served to Alexander the Great when he conquered parts of modern-day Uzbekistan. The national variants on *pilaf* are almost uncountable, and it is popular in the United States as "rice pilaf."

Radish Salad (Shalgam)

This is eaten as an appetizer during feasts.

2 TBS vegetable oil
2 TBS vinegar
½ tsp sugar
salt and cayenne pepper to taste
1 pound radishes, peeled and sliced into thin strips
2 bell peppers, cored, seeded, and sliced in thin strips

2 carrots, peeled and sliced in thin strips
1 onion, sliced in thin strips
1 cup finely shredded cabbage
1 clove garlic, finely minced

Prepare dressing by mixing oil, vinegar, sugar, salt, garlic, and cayenne.
Rub radishes and carrots with salt.
Reserve a bit of the peppers, radishes, and carrots for garnish.
Mix the remaining vegetables thoroughly. Pour on dressing and toss lightly.
Garnish with reserved vegetables and serve.

Noodles with Meat Sauce (Kespe)

This is a Kazakh staple. This particular recipe is tinged by Russian influences: dill and carrots. You may opt to buy dried egg noodles and cook according to the instructions instead of making your own from scratch, as the Kazakhs do. The greens often include cilantro, called *kinza* in Kazakh.

Meat Sauce

2 pounds mutton or beef, cubed
water to cover
salt and pepper to taste
2 carrots, peeled and chopped
4 large tomatoes, chopped, or 1 8-ounce can chopped tomatoes
1 onion, chopped

2 TBS melted fat (mutton fat preferred, or substitute butter)
2 bay leaves
2 cups *katyk* (goat's milk yogurt, or any plain yogurt)
½ cup dill, finely minced (or a mix of dill, cilantro, and parsley)

Place meat with water, salt, and pepper in a covered saucepan and bring to a
   boil.
Skim off scum and discard.
Reduce heat; simmer for 1 hour.
Add carrots, tomatoes, onion, fat, and bay leaves.
Season to taste.
Add noodles and cook until *al dente*.
Transfer to four bowls.
Place dill and *katyk* on the table for people to help themselves.
Serve very hot.

Egg Noodles

1 pound flour	¼ tsp salt
2 eggs, beaten	additional flour for rolling out
½ cup water	

Sift flour and salt into a bowl, making a crater on top.
Add beaten eggs. Mix in water a little at a time until the dough comes away
   from the side of the bowl.
Take dough out and knead on a floured board until shiny and elastic.
Let rest for 30–40 minutes, covered with a damp towel.
Roll out on floured surface about ¼-inch thick.
Slice into ½-inch-wide strips.
Allow to dry slightly, uncovered, until needed.

Stuffed Dumplings (Manty)

The term is similar to the Chinese *mantou* (steamed buns) and may well be
derived from the days the Kazakhs were a central part of the Mongol empire.
Manty are common throughout the Turkic-Mongol world, including, of course,
the Kazakhs. Grated carrot or pumpkin or a mixture of both is sometimes used
instead of meat. This is a special dish, made when there are many hands to help
wrap the dumplings.

1½ pounds flour	1 TBS oil for oiling steamer
1 tsp salt	3 cups sour cream
3 cups water	

Sift flour and salt into bowl.
Add water, a little at a time until you have a dough that comes away from
   the side of the bowl (you may need to add water or flour to get it
   right).
Knead in bowl for 5 minutes, then on a floured board until elastic and shiny.
Return to floured bowl and allow to rest for 30–40 minutes.
Roll out about ⅛-inch thick.

(continued)

Cut out pastry circles about 3 inches in diameter with a wide glass or cookie cutter.

Place a teaspoonful of stuffing in the center of the pastry circle. Fold up the edges to make a crescent. Crimp the edges firmly to seal.

Oil the top of a large steamer (metal or bamboo) to prevent sticking. (Or alternatively use a metal rack over a saucepan of boiling water.)

Place the stuffed pastries slightly apart and steam over boiling water for about $\frac{1}{2}$ hour until done (test one to check).

Transfer to a serving plate; pour over sour cream before serving.

Stuffing

1 pound minced meat (mutton or beef, or substitute grated carrot)	$\frac{1}{2}$ pound mutton fat (preferably from tail, or substitute more fatty meat or butter)
1 pound pumpkin flesh, grated	
2 onions, chopped fine	1 tsp salt

Mix meat, pumpkin, onions, fat, and salt thoroughly.

Steamed Carrot Roll (Zhuta)

Carrots are a common vegetable easily grown in Kazakhstan. Here they are used as a sweet stuffing.

$1\frac{1}{2}$ pounds flour	1 egg white, beaten, for sealing rolls
1 tsp salt	
$1\frac{1}{2}$ pints water	1 tsp oil for oiling steamer

Sift flour and salt into bowl.

Add water, a little at a time until you have a dough that comes away from the side of the bowl (you may need to add water or flour to get it right).

Knead in bowl for 5 minutes, then on a floured board until elastic and shiny.

Return to floured bowl and allow to rest for 30–40 minutes.

Roll out on floured board until $\frac{1}{8}$-inch thick.

Cover evenly with stuffing.

Roll up lightly, as for a Swiss roll, so that the filling does not ooze out.

Stick edges together with water or a little beaten egg white.

Place in an oiled *kaskan* (steamer) and steam for 25–30 minutes.

Serve warm or cold, sliced crosswise.

Sweet Stuffing

2 pounds carrot or pumpkin flesh, shredded	sugar to taste (the pumpkin and carrots may be sweet enough on their own)
3 ounces butter	

Melt butter in a large saucepan over medium heat.

Add vegetables and stir well.

Cook over low heat until tender.
Add sugar to taste.

Flavored Rice (Plov *or* Pilav)

This is a Kazakh variation—one of many across Asia—of a Persian original called *pilaf* (see box "Pilaf[s]").

2 TBS melted fat (mutton is recommended, or substitute butter)	2 large carrots, scraped and cut into julienne strips
1 onion, sliced into thin rings	2 cups rice, rinsed and drained
$\frac{1}{2}$ pound mutton or chicken breast, diced	$3\frac{1}{2}$ cups water
	1 cup dried apricots or apples, diced
	salt and pepper to taste

Heat fat over medium heat in a covered heavy saucepan.
Sauté onion until golden.
Add meat and fry until slightly browned.
Add carrots; season, and cook for an additional 5 minutes.
Pour rice over the vegetables and meat without stirring.
Carefully add water without disturbing the rice; bring to a boil.
Pierce rice in several places with the handle of a wooden spoon.
Top with dried fruit, again without disturbing rice.
Reduce heat to lowest, cover, and simmer for about 30–35 minutes.
Remove from heat, and let rest for 15–20 minutes.
While serving, ensure each helping has some of all three layers.

Sweet Fritters (Domalak Baursak)

These fried rolls are often eaten as snacks or served after meals as dessert.

1 cup cottage cheese	$\frac{1}{4}$ tsp salt
1 cup flour	8 cups water
1 egg, beaten	$\frac{1}{4}$–$\frac{1}{2}$ cup flour
1 TBS butter, melted	oil for deep-frying
1 TBS sugar	$\frac{1}{2}$ cup sour cream

In a food processor, process cottage cheese until smooth.
Add flour, egg, butter, sugar, and salt to make a stiff dough.
Remove dough and knead for 10 minutes until smooth and elastic.
Roll it out into a cylinder about $\frac{1}{2}$ inch in diameter. Cut into 2-inch slices.
Bring water to a simmer in a large pot.

(continued)

Add fritters a few at a time, and cook for 2–3 minutes after they float. Drain
  thoroughly.

Heat oil to 360°F.

Roll drained fritters in flour and slip into the hot oil a few at a time. Fry to a
  golden brown. Drain on paper towels.

To serve: arrange on serving dish, spoon sour cream over fritters, and serve.

Kazakh Cereal Bar (Zhent)

Zhent, often called Kazakh chocolate, makes a nutritious, energy-filled food for
journeys and at times of war. Though the end result bears no similarity in taste to
chocolate, it is comparable in sweetness, its provision of energy, and texture.
Irimshik, the dried curd that is one component, can be eaten on its own, much
like cheese. The original dish uses millet instead of oatmeal.

1 cup quick oatmeal flakes	¼ cup butter, melted
¾ cup *irimshik* (or substitute dry goat's or sheep's cheese or grated parmesan or other hard cheese)	½ cup sugar
	1 TBS raisins

In a food processor or blender, process cereal and cheese until well mixed.

Add butter and sugar, mixing well.

Stir in raisins.

Transfer to a flat tray to form a layer ½-inch thick, and allow to set for 1 hour.

Cut into cubes with a sharp, heated knife.

Serve as a snack.

Kazakh Tea (Chai)

Salted milk tea is drunk all over Central Asia. Sweet fritters, jam, butter or sour
cream, curds, dried fruit, and other sweetmeats are served with tea. Often in
winter, pieces of curd or dried meat are dropped into the tea, making it more of a
reviving soup.

4 cups water	2 cups milk
5 tsp loose black tea	sugar or honey to taste
4 cardamom pods	salt
1 tsp fennel seeds	butter or sour cream

Combine water, tea, cardamom, and fennel seeds and simmer over low heat
  for 3 minutes.

Add milk and simmer for an additional 2 minutes.

Strain tea into cups; add sugar or honey. Add salt, butter, or sour cream to taste.

KENYA

Kenya is an East African country, between Ethiopia and Somalia on the north and Tanzania to the south, bordered on the west by the African Rift system. The eastern coastline is hot and humid. The north is largely desert scrub. The rest of the country is largely a cool highland plateau. The Kenyan highlands are a source of various agricultural products ranging from vegetables and herbs to flowers. Much of the produce is exported to Europe and the Middle East.

Forty large ethnic groups and many more small ones make up the population, but a common staple is *ugali*, a stiff porridge made from white cornmeal (or, in some areas, sorghum or millet). Cooked to a thinner, gruel-like consistency called *uji*, it is served for breakfast. There is a dark *ugali* made from millet flour.

Foodstuffs

- Cornmeal, sorghum, millet are the main staples.
- Meat: goat and chicken are most common in the countryside. Beef and game can be found in the cities.
- Fish: fresh fish and seafood on the coast. Dried and smoked fish are used for flavoring in many households, depending on area.
- Milk and milk products are sold throughout the urban areas, less commonly in the countryside. Some ethnic groups (Maasai, Turkana, Massalit, Karomojong) who are cattle nomads subsist largely on milk or a mixture of milk and blood extracted from living cattle.
- Vegetables: greens such as spinach, onions, wild mushrooms in some areas.
- Fruit: plentiful tropical fruit; some local, some introduced. Mango, pineapples, strawberries, passion fruit have been introduced and are now raised commercially for export and local consumption. Native oranges, bananas, coconuts on the coast, baobab fruit are local fruits that are available most of the year.
- Preserved imports, particularly condensed milk and corned beef, have been incorporated into the cuisine.

Typical Dishes

- *Ugali*, a stiff porridge from cornmeal or millet, or *irio*, a more elaborate version, are the common staples.
- Grilled meat (*nyama choma*) is most popular in the cities and is made from goat, beef, or whatever is available. Grilled chicken (*mchuzi wa kuku*) is also very popular.
- *M'baazi* (cooked pea beans), which is sometimes an appetizer but may also be a main dish.
- *Samaki na nazi* (fish and coconut) is eaten along the coast.
- Common beverages include *maziwa ya kuganda* (sour milk), ginger beer, and sorrel tea. Many younger Kenyans drink large quantities of soda pops.

Styles of Eating

- People eat three meals a day if they can afford it.
- Middle-class Kenyans tend to eat like their European counterparts, and table settings include forks and spoons, glasses, and flat plates.
- In the countryside, traditional households eat around a shared dish of the staple, which is enlivened by side dishes. Food is brought to the table all at the same time, and people help themselves as they please. Often, dining is not around a table but with diners seated in armchairs, plate on one's lap.
- Breakfast consists of fresh or fried bread and coffee, and sometimes egg.
- Lunch and dinner tend to be similar: a staple with a stew of meat or vegetables, sometimes more than one stew if the person can afford it.
- Sweet things are rarely eaten, except fruit in season or during special occasions. Snacks of fruit sometimes supplement scant meals.

Corn and Beans Mash (Githeri)

Githeri is a traditional staple for the Kikuyu people of Kenya.

1 cup dried whole kernel corn (maize: the kind for tortillas is best), rinsed in cold water
1 cup dried beans (kidney, pinto, navy beans, or similar), soaked in cold water for a few hours and drained
water to cover
salt to taste

Combine corn and beans.
Add enough cold water to cover.
Bring to a boil and cook over high heat for 10 minutes.
Reduce heat.
Cover and simmer for 2 hours.
Cook until almost dry: most of the water should be absorbed or evaporated, and the corn and beans should be tender yet still intact, not mushy.
Season to taste.
Serve hot with any dish.

Corn, Peas, and Potato Staple (Irio)

This is a Kikuyu traditional staple, similar to, but more elaborate than, *githeri*.

1 cup dried peas soaked overnight
  or 1 pound frozen peas
1 large potato, peeled and diced
1 cup dried corn (maize) kernels or
  1 pound frozen corn

$\frac{1}{2}$ pound greens or spinach
salt and black pepper to taste
$\frac{1}{4}$ cup water
1 medium onion, finely chopped
  and fried brown

Boil peas in water to cover until nearly tender, about 20–30 minutes.
  Drain. (If using frozen peas, omit this step and merely add a few tablespoons water.)
In a heavy saucepan with tight-fitting lid, add the peas and all other ingredients. There should be just enough moisture in the vegetables themselves to eanable them to steam-cook. (If not, add $\frac{1}{4}$ cup water.)
Season with salt and pepper, and simmer until tender, about 20 minutes.
Mash with a potato masher until smooth and thick (or puree in blender or
  food processor).
Serve hot with roasted or barbecued meat (to make *nyamana irio*) and
  gravy.

Bean Stew

This might be served for any meal.

2 cups dried beans (any kind,
  although pigeon peas are
  most common)
1$\frac{1}{2}$ pints boiling water
2 TBS oil
1 pound stewing beef, cut into
  1-inch cubes
1 large onion, coarsely chopped
2 large potatoes, peeled and cubed

2 medium carrots, peeled and cut
  in rounds
$\frac{1}{2}$ pound kale or cabbage, tough
  ribs discarded
1 cup fresh or frozen maize kernels
1 tsp curry powder
salt to taste
$\frac{1}{2}$ pint boiling water

Add beans to boiling water in a large stewing pot.
Remove from heat and let stand, covered, for 2 hours or overnight.
Drain and simmer in water to cover for 20 minutes.
Meanwhile, heat oil in a frying pan and brown the meat.
Add onion and fry until golden, stirring constantly.
Stir in meat and onion mixture and all other ingredients to the beans.
Add boiling water and simmer for 30–45 minutes until meat is tender.
Serve with *ugali* (see Angola for the box "African Staple") as main dish.

Cooling Relish (Saladi)

This salad relish is added to and mixed with hot spicy food a little at a time to "cool" the spiciness of the dish and change its texture.

2 cups cabbage, finely shredded
$\frac{1}{2}$ cup carrots, scraped and sliced very thin
$\frac{1}{2}$ cup scallions, sliced very thin

$\frac{1}{4}$ cup green bell pepper, cored, seeded, and cut into fine strips
1 TBS lime juice

Toss ingredients together.
Serve in small individual bowls.

Pea Beans or Pigeon Peas (M'baazi)

This is a standard side dish for many Kenyan families. You can substitute any bean for the traditional pigeon pea.

1 cup dried beans, soaked overnight
1 quart boiling salted water
2 TBS vegetable oil
$\frac{1}{2}$ cup onions, chopped fine
$\frac{1}{2}$ cup green bell pepper, cored, seeded, and chopped fine

1 tsp salt
$\frac{1}{4}$ tsp crushed red pepper flakes or one whole chili pepper
1 cup coconut milk

Simmer beans for 1 hour in salted water until tender. Drain.
In a separate pot heat oil and sauté onions until brown. Add green pepper and seasoning.
Add beans and coconut milk.
Simmer gently until sauce is thickened.
Correct the seasoning.
Serve hot or cold with *ugali* (see Angola for the box "African Staple").

Barbecued Meat (Nyama Choma)

This is the favorite dining-out dish of most Kenyan families. Nairobi has hundreds, perhaps thousands, of places that serve roast meat to avid customers.

2–3 pounds of any piece of meat suitable for roasting (beef chuck ribs, rolled ribs, rump, pork shoulder or leg)

2 cloves garlic, minced
juice of 1 lemon
about 1 TBS curry powder
about 1 TBS turmeric powder

about 1 TBS coriander powder   salt and black pepper to taste
about 1 TBS chili powder

Combine garlic, lemon juice, and spices (to taste) in a large bowl. Mix well.
Add meat and rub marinade all over. Allow to marinate at least 1 hour.
Grill meat over charcoal or broil it under a grill. Use a meat thermometer to
    check for doneness.
Serve with *ugali* or with *irio.*

Mango Ice Cream

Mangoes are common fruits in season, and people consume huge amounts
raw. The pulp is available canned throughout Kenya and for export. Wealthier
households make this for dessert or for a snack.

4 or 5 ripe mangos, peeled, pitted, $\frac{1}{2}$ cup condensed milk
    and mashed (about 2 cups) $\frac{1}{2}$ tsp salt
2 TBS lemon rind shredded fine or   1 cup heavy cream
    grated $\frac{1}{2}$ cup sugar

Combine mashed mangos, rind, condensed milk, and salt.
Whip cream with sugar until it stands in stiff peaks.
Fold the fruit mixture into the whipped cream.
Pour into freezer trays or an ice cream freezer and freeze. Break up ice
    crystals after 1 hour and return to freezer for another hour. Beat the
    frozen mango cream again to break up the crystals, and return to freezer
    to freeze for 2 hours or until solid (or use ice cream churn following
    instructions).

KIRIBATI

 A cluster of 33 coral atolls in the Pacific straddling the equator, formerly known as the Gilbert Islands, Kiribati (pronounced *keer-ree-bahss*) became independent in 1979 under the new name. The atolls are sandy, with little arable land, and so edible plants are carefully gardened. The climate is tropical, mediated by cool trade winds, which keeps the temperature comfortable throughout most of the year. Kiribati has been strongly influenced by British, missionary, and more recently, Japanese food practices.

Foodstuffs

- Breadfruit and, more recently, rice are the common staples.
- The most valuable plant is the coconut, which provides food, drink, and cooking oil, among other uses.
- Fish are an important food resource. Marine foods include tuna and other large fish from the deep sea, and coastal cockles, octopus, clams, sea urchin, eels, and squid. Milkfish are today raised in ponds on some of the islands.
- Pandanus flour (*te kabubu*) and other products made from the pandanus (screwpine) fruit are important food sources. The fruit rarely ripens in other places, and it is perhaps the most unique Kiribati food resource.
- Among the more northern islands, taro and a variety of tree figs are cultivated.
- Due to the common occurrence of drought (and consequent famine), the population has evolved methods of preserving as many foods as possible—coconuts, pandanus fruit, taro, fish—by drying and fermentation.
- Introduced foods include canned tuna and corned beef, evaporated milk, and granulated sugar.

Typical Dishes

- Pancakes, on their own or with jam.
- Raw tuna with rice and soy sauce; grilled fish; fish tempura; dried, salted octopus eaten raw or grilled.
- Boiled breadfruit as a side dish, fried breadfruit chips.
- Pigs roasted in an earth oven.

- Imported instant noodles (usually chicken flavored), eaten as part of a meal with rice and sometimes brought to celebratory meals as well.
- Imported corned beef, either fried or straight out of the can.
- The most common drink is palm toddy (*karewe*), the sap of the palm. This can be concentrated into a syrup—*te kamaimai*—which is diluted with water to make a sweet refreshing drink, or fermented.

Styles of Eating

- If possible, people eat three times a day with snacks.
- People eat from their own plates from a common serving dish, with little ceremony. Food is scarce in the islands and sharing food is common.
- Breakfast: usually rice with soy sauce, washed down with a coconut toddy drink (*te kamaimai*).
- Lunch and dinner are no different in composition: rice or taro with fish or some other protein, or whatever is available, preserves or pickles.
- Snacks: dried sea worms, which are chewed like chewing gum; potato or breadfruit crisps; Chinese dried plums; ice pops made from powdered milk, mixed with coconut toddy or sugar and dyed bright colors; pancakes (which may also be part of a main meal).
- On special occasions, pork, taro, fish, and other foods wrapped in leaves and cooked for several hours in an earth oven are consumed.

Corned Beef Stew

As in many places in the world that have been exposed to European and American food ways, corned beef has become a delicacy that is often made and consumed at festivals and parties.

1 can corned beef	2 TBS tomato ketchup
1 TBS oil	soy sauce to taste

Break the corned beef up into small chunks.
Heat oil in a wok and stir-fry the beef until warmed through and slightly browned.
Add the ketchup, stirring constantly.
When the ketchup has been absorbed, add soy sauce to taste.
Serve over rice.

Ice Pops

The climate makes cold foods very attractive, and the fairly recent introduction of refrigeration means that some households can prepare a kids' favorite, with a local twist.

1 cup powdered milk

2 cups palm toddy (or $1\frac{1}{2}$ cups light sugar syrup mixed with

$\frac{1}{2}$ cup coconut water), warmed (not boiled)

food dye of your choice

Dissolve milk powder in warm toddy.

Allow to cool.

Add food coloring if desired and mix well. Cool.

Freeze in ice tray.

Serve as a snack.

KOREA

Korea is located on a peninsula in East Asia between Japan and China. It was a Japanese colony between 1911 and 1945 and subsequently suffered a devastating civil war (complicated by a UN war with China). The climate is temperate: warmer and subtropical in the south, cooler to cold in the north. The substrate of the land is largely granite, and so is not all suitable for cultivation.

The population is almost homogeneously Korean, save for a tiny Chinese minority. The country is divided into two political regimes. There is little traditional, linguistic, or culinary difference between the two states except for that imposed by differences of rule over the past half-century.

North Korea (north of the 38th parallel) is a poor, underdeveloped state, controlled by a Communist dynasty. The North has been unable to feed its population for decades. The South is a successful industrial state, whose farmers have been able, in recent years, to supply most food needs.

The traditional preferred staple is rice. The North tends to be cooler than the South, so rice does not grow well, and the staple is sometimes barley and sweet potatoes (when available).

Korean food is influenced by China through historical cultural exchanges and, to a limited extent, by Japan. There are similarities to Mongolian food, notably in the preference for meat, particularly grilled. However, Korean food is distinguished by a liberal use of chili peppers, garlic, green onions, and sesame oil.

Foodstuffs

- Staples: rice, wheat noodles, soybean products.
- Barley, millet, buckwheat, maize, potato.
- Beef, pork, chicken, fish, seafood (clams, oysters, octopus).
- Vegetables: fresh and pickled Chinese cabbage, turnips, garlic, cucumber, soybean (including sprouts), mung bean, red bean, dried or fresh wild vegetables, mushrooms, gingko nuts, day lily buds, water chestnut, eggplant, pumpkin, assorted gourds, sweet potato, assorted seaweed.
- Fruits: persimmon, apple, Asian pear, plum, peach, citrus (mandarin, clementine).
- Seasonings: chilies, garlic, green onions, sesame oil; soy sauce, soybean paste (*doenjang*).

Typical Dishes

- Stews (*chige*, also spelled *jjigae*) of meat or fish or soybean curd and seasonal vegetables such as zucchini, spinach, carrots. The most popular stew (*doenjang jjigae*) is flavored with soybean paste and is claimed as the national dish. Barbecued meats, marinated in chilies, garlic, green onions, and sesame oil, grilled at the table.
- Japanese-style dishes: noodles in soup (*udong*), seaweed rolls (*gimbap*), raw fish.
- Chinese-style stir-fried dishes of meat and vegetables.
- Salads (*namul*) of soy bean sprouts and reconstituted wild vegetables.
- Drinks: green tea, ginseng tea, rice wine (*takju*), rice liquor (*soju*), coffee, bottled fruit and carbonated drinks. Ginseng tea is consumed frequently for health.

Styles of Eating

- Three main meals daily, and snacks. North Koreans suffer from hunger and malnutrition in many cases, and rarely eat as much.
- Traditional meals are eaten with metal utensils (bowl, chopsticks, and spoon). Unlike in China and Japan, the rice bowl is not raised to the lips: rice is eaten with a spoon.

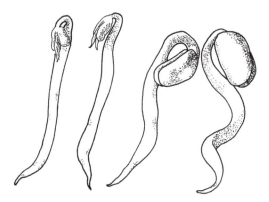

SOYBEAN AND MUNGBEAN SPROUTS

- *Kimchi* (peppery pickled vegetables), most commonly of Chinese cabbage, accompany every meal.
- Breakfast: rice, pickles, soup of beef ribs or fish, ginseng or barley tea; savory pancake with vegetables (*pajyong*); rice porridge (*juk*) with egg, fish, or meat.
- Lunch: stew (*jjigae*) of meat or seafood or *tubu* (soybean curd) with vegetables, pickles, rice, barley or ginseng tea.
- Dinner: grilled meat or fish, rice, pickles, seasoned vegetables (*namul*), tea.
- Snacks: traditional cakes (*deok*) of rice flour, millet, and other grains stuffed with red beans, persimmon, and other fruits for sweet types, and made with garlic chives and egg for savory type; Western cakes with coffee; street snacks of sausage (*sundae*), wheat noodles in anchovy soup (*guksu*), or *kimbap* (rolls of rice and shredded vegetables wrapped in seaweed, similar to Japanese *sushi* rolls, but not quite so).
- There are many types of eating venues, from itinerant peddlers and street stalls to Korean and international food restaurants, including multinational fast food chains. Little dishes of assorted accompaniments (*banchan*), for example, fresh shucked oysters, stir-fried anchovies, garlic-chive fritters, and seasoned vegetables (*namul*), come with restaurant meals, the number depending on the type (and price) of food. Pickles are a subset of *banchan*.

Barbecued Short Ribs (Kalbi-gui, *also* Galbi-gui)

Kalbi-gui are marinated overnight, usually in sesame oil, soy sauce, garlic, sugar, green onions, ginger, and other spices. Rice wine may be added for flavor

KIMCHEE

Koreans pride themselves on their *kimchee* (pickles). Pickles are so important for the Korean diet that there is a *kimchee* museum in Seoul, celebrating the thousands of varieties. *Kimchee* is made from firm vegetables—Chinese cabbage and various radishes are favorites—well flavored with salt and chilies, and there are many local variants. Other ingredients such as dried shrimp or fish are often added. In traditional Korea, *kimchee* was made in late summer. The pickles were placed in large (2–3 feet long) black glazed jars, which were well sealed and placed in an area with constant light warmth. In many rural areas it was usual, until the late 1970s, to see several *kimchee* jars half-buried in compost heaps in every yard.

and as tenderizer. The marinated meat is cooked at the table on a metal grid over a burner; traditionally, this was a clay burner with charcoal. Each diner picks a piece of cooked beef with metal chopsticks, and wraps it in a fresh lettuce leaf together with a bit of rice, pickled or fresh vegetables, or any other garnish laid out on little bowls on the table. If pork is used, the dish is called *dwaeji kalbi-gui*. This dish is for an evening meal. Serve accompanied by plain rice, pickled vegetables (*kimchee*), a vegetable salad (*namul*), and soup (see box "Kimchee").

$1\frac{1}{2}$ pounds beef or pork short ribs, about 2–$2\frac{1}{2}$ inches long	1 TBS black bean paste
2 tsp water	1 tsp sugar
2 tsp scallion, minced	$\frac{1}{4}$ tsp cayenne pepper
1 clove garlic, minced	$\frac{1}{2}$ TBS ginger, grated
3 tsp thick soy sauce	$1\frac{1}{2}$ tsp brown sugar
1 tsp sesame oil	1 tsp sesame seed, toasted
	1 tsp oil

Combine all ingredients and allow beef to marinate overnight, refrigerated.
Broil over very hot charcoal or under very hot grill.
Serve with white rice and dipping sauce on the side.

Dipping Sauce

chili sauce to taste	1 tsp sesame seed, toasted
salt to taste	1 tsp scallions, minced fine
1 garlic clove, crushed	1 tsp sesame oil

Combine all ingredients about 1 hour before use.

Noodles and Beef (Chapjae, *also* Japchae)

A dish commonly served at parties and special occasions, *chapjae* can be made with any type of vegetable in season. Vegetables are fried separately in a small amount of oil. Instead of ground beef, strips of beef, pork, or chicken can be used.

3 TBS vegetable oil
½ pound ground beef
½ pound cellophane noodles
  (available in Oriental stores),
  soaked in cold water for
  10 minutes
boiling water to cover noodles
½ bunch spinach (about 1 cup
  when cooked)
6 *shiitake* mushrooms, fresh or
  dried and soaked for 10 minutes
  in hot water, woody stem end

removed and discarded,
  chopped fine
1 onion, chopped
1 carrot, peeled and cut into
  julienne strips
1 TBS sesame seeds
1 TBS sesame oil
¼ cup soy sauce
1 TBS brown sugar
2 cloves garlic, minced
salt and pepper to taste

Heat 1 TBS oil in a wok. Brown meat. Set aside.
Blanch noodles in boiling water for about 2–3 minutes. Rinse in cold water
  immediately and drain.
Blanch spinach quickly in boiling water. Plunge immediately in cold water to
  keep color. Drain and chop roughly.
Heat remaining oil and stir-fry mushrooms, onion, and carrot until almost
  tender.
Stir in meat, spinach, and noodles, frying briefly.
Add sesame seeds, sesame oil, soy sauce, sugar, and garlic.
Adjust seasoning.
Serve hot.

Vegetable and Beef Rice Bowl
(Bibimbap)

Bibimbap is a one-dish meal of rice mixed with assorted vegetables, usually
served with pickles and soup, and a dollop of hot pepper sauce (*chojang*).

2 carrots, cut into julienne strips
2 zucchini, cut into julienne
  strips
2 cups soybean or mung bean
  sprouts, rinsed and drained
6 dried *shiitake* mushrooms,
  presoaked in hot water, drained,
  woody stems discarded, and
  sliced
salt and cayenne pepper to taste
2 cups spinach, blanched, then
  plunged into cold water,
  drained

1 cup icicle radish (*daikon*), cut
  into julienne strips
4 cups cooked rice (this can be all
  white rice, or two-thirds rice
  cooked with one-third barley)
1 pound beef, ground or thinly
  sliced
2 TBS soy sauce
1 TBS sesame oil
1 tsp sugar
about ¼ cup vegetable oil for
  frying
4 eggs

Put vegetables into separate bowls. Season with salt and cayenne pepper to
taste. Allow to rest for 5 minutes, then drain and discard excess liquid.
Mix soy sauce, sesame oil, and sugar in a bowl. Marinate meat for 5 minutes
in this mixture.
Heat 1 TBS oil in a wok. Brown meat. Set aside.
Using 1 TBS oil each time, stir-fry vegetables separately, except spinach and
radish. Set aside.
Divide hot cooked rice into four individual bowls.
Arrange vegetables and beef over the rice in pie-shaped wedges, radiating
around an empty space in the center to make room for the egg.
Heat oil.
Fry eggs (sunny side up) to desired state; lightly season with salt.
Place egg in the center, surrounded by the vegetables.
Serve with vinegar and *chojang*.

Vinegar and Hot Pepper Sauce (Chojang)

Koreans adore the bite of strong hot peppers. *Chojang* is almost always present
on the table as a relish at any meal.

5 TBS hot (peppery) soybean paste
(*kochujang*, available from
Korean stores, or substitute a
hot soybean paste available
from Chinese stores)

2 TBS brown-colored rice vinegar
(available also in Chinese food
stores)
1½ tsp sugar
½ tsp sesame oil

Mix all ingredients thoroughly.
Adjust seasoning to your liking.
Serve with any one-bowl rice dish.

Cucumber Salad (Oi Namul)

Namul are salads of fresh seasonal vegetables, or reconstituted dried wild
vegetables such as fern fronds or bellflower roots, which are usual relishes for a
meal. They are flavored with salt or hot soybean paste (*gochujang*), toasted sesame
seeds, sesame oil, vinegar, green onions, and garlic.

3 cucumbers, each 4–5 inches long
(Asian variety preferable),
sliced into thin rounds
1 TBS salt

1 garlic clove, minced
¼ tsp salt
1 tsp toasted sesame seeds (to
toast: dry fry in a skillet over

(*continued*)

low heat until the seeds start   a pinch of sugar
    to "jump")   1 tsp sesame oil
¼ tsp cayenne pepper

Sprinkle salt over cucumber slices, mix well, and let stand for 30 minutes.
Place the cucumbers in a damp cloth and gently squeeze out liquid.
Toss with rest of ingredients, adding sesame oil last.

Three-Color Dumplings (Samsaekchuak)

Red, green, and white are the Korean national colors. Three-color dumplings
are served during festivals and sometimes offered at temples. These sweet
dumplings are served as a snack with ginseng, green, or barley tea.

4 cups glutinous rice flour   2 tsp cinnamon
    (available from Oriental stores)   1 tsp honey
1 TBS salt   1 or 2 drops food coloring (red,
20 dried Chinese dates (jujubes;   green), each dissolved
    available from Chinese stores,   separately in 1 TBS water
    or substitute small dried   oil for deep-frying
    dates), pitted and chopped   ½ cup honey dissolved in
    fine   equivalent hot water

Divide rice flour into three equal parts.
Add food coloring separately to two of the three parts and mix well.
Gradually add hot water and knead each of them into a smooth, elastic
    dough.
Mix jujubes with 1 teaspoon honey and cinnamon to make the filling.
Shape the dough into dumplings about the size of a golf ball.
Make a cavity in each ball with a finger. Insert ½ teaspoon of filling and seal
    well, smoothing dough over the opening.
Heat oil to 340°F in a deep pot or a wok. Deep-fry dumplings until crisp and
    golden brown in color. Drain off excess oil on paper towels or a rack.
While dumplings are still hot, soak in honey-water.
To serve, arrange in a pyramid on a serving plate. Serve warm with tea.

KURDISTAN

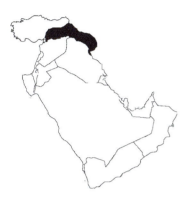

The Kurds are a Middle Eastern people speaking an Indo-Aryan language related to Persian. Largely farmers and to a lesser extent nomads, some 25 to 40 million Kurds live at the conflux of the borders of Iran, Iraq, Syria, and particularly Turkey, where they are the majority people in the eastern third of the country. The area largely populated by Kurds is about 74,000 square miles, though the country is not a recognized national or international entity.

Due to the Kurds' intermingling with other populations, many of their dishes are claimed by other countries (Turkey, Syria, Iraq, or Iran). The Kurds identify certain dishes as typically theirs, though many of those are likely adaptations or borrowings from their neighbors.

Foodstuffs

- Staples: rice, *bulghur* (cracked wheat), flat breads baked on the sides of a *tabun* (circular oven), vegetables, plain yogurt, cheese.
- Vegetables: squash, cucumbers, tomatoes, onions, peppers, eggplant, and greens.
- Fruit: watermelons, melons, figs, grapes, apricots, pomegranates.
- Flavoring: pepper, cumin, and garlic are common spices; hot peppers are used sparingly.

Typical Dishes

- *Mezes* (appetizers) and salads: marinated lamb liver fried in olive oil, served with onions and parsley (*ciger*); chopped onion, tomatoes, red peppers, cucumber, and mint (*ezme*); grilled eggplant with cultured yogurt and garlic (*alinazik*); green beans with olive oil, tomatoes, and onions (*sholik*); *bulghur* and vegetables (*kisir*); lamb kidneys with feta cheese, tomato paste (*gurchuk*); fried eggplant with green pepper, baby marrow, and garlic yogurt (*kizartma*); eggplant stuffed with vegetables served with salads (*badiljane tijikiri*); *bulghur* with mushrooms (*savare kariya*); lamb hearts stuffed with rice, meat, raisins, walnuts, and pine nuts in a curried apricot sauce (*giri-giri*).
- Soups: rice and yogurt soup sprinkled with dried mint (*yayla*); meat-stuffed *bulghur* dumplings in a sour soup (*kubbeh khamoustah*).

- Meat dishes: lamb cooked with spices, served with garlic yogurt (*haran*); spicy lamb with green peppers and onion in a tomato and garlic sauce wrapped in flat bread (*serok*); lamb with vegetables grilled on skewers (*sikh kebab*); lamb ribs cooked with pickled onions (*yagni*); sweet and sour chicken with herbs (*zozan*).
- The star of Kurdish cooking is *kubbeh* (also *kibbeh*). These *bulghur* dumplings are made in many ways, and are served in soups (red on the basis of tomatoes, or green on the basis of sour herbs), on their own, and with many different kinds of fillings. *Kubbeh* soup is a meal in itself.
- Sweet dishes: dates and nuts rolled in phyllo pastry served with ice cream or yogurt (*hurma sarma*); syrup-cooked pumpkin (*sirini*); apricots stuffed with cream and almonds (*kaysi dolma*); baked rice pudding flavored with sugar and cinnamon (*sutlatch*).
- Tea is sweetened traditionally by a sugar cube held under the tongue while sipping.

Styles of Eating

- Kurds in the towns eat three meals a day and snacks. Country people might eat only once or twice a day.
- Traditional dining is around dishes on a carpet, with everyone helping themselves to what takes their fancy. All foods are served together.
- Breakfast: bread, yogurt, or *laban*, tea or coffee.
- Lunch and dinner: main dishes such as *kubbeh*; salads; a sweet; tea or coffee. For guests, the same meal will be made more elaborate with several kinds of *kubbeh*, meat, rice, and whatever the household can afford.

Chickpea Salad

This is served at any meal as a salad.

¼ cup extra-virgin olive oil
1 TBS toasted cumin seeds
1 small red onion, finely chopped
1 clove garlic, minced
½ inch fresh ginger, grated
½ tsp salt
½ tsp pepper
⅛ tsp cayenne pepper

2 TBS fresh lime juice
1 large tomato, diced
2 cups canned chickpeas
 (*garbanzos*), rinsed and drained
 (or substitute black beans,
 kidney beans, or white beans)
½ cup chopped fresh cilantro

Heat oil in a pan and add cumin seeds; cook just till fragrant.
Add onion and garlic and sauté until onion is tender.
Add ginger, salt, pepper, cayenne, lime juice, tomato, and chickpeas, and simmer for 5 minutes or until hot.
Serve salad hot, garnished with chopped cilantro.

Okra and Stuffed Bulghur
(Kubbeh Bamya, *also* Kibbeh Bamya)

Kubbeh appear in many forms. This dish would be served either as part of the appetizers, or as a main dish.

1 large onion, minced fine	1 tsp salt
salt to taste	2 TBS oil
1 pound ground meat (mutton preferably, or beef)	1 TBS garlic, crushed
1 TBS mixed cumin and cardamom powder	1 ripe tomato, chopped
1 pound fine *bulghur* or semolina, rinsed and drained	1 pound okra, cut for more glutinous consistency, whole for less
½ pound plain flour	2 TBS tomato paste
2 tsp oil	½ TBS sugar
	¼ cup lemon juice, strained

Make the filling: season onion with salt and let stand for 10 minutes.
Squeeze to remove excess juice. Add meat and spices.
Mix thoroughly with moistened hands or in a food processor.
Make the shells: place *bulghur,* flour, oil, and salt in a bowl. Knead the mixture vigorously or pound in a mortar and pestle for about 15–20 minutes until pasty. Alternatively, blend in a food processor until smooth.
Divide the mixture into twelve portions.
With moistened fingers, roll each into a lemon shape.
To fill the kubbeh: take one in the palm of your moistened left hand.
Create a long, narrow cavity in the kubbeh with one finger, while turning the shell around with your left hand. Try not to pierce through to the exterior, but if this happens, simply moisten a finger and smooth out the crack.
Carefully push in 1 tablespoon of the meat mixture into the cavity.
Seal the cavity closed, and taper the ends gently.
Lay each *kubbeh* aside carefully.
Heat oil. Sauté garlic for 1 minute over low heat.
Add tomato and okra. Cook for 10–15 minutes until softened.
Add tomato paste and 1 cup water. Raise heat to medium and bring to a boil.
Add lemon juice, sugar, and salt to taste. Simmer for 10 minutes.
Keep the sauce simmering and carefully slip in the *kubbeh.*
Cover and gently simmer for 15–20 minutes.
Serve for the main meal.

Pine Nut–Stuffed Bulghur *Dumplings*
(Kubbeh Mahsh, *also* Kibbeh Mahshi)

Though claimed by many in the Middle East, this is considered by Kurds to be their national dish. It is said that a Kurdish woman cannot be married until she can prepare *kubbeh* properly. The end product must be firm, the exterior crisp but not dry. *Kubbeh* can be served as the main dish or as appetizers.

2 cups *bulghur* (cracked wheat)	$\frac{1}{4}$ tsp freshly grated nutmeg
1 pound lamb, finely minced	1 tsp cinnamon powder
1 large onion, peeled and finely minced	$\frac{1}{2}$ tsp turmeric powder
	3 ounces pine nuts
salt and black pepper to taste	vegetable oil for deep-frying

Soak *bulghur* in cold water for 10 minutes, then squeeze out and mix with meat, onion, spices, and seasonings.

Pound ingredients until thoroughly pasty (traditional), or run through a food processor. The result should be a firm paste.

Wet both hands, then take a small lump of the mixture (about the size of a medium egg) and form it around your forefinger to an even thickness all over. The result should be the shape of a short sausage (moisten if necessary and smooth over all cracks).

Fill each shell loosely with about 1 teaspoon of pine nuts.

Smooth the ends to seal.

Heat oil in a deep pan to moderate heat, then carefully slip in two or three shells and fry for about 5 minutes, until browned and crisp all over. Do not cook more than two or three at a time to avoid sticking and cracking.

Drain thoroughly and serve hot or cold with salad and yogurt.

Serve as appetizer in a *meze* or as main dish.

Pumpkin in Syrup (Shirini)

This is a frequently made sweet.

$1\frac{1}{2}$ cups sugar	into large chunks
1 cup water	1 cup chopped walnut meats
1 pound pumpkin, washed, seeded, peeled, and cut	

Simmer the sugar and water until sugar is completely dissolved and syrup is slightly thickened.

Add the pumpkin pieces and gently cook, without stirring, until the syrup is almost completely absorbed and the pumpkin is tender, about 20–25 minutes. Watch carefully to ensure the pumpkin does not burn.

Arrange the cooked pumpkin on a plate and garnish with walnuts.

Serve with thick yogurt as a snack.

Kurdish Tea (Chai Kurdi)

Like many Middle Eastern societies, the Kurds are very fond of sweet things, accompanied by tea. Tea is an important part of hospitality.

1 TBS tea leaves	2 cups boiling water
1 4-inch cinnamon stick	8 sugar cubes

Pour boiling water over tea and cinnamon in a teapot.
Steep for 5 minutes.
Pour into small glasses (or cups) about $\frac{1}{2}$ cup in volume.
Place a sugar cube between your teeth.
Sip the hot tea through the sugar cube.
Repeat for a second glass.

KUWAIT

Kuwait is a kingdom in the Middle East, on the shores of the Persian Gulf, sandwiched between Iraq and Saudi Arabia. It is slightly smaller than New Jersey. It has intensely hot and humid summers and short, cool winters. Much of the land is flat and arid.

Kuwait being a Muslim nation, Eid-el-Adha (Abraham's Sacrifice), Eid-el-Fitr (End of Ramadan), and Muharram (Muslim New Year) are celebrated. Kuwait enjoys a high standard of living due to the income from petroleum. Virtually all foods are imported. Large number of non-Kuwaitis, mainly from the Indian subcontinent, have brought an Indian influence to the cuisine.

Foodstuffs

- Rice, breads of wheat flour are the popular staples.
- Seafood of all kinds is very common.
- Preferred meats are lamb and camel calf.
- Dates are popular, both grown locally and imported from Iraq.

Typical Dishes

- Deep-fried, baked, and mixed dishes of vegetables and meat cooked with rice are popular.
- *Mechbous*, a spiced mixture of rice and chicken; seafood cooked with rice; grilled fish.

Styles of Eating

- Three meals a day and many snacks are currently eaten, though in the past most people ate only in the morning and late afternoon.
- Traditional meals are eaten by the entire family sitting around a common dish of rice and meat or vegetables, eaten with the right hand only. Western dining with individual place settings and cutlery is common when eating out. Male and female guests eat separately.
- Breakfast: Western-style breakfasts including cereals and bread are becoming popular. Older people still eat bread dipped in oil, with coffee or tea.

- Lunch and dinner are similar, though the evening meal is likely to be heavier. Often the main meal is a rice dish mixed with meat, chicken, or fish.
- The evening meal during the month of fasting, Ramadan, tends to be lavish, with many dishes served, particularly sweet foods.
- Coffee and tea are drunk throughout the day, often accompanied by sweet pastries.

DRIED LIME (LOOMI)

Chicken on Rice (Mechbous)

This is a characteristic dish for a main meal.

1 small whole chicken, cut into serving portions, rinsed and patted dry
salt
1 cinnamon stick
2 cardamom pods
3 whole cloves
5 black peppercorns, whole
3 cups short-grained rice
water as needed
flour as needed
oil for shallow frying

Onion-Spice Topping (Hashu)

2–3 TBS vegetable oil
2 large yellow onions, finely chopped
¼ cup seedless raisins, soaked in water and drained
¼ tsp ground cardamom
½ tsp ground *loomi* (dried lime, available from some Middle Eastern stores. Or substitute grated lime rind)
¼ tsp ground black pepper
½ tsp sugar

Tomato Sauce (Duqqus)

2 large tomatoes, chopped
2 TBS water
2 cloves garlic, crushed
1 TBS tomato paste
salt, pepper to taste

Place chicken and spices in a stockpot with enough water to cover.
Bring to a boil, reduce heat, and continue to simmer uncovered over medium heat until chicken is done but still firm (approximately 30 minutes).
Remove and drain the chicken, reserving broth.
Chill broth and skim off congealed fat. Strain to remove spices and other particles.
Prepare three cups of rice, with broth from the chicken topped up with water to make 6 cups, if necessary. Add a pinch of salt.
While rice is cooking, prepare the onion topping.
Heat oil over medium heat in a frying pan and stir fry onions until brown and almost caramelized.
Stir in raisins and spices. Cook for 1 minute. Remove mixture from pan and set aside.

(continued)

Make the tomato sauce: in the same frying pan, put chopped tomatoes, water, garlic, tomato paste, salt, and pepper to simmer until tomatoes are soft and the sauce well blended. Set aside.

Lightly dust the boiled, drained chicken with flour. Heat oil in a clean frying pan and shallow fry the the chicken over medium-high heat, turning frequently, until brown and crispy.

When the rice is done, spread it on a serving platter. Sprinkle the onion mixture over the rice and place the chicken on top. Place the tomato sauce in a bowl on the table for diners to help themselves.

Shrimp Stew (Murabyan)

Fish and seafood are popular foods. This is served for a main meal.

Main Dish

2 TBS vegetable oil
1 large onion, thinly sliced
2 cloves garlic, minced
2 tsp powdered coriander
1 TBS fresh ginger, grated
$\frac{1}{4}$ tsp black pepper
2 pounds peeled and deveined shrimp (medium size)

1 pound tomatoes, chopped roughly
1 tsp salt
4 cups water
4 cups short-grained rice, rinsed and drained

Topping

2 onions, thinly sliced
$\frac{1}{4}$ cup vegetable oil
$\frac{1}{2}$ tsp ground cardamom
1 tsp black pepper
1 tsp curry powder
1 tsp ground turmeric
$\frac{1}{4}$ tsp ground cloves
1 bunch cilantro, chopped

grated peel of 1 *loomi* (dried lime; or substitute fresh grated lime rind)
1 clove garlic, mashed with 1 tsp ground coriander
1 pound peeled deveined shrimp

Heat oil over medium heat.

Add sliced onions and sauté until golden.

Add garlic, coriander, ginger, and pepper.

Stir in shrimp and sauté for 2–3 minutes.

Add tomatoes and cook for 10 minutes until softened.

Add salt and water, and bring to a boil.

Stir in rice.

Reduce heat and simmer, covered, until all the water is absorbed, about 15–20 minutes.

Remove from heat and set aside.

Now prepare the topping. Sauté onions in oil until golden.

Add the cardamom, black pepper, curry powder, turmeric, cloves, cilantro, grated *loomi*, and garlic/coriander mixture. Mix well.

Add shrimp and sauté until cooked through (about 5 minutes).
To serve, mound the rice and shrimp mixture on a platter.
Ladle the shrimp topping over the rice.

Black-Eyed Peas in Tomato Broth

This is a side dish commonly eaten at lunchtime.

1 large onion, chopped
3 TBS olive oil
2 cloves garlic, minced
½ pound lamb, cut into small
   cubes (or minced meat)
salt and black pepper to taste
1 cup dried black-eyed peas,
   soaked in boiling water for at
least an hour, or
overnight, drained (or
use 2 cups canned)
4 stalks celery, sliced crosswise
2 ripe tomatoes, chopped
6 cups water
1 tsp tomato paste
½ tsp chili powder

Sauté onion in olive oil on medium heat until translucent.
Add garlic and sauté for 1 minute.
Increase the heat and add the lamb and seasoning to taste. Sauté until
   browned.
Add remaining ingredients and bring to a boil.
Cover and simmer for 30–45 minutes, until the meat and the peas are tender.
Adjust seasoning.
Serve over rice.

Tea (Chai)

Hot, strong, sweet tea is drunk at any time of the day, and is an essential
component of any hospitality. It is often served in small, thick-walled glasses.

6 cups water
4 cinnamon sticks
5 TBS tea leaves or 5 tea bags
2 tsp sugar

In a small pot combine water and cinnamon.
Bring to a boil. Reduce the heat to medium and simmer for 10–15 minutes.
Remove the cinnamon sticks.
Stir in tea leaves and sugar.
Boil for 1 minute. Remove from heat.
Pour into small teacups (the traditional ones used are without handles) and
   serve.

Tahina *and Date Syrup Dip* (Dibis wa' Rashi)

Traditionally, this would be eaten for breakfast. Nowadays it is served as an appetizer.

$\frac{1}{2}$ cup date syrup (available from Indian and Middle Eastern stores, or puree pitted dates with $\frac{1}{2}$ cup warm water in a food processor)

1 TBS *tahina*
1 TBS fresh lemon juice, or to taste

Blend all the ingredients together in a bowl.
Serve as an appetizer with flat bread.

Sponge Cake

This is a popular cake that may have been borrowed from the British. Served as a snack with tea.

2 eggs
6 threads saffron, soaked in 1 tsp warm water for 5 minutes
$\frac{3}{4}$ cup sugar
$\frac{3}{4}$ cup flour

$\frac{1}{2}$ tsp baking powder
$\frac{1}{4}$ tsp cardamom powder
1 TBS butter for greasing the pan
1 tsp sesame seeds

Beat eggs well in a large bowl.
Add saffron.
Gradually beat in sugar.
Sift flour with baking powder and cardamom.
Add to eggs and mix thoroughly.
Pour mixture into a well-buttered 8-inch baking pan.
Sprinkle with sesame seeds.
Bake in a preheated 350°F oven for 20 minutes.

KYRGYZSTAN

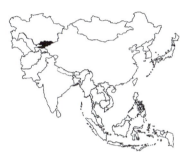 Kyrgyzstan is a large central Asian country, consisting mainly of wide steppes. The northeast is a mass of rough mountain ranges. The climate is hot in the summer (except in the higher altitudes) and very cold in the winter.

Kyrgyztan is largely settled by the forty tribes of the Kyrgyz, a Turkic-speaking people who also live in other countries of Central and East Asia. Most are currently Muslims and are forbidden alcohol and pork.

The Kyrgyz being traditionally nomads, their favorite food is meat, and cooking is simple. Chinese and Western (Russian) influences are changing the cuisine.

Foodstuffs

- Meat is primary, preferably fat-tailed sheep, horsemeat, and beef.
- Flour noodles.
- Carrots and squashes; rice and wheat flour; onions and garlic; chilies.

Typical Dishes

- Noodles and stuffed dumplings (*manty*) are staples for all meals.
- *Beshbarmak*, mutton-on-the-bone, is the classic Kyrgyz dish for guests.
- *Kesme* (noodle soup) is eaten at any meal.
- Tea, both black and green, is the common drink.

Styles of Eating

- Currently, three meals a day and snacks. Traditionally, the main heavy meal of meat and dumplings was eaten in the evening.
- Traditional dining involves a central dish or pot from which everyone is served in individual bowls. Diners sit on a ground cloth or carpet around the pot. Spoons are provided, though solids such as meat are eaten by hand. Men are served separately and first, women and children later.
- Other meals are usually breads or noodles with whatever vegetables are available, cheese, and a great deal of tea.
- Appreciation is expressed by burping loudly at the end of a meal. Hosts like to see that guests eat a lot, and considered themselves insulted if guests eat only small quantities.

Mutton-on-the-Bone (Beshbarmak)

Beshbarmak means "five fingers" in Kyrgyz. It is traditionally eaten with the five fingers of the right hand, hence the name. This is a simple dish offered to important guests. To recreate this dish for 4 diners, use 2–3 pounds stewing lamb on the bone, 2 onions, 5 cloves garlic, and 2 pounds fresh noodles, and follow the procedure given below.

1 fat-tailed sheep
salt to taste
4 large onions
1 garlic bulb, separated, cloves
   peeled

about $\frac{1}{2}$–$\frac{2}{3}$ pound fresh flour
   noodles per person

Upon the guests' arrival, a fat-tailed sheep is slaughtered.
The sheep carcass is skinned and cut up, then set to cook (cleaned small
   intestines, liver, all the variety meats, and head are included) in a large
   cauldron with salt, onions, garlic, and water to cover.
When the meat is tender, after about 1 hour or so, the noodles are added to
   boil with the meat in the same stock.
To serve, the meat and noodles are placed in separate bowls and placed on the
   ground cloth (eating is customarily done sitting around the ground cloth).
Some of the meat is shredded to facilititate eating, and mounded in a bowl.
The head, intestines, and other internal organs are brought on a separate
   tray. The guest of honor is offered the eyes.
Noodles and broth are served to each diner in a bowl. Diners help themselves
   to the meat, to be eaten with the noodles with the fingers. The broth is
   sipped directly from the side of the bowl.

Noodle Soup (Kesme)

Kesme is the Kyrgyz national dish. The meat and fat are supposed to come from the fat-tailed sheep common in the area.

2 ounces mutton fat (from tail
   preferably), cut into thin strips
$1\frac{1}{2}$ pounds lamb or mutton, cut
   into strips
1 large onion, sliced
$\frac{1}{2}$ pound radish, cut into julienne
   strips
2 ounces tomato paste

2 cubes beef bouillon dissolved
   in 4 cups hot water
5 ounces flour
2 eggs, beaten
5 ounces water
salt and black pepper to taste
1 ounce garlic, minced

Heat the fat over low heat in a heavy covered pot to render the oil. When
   sizzling, add the meat. Brown on all sides.
Add onion and radish and stir-fry until softened.

Add tomato paste and bouillon; cover the pot and simmer for 30–45 minutes
   until the meat is tender.

Meanwhile, prepare a dough: blend the flour and eggs in a food processor.
   Add water a little at a time, mixing until the mixture forms a ball.

Remove dough and knead on a floured surface for 10 minutes until shiny
   and elastic.

Roll dough out to $\frac{1}{4}$-inch thickness.

Cut into strips about $\frac{1}{2}$-inch wide.

Add noodles to simmering soup (add more stock if necessary). Cook for 5
   minutes.

Season to taste.

Place in tureen and sprinkle with garlic.

Serve hot.

Mutton Soup (Shorpo)

This is served as a main dish with *manty* (dumplings).

1 pound stewing lamb
salt and pepper to taste
5 ounces mutton fat or butter
$\frac{1}{4}$ pound onion, sliced
$\frac{1}{2}$ pound tomatoes, chopped
6 cups water

1 pound potatoes, cut into
   1-inch cubes
1 cup greens (spring onions,
   shallots, parsley, cress, or
   spinach—as desired), finely
   minced

Rub the meat thoroughly with salt and pepper.

Render the mutton fat over low heat in a heavy covered pot.

Brown the seasoned meat in hot fat.

Add onion and tomatoes and cook for 2 minutes over high heat.

Add water and potatoes. Bring to a boil.

Reduce heat and simmer for 30 minutes or more, covered, until meat is
   tender.

Serve in individual bowls, hot, garnishing each bowl with greens.

Kyrgyz Tea (Atkanchay)

Atkanchay is normally served with flat bread. It is consumed after meals or at
any time during the day.

2 cups water
1 ounce tea leaves
2 cups milk

1 ounce butter
5 ounces sour cream
salt to taste

(continued)

Boil the water and add tea. Simmer briefly.
Add milk, bring to a boil.
Add butter, salt, and sour cream. Stir and bring back to a boil.
Strain into cups to serve.

Baked Beef

Though mutton is the favorite meat in Kyrgyzstan, beef is also consumed. This dish betrays the influence of its Central Asian neighbors, as it is far more complex than most nomadic dishes.

3 TBS butter
1 large onion, chopped
1 green bell pepper, cored, seeded, and chopped
1 pound beef, cut into ½-inch cubes
1 cup yogurt
2 apples, diced
1 cup dried apricots, diced
½ cup raisins
½ cup jujubes (Chinese dates, available from Chinese stores or substitute dried dates), pitted and diced
2 tsp curry powder
1 tsp salt
2 tsp black pepper

Heat oven to 350°F.
Heat butter in a heavy skillet. Sauté onion until translucent. Add green pepper.
Add beef and sauté until it changes color.
Add yogurt, fruit, curry powder, salt, and pepper; mix well.
Place in a large, deep casserole.
Bake for 45 minutes or until beef is tender.
Serve with steamed rice.

LAOS

A small landlocked Southeast Asian country, Laos was a French colony that became independent in 1946. It is one of a few remaining Communist countries. Mostly mountainous and thickly forested, arable land is scarce. The climate is tropical, enabling sugarcane, rice, fruits, vegetables, and livestock to be raised. Fresh-water fish and crustaceans are a major food resource.

The population is predominantly Lao, who speak a language similar to Thai. Minority ethnic groups include Hmong, Liao, Meo, and others. Most are Buddhists who eschew excessive meat eating. Laotian cuisine is spice- and herb-based, influenced by neighboring Thailand, China, and France. Presentation of foods, with regard to color and texture, is very important. Laotian food is distinguished from that of its neighbors (Vietnam and Thailand) by preference for sticky glutinous rice as the staple.

Foodstuffs

- Staples: sticky rice, fish, greens.
- Rice and bean noodles.
- Water buffalo and pork (internal organs, feet, and skin), chicken, beef, eggs, wild game (python, deer, civet), preserved meat (meat and blood sausage, cured meat).
- Assorted leafy vegetables, corn, cassava, various types of eggplant, white radish, cucumber, sweet potato, green (unripe) papaya, unripe mango, bamboo shoots, banana blossom, mushrooms, riverweed—fresh-water "seaweed," called *kaipen*. Unusual vegetables such as rattan shoots, taro leaf stalks, and morning glory shoots.
- Banana, citrus (tangerines), berries, peanuts, papaya, mango.
- Seasonings: *galangal* (a ginger relative), chunky fresh-water fish sauce (*padek*) (see box "Fish Sauce"), mint, dill, chili, ginger flower bud, large-leaf cilantro, cilantro. Table condiments of hot chili, vinegar or lime juice, fish sauce, and herbs.
- Drinks: beverages, including water, are not drunk during meals. Locally grown tea and coffee are drunk at breaks; coffee is usually

LEMON GRASS

instant with condensed milk and is drunk in a glass. When coffee is finished, weak tea or water is drunk as a chaser; rice wine (*lao hai*), pink rice wine (*kao kham*), rice liquor (*laolao*), fresh fruit juices, bottled fruit drinks, carbonated fruit drinks, locally brewed beer.

Typical Dishes

- Marinated meat and/or fish, sometimes raw, with assorted greens, herbs, and spices (*laap*), is considered the national dish.
- Charcoal-grilled meat, duck or chicken.
- Dry, thick meat curries and stews (dry consistency because fingers are used for eating).
- Water buffalo meat and skin in sausages, stews, and sauces.
- Raw or parboiled or steamed vegetables, bitter- and astringent-tasting vegetables, such as marble-sized eggplant. Flavoring includes fish sauce and various herbs and chilies.
- Banana leaf–wrapped and steamed dishes: meat or fish and herbs (*knap*, also spelled *kanab*).

Styles of Eating

- Three meals and snacks daily.
- In traditional dining, a basket of sticky rice is placed between diners. Each diner uses the fingers of the right hand to take a small amount of rice, to be dipped into sauce or the many small bowls of communal dishes placed on the table (chopsticks are used for Vietnamese and Chinese noodle dishes; fork and spoon for regular rice dishes). Edible leaves (mint, lettuce) are also used to wrap morsels of rice, vegetables, and meat, to be dipped into sauce, and eaten, leaves and all. It is customary to defer to older people before eating: oldest persons take the first bites, followed by others in descending order of age. After this, everyone eats freely. It is considered impolite not to replace the cover on the sticky rice basket.
- Breakfast: croissant or baguette dipped into coffee; rice porridge; savory pancake with green herbs and vegetables from street stalls.

FISH SAUCE

A number of fish-derived sauces, or oils, are used throughout the world—notably in Southeast Asia—as flavoring agents. These include *nuoc mam* (Vietnam), *nampla* (Thailand), *patis* (Philippines), *fafaru* (Tahiti), and *shottsuru* (Japan), and others. These sauces are made commercially, for the most part, by fermenting small fish (sometimes small shrimp or squid) with large quantities of salt. The liquid, which is a mixture of oils and fermented essences, is then drawn off.

The specific methods differ from one place to another. The tastes do, too, at least for those familiar with them. To the uninitiated the sauces can all taste rather similar and rather strong (though they can become addictive in time).

The various sauces are available at Asian stores. The best way is to try different ones until you find one or more you like. It is rare to find the Japanese version, called *shottsuru* (popular until the introduction of soy sauce in the sixteenth century); and the secret of making *garum* (the ancient Roman version, once popular throughout the Mediterranean world) is lost.

- Lunch: rice with typical side dishes such as fermented pork sausage (*som moo*), green papaya salad, and marinated meat or fish (*laap*); fresh fruit.
- Dinner: sticky rice and several dishes: soup, grilled dish, dipping sauce, greens, stew or mixed dish (*koy* or *laap*), fresh fruit.
- Snacks: unripe mango eaten with vinegar and chilies; noodle soup with greens (*foe*); French-influenced baguette sandwich with paté or meat loaf and greens; Vietnamese-influenced spring rolls with greens and herbs.

GLUTINOUS (STICKY) RICE IN ASIA

Rice varies extensively in the quantity of starch in the kernel. This is exploited by farmers and cooks since different amounts of starch affect the finished product in different ways. "Sticky" or glutinous rice refers to the type of rice in which the kernel has high amounts of amylopectin (a component of starch), which makes the kernels stick to one another. In Laos and northeastern Thailand this type of rice, eaten by hand, is the major staple. In these areas the quality of rice is assessed partly by the degree to which it holds together to allow a diner to scoop sauces or other foods to the mouth, using the rice ball as a scoop.

Glutinous rice is used in a wider geographical zone—from Southeast Asia to China and Japan—to make pounded rice cakes. In this case, the cooked rice grains are pounded to make a sticky, chewy dough-like substance (similar in consistency to chewing gum), which is the basis for many types of steamed or shaped cakes. Since the pounded glutinous rice absorbs flavors and colors easily, it serves in a somewhat analogous role to marzipan in Europe: to make interesting shapes or emulate fruit and other food items.

Sticky Rice (Khao Neow)

Khao Neow is the Laotian staple, served at all main meals (see box "Glutinous [Sticky] Rice in Asia").

2 cups sticky rice (also called sweet or glutinous rice in Oriental stores)
4 (or more) cups water for soaking rice

water for steaming
bamboo steamer (available at Oriental stores) or double boiler and colander
cheesecloth or kitchen towel

Place rice in a bowl, add water to cover by 2–3 inches.
Soak for 2 hours or overnight. The longer the rice soaks, the better the flavor.
Drain rice well; transfer to cheesecloth-lined steamer basket or colander.
Boil water in a deep pot or double boiler. The water level must be well below the bottom of the steamer. Boiling water must not touch the rice.
Set steamer basket or colander over boiling water.
Cover rice and steam for 25 or more minutes until rice is tender.
Check boiling water level and replenish as necessary with *boiling* water.
Transfer rice to a covered container, either a basket or serving bowl, breaking up lumps.

(continued)

Place a clean cheesecloth or kitchen towel between the lid and rice to catch any condensed liquid. Remove cloth before serving.
Serve warm.

Fish with Coconut Milk (Sousi Pa)

This dish is served with rice for a main meal.

1 pound fish fillets (fresh-water fish with firm flesh, e.g., trout, tilapia), cut into serving pieces
1 large dried chili, stem and seeds removed, soaked in hot water for 10 minutes (optional)
5 cloves garlic
3 kaffir lime leaves (optional)
1 inch fresh galangal (or 1 tsp dried galangal powder, also called *laos*)
2 stalks lemon grass, finely sliced
1 cup coconut milk
1½ cups diluted coconut milk (i.e., mixed with an equal quantity of warm water)
1 TBS fish sauce (*padek*, stronger tasting than *nuoc mam* or *patis*)
2 TBS peanuts, dry roasted and chopped
4 sprigs fresh basil

Blend in a food processor or blender chili, garlic, kaffir lime leaves, galangal, and lemon grass to a paste, with 1 tablespoon coconut milk.
Heat the remaining coconut milk in a saucepan for 10 minutes on low heat.
Add the paste and cook, stirring constantly.
Add fish and turn carefully in sauce.
Add diluted coconut milk and fish sauce. Simmer for 10 minutes.
Add peanuts just before end of cooking.
Serve garnished with basil.

Stir-Fried Chicken (Aioan Chua Noeung Phset Kretni)

Chicken and duck are as commonly eaten as fish; charcoal-grilled chicken and duck are often sold in the markets and street stalls for quick snacks or light meals.

6 dried *shiitake* or other large Asian mushrooms, soaked in hot water for 20 minutes
2 TBS oil
4 cloves garlic, crushed
½ tsp finely grated fresh ginger
1 small chicken, chopped into small pieces
2 tsp sugar
2 tsp cilantro, chopped

Squeeze mushrooms dry. Remove and discard stems, cut into quarters. Reserve 1 cup of water from soaking, adding water to make 1 cup if necessary.

Heat oil. Fry garlic and ginger for 10 seconds, stirring.
Add chicken and stir-fry until light golden.
Add mushrooms, reserved water, and sugar.
Cover and simmer until chicken is cooked.
Sprinkle with chopped cilantro and serve with sticky rice.

Green Papaya Salad (Tam Mak Houng)

This spicy salad is also eaten in Thailand. where it is called *som tam*. It is commonly sold in markets and street stalls. There are many variations: a few additions are ground raw rice, rice noodles, spices such as bay-leaf flavored bark, herbs such as mint or dill, and bitter green shoots. This can be eaten on its own as a snack, or with rice and other dishes for a midday or evening meal.

4 medium red and green serrano
  chilies (or to taste)
2 large cloves garlic, crushed
2½ cups shredded green (unripe)
  papaya
1 cup green or string beans,
  cut in 1-inch pieces, blanched
  lightly, then cooled immediately
  in a bowl of ice water

6 cherry tomatoes, cut in half
2 TBS small dried shrimps
  (available from Asian stores)
  lettuce leaves
2 tsp peanuts, dry roasted, then
  roughly crushed

Pound chilies and garlic in a mortar to a coarse texture.
Add papaya, green beans, and tomatoes and mix well.
Add dried shrimps, peanuts, and dressing and toss.
Serve immediately with lettuce leaves for wrapping, sticky rice, and a meat
  dish.

Dressing

5 TBS lime juice
3 TBS *padek* fish sauce (or substitute other fish sauce, such as
  nuoc mam or *patis*)

3 TBS sugar
4 TBS finely ground dried
  shrimps

Combine the dressing ingredients in a small bowl and set aside.

Vegetable Stew (or Phak)

Green vegetables and herbs of all kinds are much appreciated and are perennial accompaniments to a Laotian meal. This vegetable stew is adapted from one using dried quail and an aromatic plant called *sa-kahn*. Serve this as a side dish, accompanied by sticky rice and a meat dish.

2 cups beef jerky
½ pound pork spareribs
4 cups water
a pinch of salt
5 small eggplants (about 4–5 inches long), stalk removed
5 pea-sized eggplants, stalk removed (available from Asian greengrocers)
1 green bell pepper, cored, seeded and quartered
1 green chili pepper (optional), left whole
1 stalk lemon grass
2 bay leaves, fresh preferably
3 slender (about 1 inch diameter) bamboo shoots, sliced into rings
1 sprig dill, cut into 1-inch pieces
3 spring onions, cut into 1-inch pieces
1 bunch sweet basil leaves
padek or similar fish sauce (nam pla, patis)
2 yard-long beans, cut into 1-inch pieces
1 cup crisp-fried pork skin, diced (sold at Hispanic and Oriental stores as chicharron)
1 cup cilantro, chopped
3 stalks spring onions, chopped, for garnish
1 cup cucumber, chopped
1 cup fresh mint leaves, left whole or watercress, chopped
5 romaine or cos lettuce leaves

Place jerky and ribs with water and salt to boil.
Simmer for 30–45 minutes until the stock is flavorful.
Add all vegetables and herbs except long beans and padek.
Simmer until eggplants are tender, for about 15 minutes.
Take out the eggplants and chili (if using) and process to a puree.
Return the puree to the pot; add long beans when the pot returns to a boil.
Simmer until long beans are done, for about 10 minutes.
Add the pork skin and cilantro.
Adjust seasoning, adding more fish sauce or salt if necessary.
Serve garnished with spring onions.
Eat with cucumbers, mint or watercress, and lettuce.

Sticky Rice and Mango (Khao Nieow Ma Muang)

Fruits, such as banana, mango, or papaya, are usually eaten for dessert.

1 cup glutinous rice
1¼ cups coconut milk
¼ cup sugar
¼ TBS salt
¼ tsp rice flour
2 ripe medium mangoes, peeled and sliced
a pinch of salt for topping

Rinse the rice well and drain.
Place in rice cooker and add water according to instructions, or steam according to recipe above.
Heat ½ cup of coconut milk on low heat, in a small saucepan.
Add sugar and salt and stir until dissolved.

Remove from heat and pour onto cooked rice. Stir to mix well and set aside
    for about 15 minutes.

Now make topping sauce. Heat rest of coconut milk and add salt and rice
    flour.

Stir until the salt is dissolved and sauce is thick.

Place sliced mangoes on one side of a dessert dish for each person.

Place sticky rice on the other side.

Top rice with 1 or 2 tablespoons coconut topping sauce and serve.

LATVIA

A Baltic country between Estonia and Lithuania, Latvia largely flat, and swampy in some areas. The climate is cool and the country is covered with dense forests that yield favored foodstuffs, including honey and berries.

The population is mostly Lets, who have lived in the area since well before the arrival of the Scandinavian and Slavic tribes from the East in the Dark Ages. For 700 years, Latvia was a colony of Germany, Poland, or Russia, and only recently achieved renewed independence.

Foodstuffs

- Staples: barley, rye, and potatoes.
- Meat: pork, and to a lesser extent, duck and beef. In traditional cuisine, the best parts of the animal were reserved for the Russian, Polish, or German overlords, so the Latvians learned to make use of and enjoy the less popular parts of the carcass.
- Fish: herring from the sea, and carp and salmon from the plentiful rivers and streams.
- Vegetables: beans, cabbage, turnips.
- Fruits: berries and honey from woods, as well as harvested.

Typical Dishes

- Porridges of barley and wheat.
- Many varieties of bread, particularly rye bread, which is the basis for numerous recipes.
- *Kvass*, a drink made of rye bread and fruit juices. Vodka and beer are also drunk, as is mead (honey wine). Coffee and particularly tea are drunk between meals.

Styles of Eating

- Three meals a day and snacks when possible, notably in winter.
- Families eat together at least for the evening meal. Place settings are European standard.

- Breakfast: porridge, sweetened with honey; bread with cheese or ham or pickled fish.
- Lunch, which is the main meal of the day, consists of soup, a meat dish, potatoes, and a sweet.
- Supper is like lunch, but lighter, possibly without a meat dish.

Sauerkraut Soup (Skâbu Kâpostu Zupa)

This is a starter soup for the main meal.

1 pound sauerkraut	salt and pepper to taste
½ cup bacon, cubed	water as needed
1 onion, minced fine	1 TBS flour
1 carrot, grated	½ cup sour cream
¼ cup tomato paste	1 bunch dill, finely chopped

Put sauerkraut, bacon, onion, carrot, tomato paste, and seasoning in a covered pot. Add water to cover.
Simmer until sauerkraut and bacon are soft, about 10 minutes.
Take 1 TBS stock from the pot and mix well into the flour in a small bowl to make a slurry, then add to soup. Adjust seasoning and remove from heat.
Add sour cream and dill before serving.

Potato Salad (Rasols)

Salads are eaten as appetizers in large meals, or with a meat dish.

6 potatoes, boiled in their jackets, then skinned and cut into large chunks	3 medium dill pickles, diced
	3 pickled beets, diced
	1 apple, diced
6 eggs, hard-boiled, peeled, and diced	

Mix all the ingredients.
Add dressing and mix well. Cover and refrigerate overnight.

Dressing

3 TBS mayonnaise	3 tsp vinegar
2 TBS sour cream	salt, pepper to taste
3 tsp mustard	

Blend all ingredients.

Potato and Carrot Pies (Sklandu Rausi)

Rye was the traditional crop of Latvian peasants, as it is a cold-resistant, hardy grain suitable for the climate. These vegetable-filled pies are eaten for the evening meal.

2 cups rye flour	2 TBS butter
$\frac{1}{4}$ tsp salt	$\frac{1}{2}$ cup water

Mix flour and salt. Rub butter into flour until mixture resembles coarse meal. Add water a little at a time to make a stiff dough. Knead for 10 minutes.

Roll out dough on a floured surface to $\frac{1}{8}$-inch thickness. Cut out disks about 8 inches in diameter.

Place them on greased cookie sheets.

Spread 1 heaping TBS of potato filling in the center of each disk to within $\frac{1}{2}$ inch of the edges.

Spread 1 TBS of the cooked carrots on top.

Fold over the edges to form a crescent, crimp firmly with a fork or fingers to seal.

Bake in a moderate oven (370°F) for 15–20 minutes, or until the pastries are golden brown.

Filling

1 cup mashed potatoes	1 cup cooked grated
2 TBS melted butter or cream	carrots
1 egg yolk, beaten	2 TBS melted butter
$\frac{1}{4}$ tsp salt	1 egg, beaten
1 tsp caraway seeds	$\frac{1}{2}$ tsp salt

Mix the potatoes with melted butter, yolk, salt, and caraway seeds.

Mix the carrots with melted butter, egg, and salt.

Use potato and carrot mixtures as directed.

Pea Patties

This is a side dish to accompany meat.

$\frac{1}{2}$ pound dried green peas, soaked overnight, boiled until soft, and drained	4 TBS smoked bacon, cut into cubes
$\frac{3}{4}$ cup mashed potatoes	2 TBS hemp stalks, chopped fine
1 onion, chopped fine	salt to taste
2 TBS oil	

Mash peas with potatoes. Season.

Fry onion in oil until golden. Add bacon and hemp and stir-fry for an additional 2 minutes.

Mix with peas and potatoes. Roll into balls about the size of golf balls.

Serve as snack or for midday meal with buttermilk.

Sweet Porridge (Buberts)

This is served as a snack or dessert.

2 eggs, separated
5 TBS sugar
1 tsp vanilla extract

4 cups milk
¾ cup semolina (or cream of wheat)

Beat egg yolks with 3 tablespoons sugar and the vanilla until lemon colored. Reserve.

Warm the milk over low heat in a pan, and slowly stir in semolina.

Simmer on very low heat for 5 minutes. Keep hot but do not allow to boil.

Stir in about 2 tablespoons of the warm semolina to the egg yolk mixture. Slowly add to the rest of the semolina, stirring constantly until the mixture has thickened.

Remove from heat.

Whip egg whites to soft peaks. Add the remaining sugar and continue to whip until stiff.

Fold into semolina mixture.

Serve in bowls.

Cranberry Pudding (Biguzis)

Berries were traditionally gathered from the wild, though they are now raised commercially. This is eaten as dessert or as a snack.

1 loaf fresh rye bread
3 cups cranberries
1 cup water

½ cup honey
1 cup whipping cream
sugar as needed

Crumble the rye bread into a glass bowl.

Boil the cranberries with water until the skins have popped, about 5–8 minutes.

Strain, pressing down to extract all the juices.

Add honey to cranberry juice and mix well.

(continued)

Pour honey and cranberry mixture over bread. Allow to stand for 30 minutes at least.

Whip the cream with 2 tablespoons sugar until stiff.

Serve the pudding with whipped cream, passing the sugar around for diners to add, if desired.

LEBANON

Lebanon, on the eastern shores of the Mediterranean, has loaned its name to the entire eastern coast of the Mediterranean—the Levant. It is bordered by Syria and Israel. The country is bisected lengthwise by the Lebanon mountain range, to the east of which lies the fertile Bek'aa Valley. The climate is Mediterranean, with mild winters and hot summers, enabling a wide range of crops to be grown.

The population is largely Arab, divided among numerous Christian and Muslim sects, who engaged in a bitter civil war in the late twentieth century (1980s). Minorities of Armenians and Greeks live there as well. With the exception of the prohibition on pork among Muslims, there is little culinary difference between them. Much of the Christian population is thoroughly Westernized, with close ties to France and the United States in terms of food culture. Muslims tend to be more traditional.

Lebanon's sophisticated cuisine has influenced much of the Middle East. Due to the country's favorable position, its population has traded throughout the Mediterranean Sea for millennia.

Foodstuffs

- Staples are rice, pasta, potatoes, and wheat dishes including breads (such as *lavash*) and cracked cooked wheat (*bulghur*).
- Meat: lamb is preferred; beef, chicken, and duck are also consumed. Pork is eaten only by non-Muslims. Preserved meat (by smoking, drying, salting) is an important item.
- Fish and seafood from the Mediterranean Sea, including jacks, grouper, mullets, and shrimp.
- Vegetables: tomatoes, cucumbers, lettuce, peppers, beans, maize, eggplant, squashes, sesame. Olives and pickles are important items of diet.
- Fruit: citrus, olives, plums, pears, apples, grapes, cherries.
- Flavor principles include spices, particularly cumin and coriander, onions and garlic, and *samna* (ghee or clarified butter).

Typical Dishes

- *Meze*, a series of small dishes with salads, stuffed vegetables, and small tidbits.
- Salads of fresh vegetables.

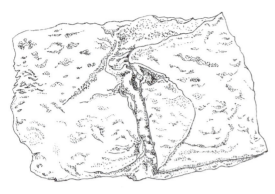

LAVASH

- *Baba ganouj*, eggplant mixed with sesame sauce.
- *Shashlik*, grilled skewered lamb.
- *Tabouleh*, parsley and cracked wheat salad.
- Stuffed vegetables.

Styles of Eating

- Three meals a day are common.
- Families generally eat together, helping themselves from a central dish (or eating European style with European place settings).
- Like most of the Middle East, breakfast can be skimpy: little more than bread, or roll, or a croissant with coffee.
- Lunch: a *meze* and some grilled meat, eaten with flat bread.
- Supper: a rice or noodle or potato dish, or several, with cooked meat, chicken, or fish.
- Lebanese have a sweet tooth, and many different kinds of pastries, often sweetened with syrup or honey, are made and consumed.
- Drinks include coffee, which is drunk in small cups; tea, beer, fruit juice, and traditional and international soft drinks. Wines and liquors, particularly anise-flavored *arak*.
- Eating out is popular, often *meze* and grilled meats. Street foods such as *falafel* are consumed in great quantities.

Home-Style Egg Dip (Tahinat el Beid)

This is served as part of a *meze* to start a meal. "Home style" usually means the ingredients do not need to be very smooth (see box "*Tahina* in Middle Eastern Cooking").

2 TBS sesame paste (*tahina*)	salt to taste
¼ cup lemon juice	1 hard-boiled egg, peeled and
½ cup water	very finely chopped
1 clove garlic, crushed	paprika to taste
2 TBS parsley, minced fine	

Put the sesame paste in a deep bowl.
Add lemon juice 1 tsp at a time (the quantity depends on how sour you want it), blending the juice in carefully before adding more (the mixture will first harden, then gradually emulsify). (This can also be done in a food processor.)
Add water also 1 teaspoon at a time, until you achieve a light sauce.
Add garlic, parsley, salt, and egg.
Sprinkle with paprika to taste.
Serve with flat bread to scoop out as part of a *meze*.

TAHINA *IN MIDDLE EASTERN COOKING*

Ground sesame seeds form a thick oily mass known as *tahina*, which is used throughout the Middle East. Thinned with water and lemon juice it forms a sauce that adds flavor to a number of dishes. It can be scooped with flat bread and eaten as is, added to other dishes (e.g., chickpea spread or eggplants), or used in cooking (e.g., *siniyah*). In Turkey *tahina* is often served sweet for breakfast with grape jelly. *Tahina* is also cooked with sugar to make a flaky confection called *halva*.

Tahina is made by grinding sesame seeds (hulled or unhulled, depending on preference; the latter yields a slightly more bitter, richer flavor), traditionally in marble grindstones. In Nablus, Palestine, a variety of *tahina* is made by grinding cumin seeds, which is used largely for cooking.

Parsley and Cracked Wheat Salad (Tabouleh)

Serve as part of a *meze* or on its own before the main dish.

½ cup *bulghur* (cracked wheat)
1½ cups parsley, chopped fine
½ cup fresh mint, chopped fine
2 spring onions, minced fine
1 large tomato, diced

salt to taste
6 TBS lemon juice
4 TBS virgin olive oil
lettuce leaves

Soak the *bulghur* in water for about 2 hours, then wash and squeeze out.
Mix well *bulghur*, parsley, mint, onions, and tomato.
Add salt to taste, lemon juice, and olive oil and mix well.
Serve in a bowl lined with lettuce leaves.
Serve with more lettuce leaves or flatbread for scooping out.

Toasted Bread Salad (Fattoush)

This may be served as part of a *meze*, though often served as a light meal.

3 pita breads (6 inches in diameter),
  each cut into eight wedges
4 cups romaine lettuce leaves, cut
  into 1-inch strips
2 cups sliced cucumbers
½ cup feta cheese, crumbled
¼ cup red onion, quartered
  and sliced

3 medium, fully ripe tomatoes
  cut into wedges
¼ cup virgin olive oil
¼ cup freshly squeezed,
  strained lemon juice
salt and pepper to taste
1 TBS parsley, chopped fresh
2 tsp mint leaves, dried, crushed

Preheat oven to 300°F.
Place pita wedges on a shallow baking pan. Toast until crisp, turning occasionally, for about 20 minutes. Remove from pan and cool.

(continued)

In a large bowl, place lettuce, cucumber, cheese, onion, tomatoes, and pita wedges.

Combine olive oil and lemon juice and season to taste.

Add parsley and mint and blend well with a fork. Pour over salad mixture. Toss until combined.

Serve as part of a *meze*.

Stuffed Cabbage (Malfuf Mahshi bi Zayt)

Stuffed vegetables come in many variations in Lebanon. This would serve as the main dish in a meal.

Rolls

24 cabbage leaves (outer leaves of Savoy cabbage are best, or Chinese cabbage)	1 tsp salt
	1 tsp dried mint, crumbled
	¼ cup lemon juice
boiling water	½ cup olive oil
3 garlic cloves, finely minced	

Stuffing

¼ cup vegetable oil	½ cup parsley, finely chopped
1 cup spring onions, chopped	1 cup tomatoes, peeled and
1 cup rice	chopped fine
1 cup canned chickpeas (*garbanzos*), drained	½ tsp ground cumin
	salt and black pepper to taste

Heat oil and fry onion for 2–3 minutes until golden.

Add the rice and stir for 5 minutes until well coated with oil.

Transfer onion and rice to a bowl, and mix well with the remaining stuffing ingredients. Season a bit stronger than usual.

Prepare the leaves: place the cabbages in boiling water for 1–2 minutes until limp.

Drain and cool the leaves in a colander.

Cut down level with the rest of the leaf the tough center rib, if necessary, to make the leaf more flexible.

To assemble the stuffed vegetables: place a generous tablespoon of stuffing on the base of each leaf, roll once, tuck in the sides and roll up to the end of the leaf. Repeat with remaining leaves.

Crush garlic with salt and blend in crumbled, crushed mint and lemon juice.

Pack the rolls flap side down in layers in a heavy pot, sprinkling some of the garlic-lemon mixture and olive oil between the layers.

Invert a plate over the topmost rolls to keep them from shifting during cooking.

Add enough cold water to just cover rolls and put lid on firmly.

Bring to a boil over medium heat, reduce to lowest possible, and simmer gently for 45 minutes.

Remove from the heat and leave aside for 30 minutes.
Serve lukewarm or cold.

Date-Stuffed Cookies (Ma'amoul Btamr)

These are served as snacks with coffee.

1 pound soft dates, pitted and
  chopped
1½ cups water
8 ounces butter
1 pound flour
4 tsp orange blossom water
  (available from Middle Eastern
and Asian shops) diluted
  in ½ cup water
confectioners' (powdered)
  sugar

Prepare the filling: cook dates in water and mash. Remove from fire and cool.
To make the pastry: cut butter into flour, then rub until mixture resembles
  coarse meal.
Mix in orange water to make a dough and knead thoroughly for 5 minutes.
Allow dough to rest for 40 minutes, covered with a damp towel.
On a floured surface, roll dough out to a 1½-inch cylinder, then cut into
  1-inch pieces.
Divide date mixture into same number of portions as the dough.
Take each dough piece and mold around your thumb to make a shell to hold
  the filling.
Fill each ball with one date portion, seal the dough, and reshape.
Ma'amoul are often decorated using a qalib (a wooden mold incised with
  traditional patterns), or you can use a small fork to etch a pattern that will
  hold the confectioners' sugar to be sprinkled on them after baking.
Warm the oven to 325°F.
Bake the ma'amoul on a buttered cookie sheet for about 15–20 minutes. They
  must not brown. They will still be soft but will firm up upon cooling.
Remove from the oven and dust with confectioners' sugar.
Cool and serve.

LESOTHO

Lesotho is a landlocked southern African country. Much of the nation is composed of hilly highlands. The climate is cool and dry in winter, hot and humid in summer.

The majority of people are of the Sotho nation, speaking the Sethotho language. The traditional sources of food were farming and cattle raising. Cattle are still very important, and every adult male owns as many heads of cattle as he can afford.

Foodstuffs

- Maize is the main staple.
- Vegetables: pumpkins and squashes, beans, peppers, tomatoes, cabbages, potatoes.
- Meat: mutton and beef, though the latter is usually only eaten on special occasions; so important is cattle ownership. Chickens and some game.
- Milk and milk products such as soured milk.

Typical Dishes

- Maize cooked into a stiff porridge (*nsima*).
- Stews of vegetables or meat.
- Grilled meat.
- Steamed corn bread.
- Drinks include beer (home-brewed and commercial), fruit juice, ginger beer, and milky tea.

Styles of Eating

- Most people eat three meals a day if they can afford it.
- Families usually share the pot of *nsima*, picking a ball of the porridge and making a small scoop with the thumb to convey the stew to the mouth.
- Urban people eat using European settings and cutlery.
- All meals are based on the staple *nsima*, accompanied, if possible, by a stew or sauce of vegetables.
- Breakfast: thin porridge, slightly salted, and leftovers, with coffee or milky tea.
- Lunch and dinner tend to be similar: *nsima* with a meat or vegetable dish, or both if one can afford it.

Stir-Fried Vegetables (Chakalaka)

This is served as a side dish with the staple.

2 TBS oil
1 onion, chopped
3 bell peppers, cored, seeded, and
  chopped
3 carrots, scraped and chopped

3 tomatoes, chopped
hot chilies to taste, seeded and
  minced
salt to taste

Heat oil and stir-fry all ingredients at high heat for 4–5 minutes each, starting
  with the onion, then the peppers, carrots, and finally the tomatoes and
  chilies.
Season.
Serve with *nsima* (maize porridge) or rice.

Stewed Cabbage and Potatoes

Another common side dish served with the staple.

2 TBS vegetable oil
1 large onion, chopped
1 TBS curry powder
10 ounces potatoes, peeled and
  chopped into large chunks

water as needed
10 ounces white cabbage,
  shredded roughly
2 tomatoes, chopped roughly
salt and pepper to taste

Heat oil and sauté onion.
Add curry powder. Cook for a few moments, stirring constantly until well
  blended.
Add potatoes and water to barely cover. Cook for 15 minutes or until the
  potato is almost done (the exterior is done, but the center needs a bit more
  cooking).
Add the cabbage and cook until the potatoes are completely tender.
Stir in the tomatoes. Season with salt and pepper, and remove from
  heat.
Serve with any meat dish and *nsima*.

Braised Mashed Vegetables (Moroko)

This dish is often made to accompany a meat dish or is served on its own.

1 pound spinach or similar greens, roughly chopped
1 pound potatoes, peeled, quartered, and soaked in cold water

about 3 cups chicken stock (or 2 chicken stock cubes dissolved in 3 cups warm water)

Place the greens in the bottom of a large covered pot.
Layer the potatoes over the greens.
Add stock to cover the vegetables by one inch (top up with water if there is not enough stock)
Bring to a boil, then reduce heat and cover.
Cook for 25–30 minutes or until potatoes are tender. Add stock if necessary to prevent the pot from getting dry.
When the potatoes and greens are fully cooked, mash them together with a potato masher, or in a food processor.
Serve hot.

Curried Meat

Many Sotho men work in the gold and diamond mines in South Africa, and they brought back with them a taste for curry, a common South African flavoring.

3 TBS oil
1 pound stewing mutton or beef, cubed
2 cups water
1 TBS curry powder

salt to taste
½ pound cabbage, shredded roughly
½ pound squash in large chunks

Heat oil in a heavy covered pot and sauté the meat quickly until brown on all sides.
Add water, cover, and slowly simmer the meat until tender, about 30–45 minutes.
Stir in the curry powder, salt, and vegetables.
Cook the vegetables for 15–20 minutes until the squash is tender.
Serve with *moroko* and *nsima*.

Peanut Bread

As in much of Africa, peanuts are a major source of protein and flavoring. This bread is a Sotho version of a bread common in much of southern Africa, eaten for breakfast or as a snack.

1 cup flour

½ cup rolled oats

½ cup cornmeal

½ cup dry milk powder

½ cup sugar

1 TBS baking powder

1 tsp salt

⅔ cup natural unsweetened
   peanut butter

1½ cups milk

1 egg, well beaten

Combine dry ingredients.

Cut in the peanut butter until the mixture resembles coarse meal. (This can
   be done in a food processor.)

Mix in milk and egg.

Turn mixture into a greased 8×10-inch pan.

Bake for 45 minutes to 1 hour at 275°F.

Serve as snack.

LIBERIA

Liberia, in West Africa on the Atlantic coast, was founded by slaves freed from the United States in the early nineteenth century. The climate is tropical, and the terrain is flat with rolling hills. Staples such as cassava, yams, fruits, and vegetables are grown.

The freed slaves settled all along the coast, rarely paying any attention to the interior, so there are major differences between the culture and cooking of the descendants of former Americans in the coastal areas and the inland natives.

Cooking for some households is influenced by American elements, with the majority similar to other West African styles: staples served with vegetable- or peanut-based sauces, with or without meat or fish.

Foodstuffs

- Rice is the preferred staple, eaten twice a day in any household that can afford it. This is often restricted to wealthier, American-descended households, and along the coast.
- Cassava, taro, hot red peppers, sweet potatoes, yams, and green bananas are common staples and appear in many dishes, particularly those from up-country, away from the coast.
- Vegetables: greens, eggplant, okra, peanuts, and ginger.
- Meat: goat, chicken, and sometimes beef.
- Fish: marine fish are caught by coastal fishermen in small boats. Rivers yield crustaceans, frogs, and river fish, some of which are dried and smoked.

Typical Dishes

- Check rice: a combination of rice and okra.
- Goat soup: the "national soup" served extensively, and almost always features in formal occasions.
- Country chop: meats, fish, and greens fried in palm oil, Liberia's best-known dish.
- Jollof rice: rice cooked with meat and various vegetables.
- Rice bread with mashed bananas.
- American pastries—coconut pie, sweet potato pie, and pumpkin pie—are extremely popular.

- Peanuts are extensively used in both sweet and savory cooking.
- Drinks: fruit juices, carbonated bottled drinks; ginger beer, palm wine, both drunk with meals.

Styles of Eating

- Three meals a day are preferred, though, given the poverty in the country, many people do without.
- In traditional African households, food is eaten with the fingers, though European place settings are common in urban areas. All food is brought to the table at once, and diners help themselves to whatsoever they choose. Soup is served in small bowls; all other dishes are eaten from the same plate.

COLLARD GREENS

- Breakfast is usually some form of porridge, or sometimes bread, with coffee.
- Lunch and dinner are not differentiated, though only one of these is likely to include meat or fish.
- Roadside restaurants called "cook shops" feature Jollof rice and various stewed dishes.

Chicken Peanut Soup

This usually serves as a main dish.

1 chicken, cut into serving pieces	2 tsp tomato paste
1 TBS salt	1 sprig parsley, chopped
5 pints cold water	$\frac{1}{4}$ tsp black pepper
3 tsp shelled, roasted, ground peanuts (or substitute natural unsweetened peanut butter)	1 small potato, peeled and diced

Place chicken, salt, and water in a pot. Cover and bring slowly to a boil. Skim froth if necessary.

Simmer gently for 20 minutes.

Mix peanut butter with $\frac{1}{4}$ pint chicken stock from the pot and add to the chicken.

Add remaining ingredients and cover.

Simmer gently for about 1 hour.

Serve hot with rice.

Liberian Jollof Rice

Like several other West African countries, Liberia claims Jollof rice for its own. This is a popular festive dish.

4 TBS oil
1 chicken, cut into serving pieces
½ pound smoked ham, cubed
2 onions, sliced
salt and black pepper to taste
¼ tsp allspice powder
2 14-ounce cans chopped
   tomatoes

6 ounces tomato paste diluted
   with an equal volume of
   warm water
¾ pint stock
¼ pound French beans, cut into
   2-inch lengths
8 ounces rice
1 tsp salt

Heat oil in a casserole or a large sauté pan and brown chicken, turning pieces
   when done on one side.
Add ham, onions, salt, pepper, and allspice.
Cook until onions are tender, stirring occasionally.
Add tomatoes, tomato paste, and stock. Mix well.
Add French beans. Cover and simmer until beans are tender (10 min-
   utes or so).
In a separate pot, cook rice for 10 minutes in double the volume of lightly
   salted water. Drain well.
Add rice to meat and vegetables and mix well.
Continue to simmer over lowest heat, covered and well sealed, for 10
   minutes.
Remove from heat, and let rest undisturbed for 10–15 minutes.
Serve as main dish in a festive meal.

Monrovia Greens

Most meals are accompanied by some form of greens with the rice. Meat is less likely.

2 pounds collard greens (or
   spinach or kale, removing hard
   stalk parts of kale), washed and
   cut in small pieces
½ pound smoked salted fish, cut
   in 1- to 2-inch pieces (or
   substitute smoked bacon)

1 large onion, sliced
salt, black pepper, chili pepper
   flakes to taste
1 quart water
2 pounds cabbage, cut into
   halves and then eight wedges
1 TBS palm oil

Combine greens, salted fish, onion, salt, pepper, chili flakes, and water in a
   large pot.
Simmer gently for 30 minutes.

Add cabbage and palm oil.
Cook for 15 minutes, or until vegetables are tender.
Correct the seasoning.
Strain before serving if water has not been completely absorbed.
Serve with a meat dish and rice.

Cassava Cake

Cassava is used in inland communities as a staple. In urban areas it is more likely made into a cake as dessert or a snack.

$\frac{1}{2}$ pound cassava (yucca), peeled and grated	8 ounces sugar
$\frac{1}{4}$ pint milk	$2\frac{1}{2}$ ounces desiccated coconut
1 tsp vanilla extract	2 ounces flour
1 egg, beaten	$2\frac{1}{2}$ level tsp baking powder
3 ounces butter	$\frac{1}{8}$ tsp salt

Mix cassava with milk, vanilla, and egg, and allow to stand for 5 minutes.
Cream butter and sugar, and add cassava mixture and coconut. Mix batter well.
Sift flour, baking powder, and salt, and add to batter.
Turn batter into a buttered and floured 8-inch round cake pan.
Bake for about 40 minutes in a preheated 350°F oven, or until cake tests done.
Remove from oven, cool, and cut into squares or bars.
Serve as snack.

Liberian Cake

This is an American-influenced snack or dessert commonly made in coastal Liberia.

$\frac{1}{2}$ cup corn syrup (or substitute molasses thinned with hot water)	$\frac{1}{2}$ tsp baking soda
$\frac{1}{4}$ cup milk	$\frac{1}{4}$ tsp baking powder
3 ounces butter	$\frac{1}{4}$ tsp cinnamon
3 ounces sugar	$\frac{1}{4}$ tsp ground allspice
1 tsp lemon rind, grated	$\frac{1}{4}$ tsp ground mace
2 eggs	$\frac{1}{8}$ tsp powdered cloves
1 cup plain flour	$\frac{1}{3}$ cup seedless raisins, chopped
	2 TBS shredded coconut

Mix syrup and milk and reserve.
Cream the butter, sugar, and lemon rind until light and fluffy.

(continued)

Add eggs one at a time, mixing well into the creamed mixture.

Sift together the flour, baking soda, baking powder, and spices, and add to the egg mixture alternately with the mixture of milk and syrup (start and end with dry ingredients).

Stir until smooth.

Stir in raisins and coconut.

Pour batter into a greased and floured 9 × 5 × 2-inch loaf pan.

Bake for 35–40 minutes.

Allow to cool for 10 minutes in the pan, then turn out onto a cake rack.

LIBYA

Libya is a mainly desert country on the southern shores of the Mediterranean, between Tunisia and Egypt. Except for a narrow coastal strip, the country is largely part of the Sahara desert, mostly flat plain and rolling hills. The climate is hot and dry all the year round, hence much food is imported, including staples such as wheat and rice.

Most of the inland people were traditionally nomads, living off camels, sheep, and dates. The coastal people had been urbanized since Roman times. Since the discovery of oil in the mid-twentieth century, Libyans have become predominantly urbanized. The population is virtually all Muslim Arab.

The cuisine is characteristic of Middle Eastern and Arab cookery.

Foodstuffs

- Staples are wheat bread and rice. Couscous features in many meals.
- Lamb is the favorite meat. Beef and chicken and, among nomads, camel are also eaten. Pork is forbidden.
- Fish: Mediterranean fish along the coastline.
- Fruit: locally raised dates, citrus, grapes, olives.
- Vegetables: peppers, tomatoes, cucumbers, carrots.
- Dairy: milk and milk products including yogurt, soft cheeses, and buttermilk.

Typical Dishes

- Roasted or baked lamb and lamb soup are favorite dishes and are served to guests when possible.
- Couscous and couscous stews, with Libyan twists.
- Stuffed vegetables, including cabbage, potatoes, onions, peppers, tomatoes, and grape leaves (*abrak*).
- Pastries, often made of *brik* (puff pastry) and filled with dates, almonds, or other nuts.
- Tea flavored with mint or desert thyme can be drunk at all hours.

Styles of Eating

- Three meals a day are common on the coast. Further inland, nomads tend to eat only twice a day.
- Families may eat together, sharing food from a common dish. The traditional way of eating is with the right hand only, which is washed before and after dining.
- Males and females generally eat separately (a gender separation is maintained throughout life).
- Breakfast: bread, yogurt, raw vegetables, coffee, cheese, a handful of dates.
- Lunch: usually light, a pocket bread with filling.
- Evening meal: heaviest of the day, with rice, couscous, a stew or some roast meat, fish, vegetable salads, cooked vegetables. Soup is often drunk from glasses, as a prelude to the main meal.
- As in many North African countries, coffee and sweetmeats of various sorts, often sweetened with dates, are highly esteemed as snacks and to entertain guests. Snacks are common in the many cafes that also serve as centers for social life for men.
- Coffee preparation and serving is a major art, and, in traditional nomad tribes, coffee was often prepared by specialists (see Eritrea for the box "Coffee Ritual"). A man's adulthood is determined, among some tribes, by his ability to pour coffee accurately from a pot held over a tiny coffee cup as much as 2–3 feet below.

Libyan Lamb Soup (Shorba)

Lamb is a favorite meat in Libya, and many meals start with this soup.

4 TBS olive oil
$1\frac{1}{2}$ pounds boneless, lean cubed stewing lamb
1 onion, chopped
4 TBS tomato paste
salt, dried chili flakes to taste

$1\frac{1}{2}$ pints water
6 ounces vermicelli noodles, uncooked
3 TBS chopped fresh mint
$1\frac{1}{2}$ TBS lemon juice

Heat oil in a deep pot and brown meat and onion for 5 minutes, stirring frequently.
Add tomato paste, salt, chili flakes, and water.
Cover and simmer for 1 hour, or until meat is tender.
Add noodles, and additional water, if needed.
Cook, uncovered, until noodles are tender, for about 8–12 minutes.
Add mint and lemon juice just before serving.
Serve as a starter.

Libyan-Style Couscous Stew (Couscous b'Lahm)

Couscous—steamed grain (see Algeria for the box "Couscous")—is the common staple throughout North Africa.

¼ cup olive oil
1 pound boneless, lean stewing
   lamb, cubed
3 large onions, sliced ½-inch thick
1 large tomato, cubed
chili flakes to taste
¼ tsp ground allspice
1 tsp turmeric powder
1 tsp salt

¼ cup tomato paste
1½ cups boiling water
2 medium potatoes, peeled and
   quartered
7 ounces canned chickpeas
   (*garbanzos*)
couscous for four (see Algeria
   for the box "Couscous")

Heat oil in the bottom half of a large couscousier or heavy saucepan. Brown
   the meat on all sides.
Add half of the onions and the tomato.
Continue cooking over low heat for 10 minutes.
Add chili, allspice, turmeric, salt, tomato paste, and water.
Cover and simmer for 30–40 minutes.
Add potatoes and the remaining onions.
Simmer for 20–25 minutes, adding more water, if needed.
Add the chickpeas with their liquid and simmer for 10 minutes, or until
   heated through.
Mound the cooked couscous in a large bowl or basin. Arrange the meat
   and vegetables over the cereal, and ladle some broth over the
   couscous.
Let the dish stand for 5 minutes to allow the grain to absorb the broth.
Serve some of the broth in a bowl for diners to add while eating, as
   wished.

Stuffed Grape Leaves (Abrak)

The grape leaves intended for stuffing are picked while young and tender,
early in the morning, and pickled in brine. They have been used in Mediterranean cooking for centuries.

¾ cup rice
boiling water as needed
½ cup minced lamb
1 medium onion, finely chopped
½ cup tomatoes, chopped
½ cup butter, melted
salt, pepper to taste

5 TBS parsley, minced
40 prepared grape leaves
   (available in jars or cans from
   Greek and Turkish stores),
   softened in boiling water for
   5–8 minutes, then drained
juice from 1 large lemon

Prepare the stuffing: add rice to ½ pint boiling water.
Boil for 5 minutes, drain, and place in a large bowl.
Add the lamb, onion, tomatoes, a quarter of the melted butter, salt, pepper,
   and parsley to the rice. Mix well.

(*continued*)

To assemble the stuffed leaves: place the leaf with its base nearest you on a flat plate or chopping board. Place about 1 tablespoons rice stuffing on the base of the leaf. Snip off any remaining leaf stalk.

Fold the base over once to enclose the stuffing. Fold both sides over.

Roll the leaf securely from base to tip (packages should be about $\frac{1}{2}$ inch × 2 to 3 inches).

Grease a heavy saucepan with a tight-fitting lid with some of the butter and place grape leaf rolls in the pan, loose edges down.

Pour over the remaining butter and lemon juice. Add boiling water to just barely cover.

Place a small plate face down on the topmost leaves to prevent them moving around while cooking.

Cover tightly and cook over low heat for 35–45 minutes.

Remove from heat and leave undisturbed for about 15–20 minutes in the pan.

Serve hot or cold as appetizers.

Stuffed Onions (Basal Mahshi)

Various forms of stuffed vegetables are one of the Middle East's most common foods, available in a variety found nowhere else. This Libyan version has cousins all over the Levant.

4 large onions (approximately $1\frac{1}{2}$ pounds), peeled	1 TBS olive oil
$\frac{1}{2}$ pound ground lamb or mutton	8 ounces chopped tomatoes (or canned tomatoes)
2 cloves garlic, finely minced	$\frac{1}{2}$ tsp sweet paprika powder
1 egg, beaten	$\frac{1}{2}$ tsp fenugreek powder
$1\frac{1}{2}$ ounces flour	1 bay leaf
salt and pepper to taste	

Cut a thin disk from the base of each onion so they can stand upright in a small heavy pot.

Cut a disk off the top, and remove the center (with a tsp or an apple corer) to create a shell for stuffing, with a wall about 2–3 onion layers thick.

Reserve the onion centers and keep the top disks to serve as lids. Salt and pepper the shells and set aside.

Finely mince the onion centers and mix with the meat, garlic, egg, flour, and seasoning. Fill onion shells with the mixture. Top with the lids.

Heat oil in a pot small enough to hold all the onions upright. (If not, have some small heat-proof bowls ready to wedge onions into place.)

Add tomatoes, salt, pepper, paprika, fenugreek, and bay leaf.

Let boil for 2 minutes. Remove from heat.

Place stuffed onions upright in the pot. Tuck in the bay leaf among the onions. (Wedge the onions into place with small bowls if necessary.)

Baste onions with some tomato sauce.

Return to the heat and simmer gently for 1 hour, covered.
Serve with rice.

Date Sweet (Halwa d'Tmar)

Dates, fresh, dried, and cooked, have been a staple of Libyan life for centuries, and various types of dates are still hugely popular.

10 ounces dates, pitted and
  chopped very fine
4 ounces walnuts, chopped
4 ounces dried figs, chopped

$\frac{1}{4}$ tsp anise seed
$\frac{1}{4}$ tsp coriander powder
2 tsp honey
$\frac{1}{2}$ tsp orange blossom water

In a bowl, mix thoroughly the dates, walnuts, figs, spices, honey, and orange blossom water.

Pat into a 6 × 6-inch baking pan or glass dish and press lightly to level the surface.

Chill in the refrigerator for at least 2 hours, preferably overnight.

Cut with a sharp knife into small squares or lozenges and serve.

LIECHTENSTEIN

 Liechtenstein is a small, independent principality between Switzerland and Austria that used to be part of the Austro-Hungarian empire. It is mostly mountainous, with a broad valley, with cold winters and moderately warm summers ideal for cows and milk production.

The population is German speaking. The cuisine is very similar to that of the neighboring areas of Austria and Switzerland, with milk products very important in the diet.

Foodstuffs

- Bread, potatoes, cabbages, and greens are the major vegetable products.
- Meat, particularly beef, is eaten frequently. Chicken and pork also feature in many dishes.
- An extensive dairy industry means that milk products, including butter, cheeses, and cream are major items on the menu.

Typical Dishes

- Hearty soups and stews.
- Baked and roasted meats.
- Sandwiches and various types of breads.
- Pastries similar to Austrian varieties are common.
- Wine and beer are common drinks during the meal. Milk is drunk by most people.

Styles of Eating

- Three meals a day and snacks.
- Table settings are European standard. Meals tend to be formal.
- Breakfast: *muesli* with flavored or unflavored yogurt; cheese and cold cuts; various types of bread; coffee, milk, or cocoa.
- Lunch: light meal, often a meat sandwich or a bowl of soup with bread and butter.
- Evening meal: usually a substantial meal of at least three dishes—an appetizer; a main dish of meat, vegetables, and a carbohydrate such as potatoes; and a dessert, often topped with cream.

- Many people stop at mid-morning and mid-afternoon for a coffee and pastry, often topped with whipped cream.

Beef Soup with Liver Dumplings (Leber Knödelsuppe)

Liver is a common ingredient. Serve this as a light meal with bread and salad, or as a first course.

2 TBS butter	1 egg, lightly beaten
1 onion, very finely minced or grated	$\frac{1}{4}$ tsp salt
	$\frac{1}{4}$ tsp pepper
$\frac{1}{2}$ cup calf or chicken liver, minced or finely chopped	$\frac{1}{4}$ tsp nutmeg
	6 cups well-flavored beef broth
1 thick slice stale bread, soaked in water, then squeezed dry	3 TBS fresh parsley, minced, for garnish

Heat butter in a frying pan and sauté onion until golden.
Remove from heat and transfer to a bowl.
Add the liver, bread, egg, salt, pepper, and nutmeg. Mix well.
Allow to rest 10 minutes refrigerated, covered with plastic film.
Shape mixture into marble-sized dumplings. (If the mixture is not firm enough, add a bit of flour or bread crumbs.)
Bring the beef broth to a simmer in a large saucepan.
Slip dumplings in and allow to simmer, covered, for about 10 minutes or until the liver is done.
Serve dumplings and soup in individual bowls, sprinkled with parsley.

Meatball Sandwich (Frikadellen Broetchen)

This is a variation on your usual hamburger. Serve with sauerkraut or pickled cucumber or pickled beet.

4 cooked meatballs, any type, or hamburgers, chopped small	2 tsp mustard
	salt and pepper to taste
4 eggs, hard-boiled, peeled, and chopped	4 crusty buns, each sliced in half

Mix chopped meatballs, eggs, and mustard, and season to taste.
Spread on one half of a bun.
Top with the other half.

LITHUANIA

A Baltic country between Estonia and Russia, Lithuania is one of the three Northern European countries (the others are Latvia and Estonia) speaking distinct singular languages but sharing a common culture and ecology. The country is largely flat and is covered by forests. Climate is cool and damp, colder in winter, and cold-resistant staple grains such as rye are grown.

The majority of the population is of Baltic origin, with a significant Russian minority, a residue of the Russian empire, which ruled Lithuania for centuries.

The cuisine shares many elements with Russian and Estonian cooking.

Foodstuffs

- Rye, oats, and barley are the major crops, supplemented in modern times by wheat.
- Pork is the most important meat, and may be fresh, smoked, or pickled in brine. Beef is also eaten.
- Fish from the Baltic and fresh-water fish from the rivers are much prized. Pickled and smoked herring are traditional winter foods.
- Cabbage, potatoes, peas, onions, mushrooms are common vegetables. Wild greens and particularly mushrooms are a standard item of diet, and Lithuanian forests and fields boast several hundred varieties of wild mushrooms.
- Milk products, notably buttermilk, cream, and butter are part of many dishes.

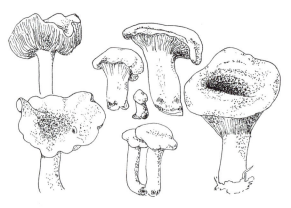

WILD MUSHROOMS

Typical Dishes

- Dumplings, stuffed with meat or with berries.
- Herring, fresh and preserved, cooked in various ways.
- Soup is the main dinner and supper food and is traditionally eaten every day.

Styles of Eating

- Three meals a day are common.
- Modern Lithuanians eat with standard European table settings.
- Breakfast: porridge (traditional), rye bread and butter, buttermilk, tea or coffee.
- Lunch: heavy meal with soup, bread, and possibly a fish or meat dish with potatoes or cabbage.
- Evening meal: similar to lunch; a soup may be the center, but without a meat or fish dish.
- Drinks include *kvass* (a drink made of rye bread or berries; see box "*Kvass*"), beer, and tea, drunk Russian style with a cube of sugar held between the teeth; buttermilk; fruit juices.

KVASS

Kvass is the most common traditional drink throughout eastern and northern Europe. It was made by most traditional households on a regular basis. Basically it is a process of recycling bread, though there are a number of flavoring variations. It is, in fact, a variation on the drink that most people in these regions consumed throughout the Middle Ages and later. *Kvass* is also available as a bottled soft drink at Russian and Baltic stores in some areas.

Latvian Gira

Gira is a form of *kvass* which exploits a common ingredient in Latvian cooking: honey.

1 pound rye bread
1 gallon hot water
1 ounce sugar
1 pound honey
$\frac{1}{2}$ ounce yeast

Slice bread and toast it until brown. Place in large glass or stainless steel bowl.
Pour water over bread.
Allow to rest for 6 hours, covered loosely.
Pass through a sieve into a glass covered jar.
Add sugar, half the honey, and yeast.
Place in a warm place for 24 hours.
Add the rest of honey and mix well.
Chill and consume immediately.

Romanian Cvas

This recipe is the most basic form of *kvass*, common throughout eastern Europe.

2 pounds rye bread, sliced thin
1 pound sugar
12 quarts boiling water

(continued)

rind of half a lemon, whole
1 ounce yeast

Dry the thinly sliced bread in the oven.
Add sugar to boiling water and pour on top of the dried bread in a 15-quart glass jar.
Add rind.
Cover with a napkin and let stand for 4–5 hours.
Strain through cheesecloth or a fine sieve.
Add the yeast dissolved in a little of the liquid. Mix, cover with a napkin, and let stand for
    another 4–5 hours until the drink starts to foam.
Strain a second time and chill. Serve immediately.

Russian Fruit Kvass

Russians drink large amounts of "standard" *kvass* made on a rye bread base. However, they also
make fruit "*kvass.*"

1 pound apples
2 ounces raisins
1 pound sugar
1 gallon water, boiled
$\frac{1}{2}$ ounce yeast

Rinse and core apples. Chop fine. Place in a large steel, enamel, or ceramic bowl.
Add raisins and sugar and pour hot water.
Allow to cool.
Add yeast and allow to stand in a warm spot for 12 hours.
Strain, discard must, and serve cool.

Mint Kvass

This is another Russian variation on *kvass.*

1 pound stale black rye bread
6 quarts water
2 TBS active dry yeast
1 cup sugar
$\frac{1}{2}$ cup lukewarm water
3 TBS fresh mint leaves
4 TBS raisins

Preheat oven to 180°F.
Place the bread in the oven for about 1 hour, until it is thoroughly dry. Chop bread coarsely.
Bring 6 quarts water to a boil in a large pot. Add bread.
Remove from heat, cover loosely with a clean kitchen towel, and set aside overnight.
Strain through a fine sieve or cheesecloth into another large pot, squeezing soaked bread to
    extract all liquid. Discard solids.
Sprinkle yeast and $\frac{1}{4}$ tsp sugar over $\frac{1}{2}$ cup lukewarm water.
Stir to dissolve the yeast completely. Set aside in a warm, draft-free spot for about 10
    minutes or until the mixture doubles in volume.

Stir the yeast mixture, remaining sugar, and the mint into the bread liquid.
Cover with a towel, and set aside for 8 hours.
Strain the mixture again.
Bottle into 2 or 3 quart-sized bottles or a gallon jug to about $\frac{2}{3}$ of the way to the top.
Divide raisins among the bottles and cover the top of each bottle with plastic wrap, secured with a rubber band.
Place in a cool, but not cold, spot overnight, or until the raisins have risen to the top and the sediment has sunk to the bottom.
Carefully draw off the clear liquid and consume immediately.

Zeppelins or Stuffed Dumplings (Cepelinai)

Cepelinai are giant dumplings named for Zeppelin air ships. They are a Lithuanian specialty, served as a main dish.

Meat Stuffing

2 TBS oil
$\frac{3}{4}$ cup onions, minced fine
8 ounces ground pork

salt and black pepper to taste
1 TBS fresh dill, minced

Heat oil and fry onions until translucent.
Add pork and briefly fry until it changes color. Remove from heat.
Season with salt, pepper and dill.
Knead mixture thoroughly and set aside until needed.

Dough

3 pounds raw potatoes, peeled, grated fine, and squeezed to expel liquid
2 pounds mashed potatoes
4 tsp cornstarch or potato flour
$1\frac{1}{2}$ tsp salt

1 cup sour cream for serving
$\frac{1}{2}$ cup crisp fried onions,
$\frac{1}{4}$ cup crisp bacon bits for garnish

In a large bowl, mix the raw and mashed potatoes, starch, and salt.
Knead thoroughly.
With moistened hands, take a fistful of the potato dough and press it flat on your palm, $\frac{1}{2}$-inch thick and $\frac{3}{4}$ the length of your hand.
Place a walnut-sized piece of the stuffing in the center of the pressed dough.
Bring the dough over the stuffing to fully enclose it. Add more dough if necessary. Taper the sides.
The finished dumpling should be as big as your fist and shaped like a lemon.
Slip the dumplings, a few at a time, into plenty of salted simmering water and simmer for approximately 25 minutes, counting from when they start floating.

(continued)

Drain and keep warm while cooking the rest.
Serve with sour cream, fried onions, and hot bacon bits.

Pork Cooked in Buttermilk (Rûgusiame Piene Virta Kiauliena)

This stew is a popular main dish, served with boiled potatoes.

1¼ pounds boneless pork pieces, roughly ½-inch thick and 2 inches square
1 cup buttermilk
¼ tsp salt
1 bay leaf
4 garlic cloves, minced
2 onions, chopped
2 TBS butter
2 tomatoes, chopped (or ½ cup canned chopped tomatoes)

1 carrot, pared and finely sliced
3 celery stalks, finely sliced
2 leeks, white part only, finely sliced
1 parsnip, pared and finely sliced
salt and pepper to taste
1 TBS flour

Cover meat with buttermilk. Add salt, bay leaf, and garlic; cover pot and cook on low heat.
Meanwhile, in a heavy saucepan with a tight-fitting lid, fry onions in butter until translucent.
Add tomatoes, carrot, celery, leeks, parsnip, and cook for 5 minutes, stirring constantly.
Add meat and buttermilk mixure to the vegetables and simmer on low heat for about 20–30 minutes, until meat is tender.
Adjust seasoning.
Mix 2 tablespoons of the cooking liquid with the flour until smooth. Pour the flour mixture into the stew and cook, stirring, until the stew thickens.
Serve with boiled potatoes and sauerkraut.

Mushrooms in a Blanket (Kepti Grybai Tedthloje)

Mushrooms, especially during the season, can be served at any meal.

1 pound fresh mushrooms
2 TBS flour
a pinch of salt
1 egg, beaten

2 TBS flour
4 TBS bread crumbs
3 ounces butter

Clean mushrooms. Cut in half lengthwise and dust with salted flour.
Dip mushroom halves into egg and roll in bread crumbs.
Fry breaded mushrooms in hot butter.

Place fried mushrooms on a baking sheet and bake in preheated oven at
    250°F, for about 10 minutes.
Serve as side dish, or with bread as a snack.

Herring in Sour Cream (Grietinîje Virta Silkê)

Baltic herring is a major mainstay for the winter, as most of the fishing catch is
salted or smoked. Fresh herring is consumed only so long as the fishing season
lasts and is a major seasonal delicacy.

4 fresh herring fillets
2 cups sour cream
a pinch of pepper

1 onion, sliced thin
1 bunch fresh dill, finely
    chopped

Cut herring into bite-sized pieces.
Pour sour cream into a heavy-bottomed frying pan, and add herring and
    pepper. Cook on low heat until sour cream thickens and turns yellow.
Arrange herring pieces on a serving dish, cover with the cooked sour cream
    and sliced onion. Sprinkle with dill.
Serve with bread or hot potatoes as a snack or for a light lunch.

Onions Stuffed with Beets (Burokëliais Ádaryti Svogûnai)

Vegetables can serve as the main dish, along with rye bread for supper, or as a
side dish for lunch.

4 large onions, peeled and
    trimmed (parboiled for 2
    minutes before being stuffed, if
    desired)
1 pickled beet, diced

salt to taste
$\frac{1}{4}$ tsp pepper
a pinch of sugar
4 TBS juice of pickled beets

Scoop out the onion centers, leaving walls about three onion layers thick.
Chop onion centers and mix with beet, salt, pepper, and sugar.
Fill onions with beet mixture.
Place filled onions on a serving platter.
Pour beet juice over.
Serve with meat dishes.

LUXEMBOURG

Luxembourg is a small landlocked country between Germany, France, and Belgium. The country is partly mountain, partly lowland plain. Weather is cool and often rainy.

The cuisine borrows from all neighboring countries and adds twists of its own. Many dishes are flavored with or based on the fruits of local orchards: plums, peaches, apples, grapes.

Foodstuffs

- Potatoes, grain dumplings, and fritters are favorite carbohydrates.
- Pork is the favorite meat. Beef and lamb are consumed, as well as geese and chicken.
- Fish from the Moselle River as well as sea fish brought from the other Low Countries.
- Vegetables: cabbage, carrots, peas and beans, asparagus, carrots, endive.
- Fruit: Luxembourg's orchards are famous for pears, plums, and particularly grapes, many of which go into making the famous Moselle wines.

Typical Dishes

- Soups, including bean soup (*Bou'neschlupp*) and nettle soup (*Brennesselszop*).
- Fish dishes, including the famous *friture*.
- Black pudding (*treipen*), ham in hay, and pork in aspic (*jhelli*).
- Crisp carnival pastry (*verwurrelt gedanken*), plum tart (*quetscheflued*).

Styles of Eating

- Most people eat three meals a day and snacks, stopping at mid-morning for a bite and in late afternoon for a bite and a drink.
- European place settings, including forks, spoons, and knives for different courses. Dining can be formal.
- Breakfast: a large cup or bowl of milky coffee and a slice of fresh bread, or rolls, cold cuts, cheese.
- Lunch: a relatively light meal, often a soup and a salad with bread.
- Evening meals: the major meal of the day, which can include an appetizer, a soup, a main course of meat and a carbohydrate, and some cooked vegetables.

Dessert follows, which is fruit or a cooked dish, often smothered in whipped cream.
- Snacks are often creamy cakes and coffee.

Green Bean Soup (Bou'neschlupp)

A soup is often the main dish during lunch.

2 pounds green or wax beans or snap beans
½ pound potatoes, peeled and diced
½ pound onion, diced
4 cups bouillon (or 2 bouillon cubes dissolved in 4 cups water)

4 slices bacon, chopped
salt, pepper to taste
½ pint sour cream

Simmer vegetables in a pot with bouillon and pepper until soft, about 25 minutes. Add water if necessary.
Meanwhile, in a frying pan, dry fry the bacon briefly.
Add bacon to vegetables.
When vegetables are done, remove from fire.
Adjust seasoning (salt may not be needed because of the bouillon and bacon).
Add sour cream, stirring briefly so that the cream is in swirls.
It is traditional to add a sausage to each soup plate, if desired.

Fried Moselle Fish (Friture de la Moselle)

This is a typical dish of the Moselle region, which produces a famous white wine. *Friture* are traditionally eaten with the fingers. Supply a bowl of fresh lemon water for washing hands.

½ pound cleaned and scaled small fresh-water fish (or fish fillets sliced into strips) per person
juice of 1 lemon
½ tsp salt
¼ tsp white pepper
5 ounces flour
oil for deep-frying (traditionally, a mix of ¼ pork fat and ¾ vegetable oil)

a bunch of parsley
2 lemons, quartered
1 lemon squeezed into individual bowls of fresh water

(continued)

Mix the fish and lemon juice, turning well in a large bowl.

Place fish in a second bowl and toss with salt and pepper.

Make sure the fish are well coated.

Place flour in a paper bag, close bag, add fish, and shake until well coated.

Heat oil in a deep fryer to 356°F.

Cook the fish by portion until golden brown. Drain on paper towels and keep warm while preparing the rest.

Serve on a warmed plate and garnish each with a lemon quarter and a sprig of parsley.

Offer diners the bowl of lemon water after dining to cleanse their hands.

Ham in Hay (Haam am Hée)

This recipe comes from the very north of Luxembourg and is almost impossible to replicate in an urban environment.

fresh, clean organic (not sprayed by any pesticide) hay
about 1 gallon water

2–3 pounds smoked ham in one piece

Take the largest pot you can find and fill one-third to one-half with fresh hay.

Pour sufficient water so that it is half the depth of the hay.

Lay the ham directly on the hay making sure it does not touch the water.

Cover the pot and bring to a boil. Allow to cook for 20 minutes per pound. Check after 10 minutes, and add hay if necessary to keep the ham out of water, or water if too much has evaporated.

Serve on a bed of hay with fried potatoes and salad.

Buckwheat Dumplings (Staerzelen)

Buckwheat is cold hardy and can grow in barren soil, making it a commonly raised grain in northern Europe. This dish is typical of the Ösling area.

1 quart salted water
1 pound buckwheat flour (available from health stores and Japanese stores)
1 cup of hot lard or melted butter

1 pint cream or whole milk
6 ounces smoked bacon, diced and lightly fried

Boil the water. As soon as it comes to a boil, sprinkle in the flour in a steady stream.

Stir once and transfer the doughy mass at once to a bowl (it will be quite solid).

Dip a tablespoon in the hot fat, take a spoonful of the dough and, with the
  help of another spoon, shape a round dumpling.
Place the dumplings gently in a mound in a prewarmed serving bowl.
Pour cream or milk over the mounded dumplings and garnish with bacon.

Potato Fritters (Gromperekichelcher)

This is served to accompany a meat dish or as a light meal on its own.

2 pounds potatoes, peeled and
  coarsely grated
1 bunch parsley
2 shallots
3 onions

2 TBS flour
4 eggs, beaten
salt and pepper to taste
oil for frying

Squeeze potatoes in a kitchen towel or cheesecloth to extract liquid.
Chop parsley, shallots, and onions together and mix with the potatoes.
Add flour and mix in.
Add the eggs.
Season to taste.
Heat about $\frac{1}{4}$ inch of oil until moderately hot in a heavy frying pan.
Drop 1 heaping tablespoonful of the mixture, and flatten out to about
  $\frac{1}{4}$-inch thick. Repeat, cooking two to four at a time (depending on size of
  frying pan). Fry until golden on both sides, turning over when necessary.
Serve with apple sauce and sour cream.

Plum Tart (Quetscheflued)

This is a dessert showcasing the famous orchard fruits on the hills above the
Moselle.

$\frac{1}{2}$ ounce dry yeast
3 TBS sugar
2 cups milk at room temperature
$\frac{1}{4}$ tsp salt
2 TBS butter, melted

1 egg, beaten
$\frac{1}{2}$ pound flour
1–2 pounds Damson plums,
  cut in half, pits discarded
sugar for serving

Heat oven to 370°F.
Mix yeast, sugar, milk, salt, butter, and egg.
Allow to rest for 5 minutes.
Mix into flour with wooden spoon (or in a food processor).
Knead flour on a floured surface until smooth and elastic.

(continued)

Place dough in a warm spot, covered with damp towel, for 1 hour.

Spread the dough onto a 12-inch buttered pie or tart pan.

Cover the dough closely with the plums in a circular or other pattern.

Bake until pastry is golden on the edges, about 30 minutes.

Sprinkle with sugar before serving (alternatively, do so ten minutes before the end of baking so that the sugar gets caramelized on the fruit).

MACEDONIA

A landlocked Balkan country, Macedonia was part of the Turkish Ottoman Empire from the fifteenth to nineteenth centuries and subsequently part of Yugoslavia until 1991 (the full name of the country is Former Yugoslav Republic of Macedonia: FYROM). Macedonia is rugged and mountainous, with several lakes, but its moderate climate is ideal for food crops such as wheat, grapes, and olives.

The population is divided between Christian (Slavic) Macedonians and Muslim Albanians. Macedonian cuisine is influenced by Greek, Turkish, and Slavic cooking.

Foodstuffs

- Staples: bread, potatoes.
- Lamb/mutton (preferred), pork (not for Muslims), beef, poultry, preserved meat (smoked), internal organs, dairy products (yogurt, sour cream, cheese), chicken eggs.
- Potatoes, olives, maize, beans, cabbage, tomato, chili pepper, beets, cucumber, eggplant.
- Grapes, watermelon, apple, plum, cherry, quince.
- Seasonings: mint, parsley, paprika, bay leaf, garlic, oregano.

Typical Dishes

- Meat dishes: grilled skewered lamb cubes (*muchkalica*) or meatballs (*kjebapchinja*); lamb roasted with vegetables (*pecheno jagne so zelka*).
- Baked casseroles: mixed meat and vegetables (*turli tarva*); pork, mushrooms, and wine (*selsko meso*); baked beans (*tavche gravche*).
- Fish dish: fried trout with lemon and sour cream (*pastrmka*).
- Vegetable dishes: sweet pepper spread (*ajvar*); pickles (*turshija*); stuffed peppers, cabbage, grape leaves; Turkish-influenced eggplant casserole (*musaka*).
- Salads: cucumbers, tomatoes, and onions with feta cheese (*shopska*); baked chopped eggplant, tomatoes and bell peppers (*pindzur*).
- Turkish-influenced rich sweets: multilayered nut-filled pastry drizzled in syrup (*baklava*).

- Drinks: coffee drunk black, thick, and sweet (*Tursko kafe*), bottled local and international fruit drinks, local beer, local grape liquor called *rakija*, and local wine.

Styles of Eating

- Three meals and snacks daily.
- Meal times are long: food and drink are less important than company and conversation.
- Breakfast: cheese-filled flaky pastry (*burek*), yogurt or coffee.
- Lunch (around 2 p.m.): Macedonian pizza (*pastrmajlija*—meat and egg-topped pizza base without tomato sauce); grilled meats with fried potatoes and *shopska* salad.
- Dinner (soon after 6 p.m.): lamb soup, roasted potatoes, stuffed cabbage, beetroot and lettuce salad with horseradish and sour cream, fresh fruit or sweet such as *baklava*.
- Snacks: sweet (walnut) or savory pastry (*burek*); homemade fruit jam (*slatko*) of quince, grape, or cherry offered on teaspoon with water when guests visit.
- Turkish coffee is served on most social occasions.
- Many bars and cafes are there for socializing; many eating places specialize in traditional food such as *burek* (savory pastries) or grilled meats.
- International fast food chains are located in shopping malls in towns; Italian restaurants are opening up.

Cucumber Salad (Tarator)

Tarator is a traditional appetizer, served with fresh bread and feta-like sharp white goat's or sheep's cheese (*sirenje*).

2 cucumbers, washed and sliced very thin	3 cloves garlic, crushed, then minced fine
1 TBS salt	1 ounce walnut meats, crushed
2 cups plain yogurt	2 TBS parsley, minced

Place cucumbers in a bowl and sprinkle with salt.
Let stand for 10 minutes, then drain.
In a separate bowl, mix yogurt, garlic, walnuts, and parsley.
Blend all ingredients together in a serving bowl.
Chill for 20–30 minutes before serving.

Eggplant Salad (Pindzhur)

This is a traditional Macedonian starter, of which there are many variations. It is also served with fresh bread and *sirinje* or *brinza* (another sharp white) cheese.

1 pound tomatoes, whole
3 fresh green bell peppers, cored and halved
1 large eggplant, stalk intact
salt and black pepper to taste
2 garlic cloves, finely minced
3 TBS olive oil

Preheat oven to 350°F.

Place tomatoes, peppers, and eggplant in a baking pan (peppers with skin up).

Bake uncovered for about 40–50 minutes or until peppers are blistered and eggplant and tomatoes collapse into themselves. Cool slightly.

Peel tomatoes and peppers. Make a slit in the eggplant and scoop out all the flesh with a spoon (do not worry if some skin goes along with it).

Chop together or put into a food processor and blend in two or three quick bursts.

Add salt and garlic and give it one more burst.

Before serving heat oil slightly (5–10 seconds at low in the microwave).

Place mixture in a serving bowl, pour oil and stir.

Meatballs (Kjoftinja)

These Turkish-influenced meatballs are a common dish, more popularly made with lamb. These are served with mashed or fried potatoes, with a vegetable dish or salad for a midday or evening meal. Sour cream is usually served on the side.

1 pound ground beef (turkey, pork, or chicken)
1 onion, finely chopped
3 cloves garlic, minced
$\frac{1}{4}$ tsp salt
$\frac{1}{4}$ tsp pepper
1 TBS fresh or $\frac{1}{4}$ tsp dried oregano
1 TBS fresh or $\frac{1}{4}$ tsp dried mint
2 slices stale bread, crumbled
$\frac{1}{2}$ cup milk or water
1 egg, beaten
flour
vegetable oil

In a large bowl, mix meat, onion, garlic, salt, pepper, oregano, and mint.

In a small bowl let bread soften in milk or water for 10–15 minutes.

Stir egg and bread into meat mixture.

Mix thoroughly and shape into golf-size balls.

Roll meatballs in flour; shake off excess.

Heat about 1 inch of oil in a frying pan over medium heat.

Fry meatballs without crowding, turning them to brown on all sides.

Keep fried meatballs warm in a low oven, absorbing excess oil on paper towels.

Place the meatballs in a warmed covered serving dish.

Serve with mashed potatoes and vegetable dishes.

Stuffed Peppers (Polneti Piperki)

Peppers are widely grown, finding their way into salads and many vegetable dishes. Serve these together with a meat dish and mashed or fried potatoes for dinner.

5 green bell peppers (4 kept
   whole, 1 finely chopped)
a large pot of boiling salted water
3 TBS butter
1 onion, finely chopped
2 cloves garlic, minced

1 8-ounce can tomato puree
½ cup smoked lean bacon or
   ham
salt and pepper to taste
2 cups bread crumbs
2 eggs, beaten

Slice the top end (the stem end) off each whole pepper, leaving a cylinder.
   Remove core and seeds; rinse.
In the pot of boiling water, parboil peppers for 5 minutes, remove and drain.
In a skillet over medium heat, melt butter; sauté onion until translucent.
Stir in garlic and chopped pepper; cook until pepper is soft.
Stir in tomato puree and smoked meat; season to taste with salt and pepper.
Lower heat to lowest possible and simmer for 10 minutes.
Turn off heat; stir in bread crumbs (reserve 2 tablespoons for sprinkling) and
   eggs.
Fill pepper shells with mixture.
Sprinkle tops with crumbs.
Bake in the oven at 350°F for 25–35 minutes or until stuffing is well
   browned.

Rice Pudding (Sutlijash)

This is a Turkish-influenced sweet served with the main meal.

4 cups milk
⅔ cup sugar
1 TBS unsalted butter
rind of 1 lemon (cut, not grated)
1 stick cinnamon
4 cups water
a pinch of salt

½ cup short-grain white rice,
   washed and drained
3 egg yolks, beaten until frothy,
   in a small bowl
1 TBS ground cinnamon, ¼ cup
   toasted almonds flakes for
   garnish

Slowly warm the milk, sugar, butter, lemon rind, and cinnamon to blood
   heat. Set aside for half an hour.
Bring water to a boil in another pan.
Add salt and rice to water, reduce the heat to lowest possible; simmer until
   rice is tender, for about 15 minutes.
Remove rice from heat. Drain.
Stir rice into milk mixture. Simmer uncovered over medium heat.

Stir rice frequently until thickened, for about 20 minutes.

Discard lemon rind and cinnamon.

Turn down the heat under the rice mixture to lowest possible.

Take $\frac{1}{2}$ cup of the hot rice mixture and stir slowly into the yolks.

Pour the yolk and rice mixture into the rest of the pudding.

Stir continuously, until the pudding thickens, for about 5 minutes.

Turn off heat and let cool to room temperature.

Spoon pudding into glass or other pretty dessert bowls.

Sprinkle with cinnamon and toasted almonds and serve.

MADAGASCAR

An island nation with a unique ecology off the coast of southern Africa, Madagascar was settled originally by people from Southeast Asia and, later, Africa. From the eighteenth to twentieth centuries, Madagascar was a protectorate of France. The climate is tropical along the coast and cooler toward the central mountain range; the south is arid.

The population mostly consists of subsistence farmers raising many varieties of rice, fruits, and vegetables. Madagascar is a major source for the vanilla bean, and many dishes feature vanilla flavoring. The population is largely Christian with a Muslim minority.

Malagasy cuisine has French, African, Indian, and Malay influences.

Foodstuffs

- Staples: rice (many types grown locally, including red, white, and black varieties), *zebu* (beef).
- Pork, fish, seafood (mangrove crab, mussel, sea urchin, oyster, shrimp, lobster), chicken, duck, turkey, eggs, wild game.
- Cassava, corn, taro, sweet potato, potato, beans (including unusual round Bambara beans, also known as groundnuts, or *Voandzeia subterranea*).
- French-influenced baguette.
- Banana (many types), mango, coconut, oranges, pineapple, peanut, lychee, peach, apricot, grape, passion fruit, star fruit, many tropical fruits, strawberry.
- Seasonings: vanilla, ginger, garlic, clove, pepper, cinnamon (all locally grown), coconut milk (for coastal dishes), curry powder. A table condiment is *sakay*, a hot chili sauce (not used for cooking).

Typical Dishes

- Clear soups and stews of mostly green vegetables or legumes with a little meat.
- French-influenced dishes: beef cooked in garlic or green onions as a *confit* (potted or preserved meat), roast breast of duck, *foie gras* (goose liver).
- Malay-Indonesian-influenced dishes of vegetables, fish, or seafood cooked in coconut sauce.
- Poultry dishes: chicken clear soup (bouillon) flavored with ginger; duck in vanilla and tomato sauce.
- Sun-dried meat or fish (*kitoza*).

- Seafood dishes: fried fish or small shrimps; French-influenced cream sauce with lobster, shrimps.
- Indian-influenced dishes: side dishes or relishes (*achard*) of curry-flavored vegetables.

Styles of Eating

- Three meals and snacks daily.
- Food is served on a mat on the floor. In cities individual plates are used; the eating utensil is a large spoon but no knives or forks are used. There are no courses as such.
- Malagasy people eat light dishes (leafy vegetables, beans, and little or lean beef) every day; rich dishes (with pork, fatty beef, or coconut milk) for weekends, celebrations, and holidays.
- Rice is eaten at all meals, but rice varies in consistency from soft to dry, to complement accompanying dish. Dry dishes go with softer rice.
- Vegetables, in the form of salads, soups, and stews, are almost always served with one or another of the many varieties of rice.
- Breakfast: traditionally, soft-cooked rice and dried beef (*kitoza*). In urban areas, baguette or other bread, butter, honey, jam, hot drinks (coffee, tea, milk, chocolate). Recent trend is small sweet rice cakes (*mofogasy*) with coffee.

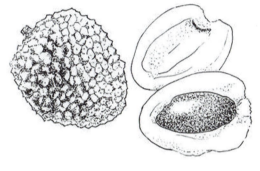

LYCHEE

- Lunch: rice; clear beef soup with greens (*romazava*); tomato and green onion relish; curried mixed vegetables; mango or other fruit in season.
- Dinner: rice; pork stew with cassava leaves (*ravitoto*); hot chili paste; fruit salad or banana fritters.
- Snacks: sweet steamed rice and fruitcakes wrapped in banana leaves (*koba ravina*); grilled skewered beef (*masikita*); Indian-style filled pastries (*samossa*).
- Desserts: sweet fritters of banana or sweet potato; tropical fruit salad; rice cakes.
- Drinks: citronella tea; burnt rice tea (*ranovola* or *ranon'ampango*); tropical fruit juices; palm toddy; local beer, rum, wine from local fruits and grapes.

Beef Soup with Greens (Romazava)

This is the national soup, whose name translates as "clear soup." This is ideally made with seven kinds of greens, and among them must be a "hot" or "prickly" vegetable (*brède mafana*), the Para (Brazilian) cress, for which watercress is a poor substitute.

2 TBS oil
2 pounds stewing beef, cubed
1 clove garlic, minced

1 onion, finely chopped
1 inch fresh ginger, sliced into julienne strips

(continued)

1 tomato, diced
salt and pepper to taste
water
1 pound mixed green vegetables
    (watercress, spinach, Chinese

cabbage, chard, pea shoots),
    washed and cut into
    1-inch slices

In a saucepan over medium heat, heat oil and quickly sear the beef.
Add garlic, onion, ginger, and tomato; season with salt and pepper.
Add water to completely cover the meat.
Allow to boil for about 10 minutes, skimming continuously.
Lower the heat to lowest possible; cover and simmer for 1 hour or until tender.
Add greens except for watercress; cook for another 10 minutes. Add watercress just before serving to preserve its peppery flavor.
Serve with white rice, a tomato relish, and a hot pepper relish.

Stewed Pork and Cassava Leaves (Ravitoto sy Henakisoa)

This is another national favorite. The African influence is evident in the use of cassava leaves, for which spinach has been substituted here. Some South American stores may carry frozen cassava leaves. Serve this with rice and side dishes of tomato relish and other vegetables for dinner.

2 TBS oil
1 onion, finely chopped
1 clove garlic, minced
2 stalks fresh thyme
2 pounds boneless pork shoulder
    and belly, cubed
1 TBS tomato paste

salt and pepper to taste
water
1 pound frozen spinach,
    defrosted and pureed in
    blender
2 cups coconut milk,
    unsweetened

Heat oil over medium heat and fry the onion until translucent. Add garlic and thyme and fry until fragrant. Transfer to a small bowl.
Add 1 more TBS oil if necessary. Increase heat and brown the meat in the hot oil, stirring frequently for 4–5 minutes.
Stir in tomato paste; continue to cook for 2 more minutes.
Season with salt and pepper to taste.
Add water to cover the meat; cover and bring to a boil.
Reduce heat; simmer for 45 minutes or until pork is very tender.
Stir in pureed spinach and coconut milk.
Simmer for 5–7 minutes.
Serve with side dishes of tomato relish and other vegetables.

Chicken with Garlic and Ginger (Akoho sy Sakamalao)

The combination of garlic and ginger in this dish is typical of Malagasy flavoring. Serve with rice, accompanied by a soup or a vegetable dish for a midday or evening meal.

8 large chicken drumsticks or 4
    quarters, skin removed, flesh
    slashed in several places
2-inch piece fresh ginger, peeled
    and grated

6 cloves garlic, finely minced
$\frac{1}{4}$ tsp salt
oil

Rub ginger, garlic, and salt into the chicken.
Leave to marinate for at least 30 minutes or longer, refrigerated in a covered
    container.
In a skillet over low heat, slowly heat enough oil for shallow-frying.
Fry chicken, covered, until done, for about 45 minutes.
Turn chicken to cook all sides evenly.
Serve hot.

Shredded Beef (Varenga)

Cattle have a mystical value in Malagasy life, and the meat of the zebu, a
type of African cow, is commonly eaten. Serve this Malagasy jerky with rice
cooked slightly soft and one or more vegetable dishes or relishes for an evening
meal.

$1\frac{1}{2}$ pounds boneless beef, cut in
    small pieces
2 level TBS salt

1 clove garlic, crushed
1 onion, sliced
water to cover

In a large saucepan, place beef, salt, garlic, and onion.
Add water to cover meat.
Cover and bring to a boil.
Lower heat and simmer for 2 hours, or until meat can be shredded with a
    fork. Add more water if necessary during cooking period.
Shred meat and transfer to a 7 × 11-inch baking dish.
Bake in a 400°F oven for $\frac{1}{2}$ hour, or until meat is browned.

Rice and Vegetables (Vary Amin'Anana)

This dish makes a complete but light meal for lunch. It can be served accompanied by another vegetable dish or relish.

2 TBS oil
$\frac{1}{4}$ pound ground beef
1 tomato, cut in $\frac{1}{2}$-inch chunks
4 scallions, cut in 1-inch pieces

$\frac{1}{4}$ pound mustard greens,
    chopped
$\frac{1}{4}$ pound spinach, chopped

(continued)

¼ pound watercress, cut in
    small pieces
1 cup water

½ cup rice, uncooked
½ tsp salt
½ tsp pepper

In a covered saucepan, heat oil over medium heat.
Brown meat, stirring frequently.
Add tomato and scallions, and reduce heat.
Stir in greens; cook until greens soften (5–10 minutes).
Add water, rice, salt, and pepper.
Cover pot and simmer on lowest heat until rice is thoroughly cooked and all
    the liquid is absorbed, for about 20–25 minutes.
Adjust seasoning and serve hot.

Tomato and Green Onion Relish (Lasary Voatabia)

This relish is a table accompaniment for soups or stews.

½ cup green onions, chopped fine
1 cup diced tomatoes
1 TBS water

1 tsp salt
⅛ tsp chili flakes

Mix all ingredients in a bowl.
Refrigerate for at least 30 minutes.
Divide into four small bowls, one for each diner, and serve with the main
    dish.

Hot Pepper Sauce (Sakay)

Although this sauce is a frequent table accompaniment to most dishes, Malagasy food is not peppery hot, and this sauce is not used for cooking. The original recipe for this sauce uses several kinds of chili peppers.

2 fresh red chili peppers, cored
    and seeded (or 5–7 drops
    prepared chili sauce, e.g.,
    Tabasco)
1 red bell pepper, cored, seeded,
    and sliced

1 TBS fresh ginger, grated
2 garlic cloves, crushed
5 (or more) TBS oil

Place all ingredients in a food processor or blender.
Process until pureed, adding more oil if needed.
Place in a small bowl as an accompaniment to dishes.

Fruit Salad (Salady Voankazo)

The range of many excellent fruits makes fruits and fruit salad the natural choice for dessert. A Malagasy touch is the use of locally grown vanilla during preparation and then again just before serving.

1 small, fresh, ripe pineapple, cut in 1-inch cubes
1 cup oranges, peeled, white parts discarded, and very thinly sliced
½ cup lychee pulp (or substitute pulp of canned lychees)

½ cup sugar
½ cup water
¼ tsp salt
2 TBS lemon juice
2 TBS vanilla extract

Combine all fruits in a bowl and mix well.
Bring sugar, water, salt, and lemon juice at a rolling boil for 1 minute.
Remove from heat.
Add vanilla extract to the syrup.
Pour the piping hot syrup over the fruit.
Chill in the refrigerator for 1 hour.
Before serving, sprinkle some more vanilla extract on each serving.

MALAWI

Malawi is a long, narrow landlocked country in southern Africa. The terrain is rolling hills, dipping down toward Lake Malawi. In the high plateaus, the climate is cool subtropical. Malawi was a British colony until the middle of the twentieth century.

Malawians are predominantly of the Chewa ethnic group, with minorities of Nyanja and Tumbuka. Although the majority are Christian, 15 percent are Muslims, largely in the north. Malawi cooking is simple and basic.

Foodstuffs

- Staple: cornmeal.
- Beef, goat, chicken, fresh-water fish, dried meat, wild game including birds.
- Potatoes (both sweet and white), cassava, sorghum, millet.
- Beans (many types), peas (cowpea, pigeon pea, chickpea), tomato, carrot, squash, cabbage, green vegetables (leaves of cassava, sweet potato, bean, pea).
- Banana, plantain, mango.
- Seasonings: tomato, onion, ground peanuts.

Styles of Eating

- One to three meals and snacks daily. (Note that meals without the staple cornmeal paste, no matter how filling or heavy, are considered snacks.)
- Hands are ritually washed with soap before and after eating by pouring water from a jug, oldest persons first. Other family members go around to assist. Families eat together, usually sitting on the floor or at a table. All share one common plate of cornmeal porridge (*nsima*) and one bowl of side dish.
- A piece of *nsima* is taken with the fingers of the right hand. This is slowly shaped with the same fingers and palm into a round ball. The ball is dipped into the side dish and brought to the mouth.
- It is considered polite to eat slowly and contribute to the conversation.
- Breakfast: thin cornmeal porridge with ground-up peanuts; tea.
- Lunch: *nsima*; green vegetable or pumpkin side dish.
- Dinner: *nsima*; fire-dried wild game or dried small fish.
- Drinks: tea; cornmeal drink commercially flavored with banana, chocolate, or orange (*mahewu*), or homemade; ginger ale and other international

- bottled drinks; home-brewed beer; local vodka and coffee liqueur.
- Snacks (homemade or sold in streets): corn on the cob, fresh fruits, cashew nuts.
- Western-style fast food such as burgers, pizza, and fried chicken are available in cities.

Cornmeal Porridge (Nsima, Ufa)

Nsima is actually more of a thick paste and resembles very firm mashed potatoes when served. It is usually eaten twice a day at lunch and dinner. During shortages, or if unaffordable, *nsima* is eaten once a day: for dinner in the late afternoon. A side dish of

BAOBAB LEAF

greens or other vegetables is the usual accompaniment: pumpkin, pumpkin leaves, or other vegetables or meat. Small dried fish from the lake, beef, goat, wild game, or, for a celebration, chicken (the most expensive form of protein) can also be made into side dishes. It is usual for most people to have just one side dish for everyday family meals.

2 cups white cornmeal	4 cups water

In a large saucepan, heat water until lukewarm.
Slowly trickle cornmeal (altogether about $\frac{2}{3}$ cup) into the water, stirring continuously with a wooden spoon to make sure lumps do not form.
Bring to a boil, stirring continuously.
Reduce heat, cover, and let simmer gently for 3–5 minutes.
The mixture will thicken to look like a thin transparent porridge.
Sprinkle the remaining cornmeal, a spoonful at a time, stirring continuously.
Keep stirring until the *nsima* is smooth and well cooked.
Let rest, covered, for 2–3 minutes.
Arrange *nsima* in three (or more) large mounds on a warmed serving platter.
   Place in the middle of the table or on a cloth on the floor and serve.

Cabbage in Peanut Sauce (Kutendela)

The usual vegetables made into a side dish are the top young leaves (shoots) from cassava, squash, pumpkin, bean, or sweet potato plants. Greens gathered from the wild (ferns, baobab leaves) are also commonly cooked. Other greens such as collards, kale, spinach, or Chinese cabbage may be used. *Kutendela* is peanut powder, here substituted by readily available peanut butter.

1 TBS oil	1 pound cabbage, shredded
1 onion, finely chopped	
1 large tomato, diced	1 cup water

(continued)

1 cup peanut butter (unsweetened if possible), in a small bowl

¼ cup warm water
salt to taste

In a saucepan, heat oil over medium heat.
Stir in onion and fry until softened.
Add tomato and fry for 2–3 minutes.
Add cabbage and 1 cup water, stirring well.
Cover and bring to a boil.
Reduce heat.
Dilute peanut butter with warm water and stir well into cabbage (add a bit more water if necessary, but do not thin the peanut sauce; it should be like thick gravy).
Taste the peanut sauce, adding salt if necessary.
Keep stirring until peanut sauce boils and cabbage is tender, for about 7–10 more minutes.
Place in one large or two small bowls.
Serve hot with *nsima*.

Sweet Potato Biscuits (Mbatata)

These sweet snacks in between meals are most likely to be made in urban areas.

4 TBS butter
¼ cup milk
¾ cup cooked, mashed sweet potato

1¼ cups sifted flour
2 tsp baking powder
½ tsp salt

Preheat oven to 350°F.
In a small saucepan, melt butter in the milk.
Pour over sweet potato and mix thoroughly.
Combine flour, baking powder, and salt, and blend into sweet potato mixture.
Turn out onto a floured surface.
Knead lightly and roll out ½-inch thick.
Cut out with a cookie cutter.
Lightly grease a baking sheet.
Place biscuits without crowding; bake for 15 minutes or until golden.
Serve warm or cold.

Peanut Puffs (Mtedza)

This is a common street food, sold from street stalls or by vendors in the cities.

½ cup butter
2 TBS sugar
¾ cup finely chopped peanuts

½ tsp vanilla
1 cup flour
powdered sugar

Preheat oven to 325°F.
Cream butter and sugar.
Stir in peanuts, vanilla, and flour.
With floured hands, roll into marble-sized balls.
Place without crowding on a lightly greased baking sheet.
Bake 20–25 minutes or until lightly golden.
Remove from oven and, while still hot, roll in powdered sugar.

Banana Fritters (Zitumbuwa)

Bananas are plentiful and often made into snacks.

3 ripe bananas, mashed
1 pinch salt
1 tsp sugar

½ cup white cornmeal or flour
oil for frying

Mix bananas well with the salt, sugar, and cornmeal or flour.
Heat over medium heat about ⅛ inch of oil in a skillet.
Place 4–5 spoonfuls of the mixture to fry in the hot oil.
Turn over when golden brown, and fry for another 2–3 minutes more.
Drain on paper towels; serve hot or cold.

MALAYSIA

Malaysia, a constitutional monarchy in Southeast Asia, was a British colony until independence in 1957. Its coastal plains have a tropical and humid climate that favor rice and coconut production while the milder temperatures in the hills and mountains are ideal for tea. The coasts provide abundant fish and seafood.

The population is divided among Malays (about 40 percent), Chinese, and Indians, mostly descendants of plantation workers brought in by colonial British. Islam is the dominant religion; Buddhism, Hinduism, Taoism, and Christianity are also practiced.

In general, peninsular Malaysian food is similar to Indonesian food in the use of many spices, hot chilies, and coconut milk, but with more pronounced Indian and Chinese elements. Mixed marriages between Chinese and Malays resulted in a distinctive style of cooking called *nyonya*, combining Malay and Chinese elements. This style of cooking is prevalent in neighboring Singapore as well. The cooking in northern Malaysia (close to Thailand) reflects the fiery hot, sweet, and sour tastes of Thai cuisine. Eastern Malaysian cooking, that is, that of diverse indigenous ethnic groups (Iban, Kenyah, Bidayoh, Penan, Kelabit, etc.), is different from the rest of Malaysia.

Foodstuffs

- Staples: rice, noodles.
- Indian-style flat breads (*roti*).
- Fish, seafood, chicken, pork (not for Muslims), beef (not for Hindus), eggs.
- Long beans, eggplant, squash, okra, leafy greens, various gourds, bitter melon, various types of Chinese cabbage, Chinese flowering broccoli.
- Soybean products (tofu, soy sauce, fermented black beans).
- Seasoning: wide range of spices (cinnamon, nutmeg, coriander, cumin, cardamom, star anise, turmeric, etc.), tamarind, hot chilies; *sambal belachan* (chili and shrimp paste, an indispensable table condiment).
- Drinks: rose syrup drinks with milk or lemon; tea; coffee; fruit juices; coconut water. Alcoholic drinks for non-Muslim indigenous groups in Sabah and Sarawak—*tapai* (rice beer) and *leheng* (sweet toddy).

Typical Dishes

- Curried stews of chicken, meat, and vegetables with or without coconut milk.
- Roast or grilled meats: roast suckling pig (for non-Muslims), roast duck, charcoal-grilled skewered chicken pieces (*satay*) with spicy peanut sauce.
- Soups of meat, seafood, and vegetables: pork and herb soup (*bak kut teh*).
- Noodles with or without soup: spicy noodles with meat, fish, or seafood with or without coconut milk (*laksa Penang*); fried noodles with seafood (*char kuay teow*).
- Fish and seafood: hot and sour fish (*ikan asam pedas*), chili-vinegar marinated fish (*acar kunyit ikan*).
- Vegetable dishes: blanched vegetables with shrimp paste dressing (*lalap, pecal*).
- Rice dishes: cooked in coconut milk (*nasi lemak*), with assorted herbs and shredded fish (*nasi ulam*).

Styles of Eating

- Three meals and snacks daily.
- Muslim Malaysians and Indians eat with their right hand or with a fork and spoon. Chinese Malays use chopsticks or fork and spoon. The spoon is used to convey food to the mouth while the fork pushes food onto the spoon.
- Breakfast: rice porridge eaten with Chinese-style fried bread; noodles with meat or fish and vegetables, usually eaten out.
- Lunch: noodles or filled *roti* (Indian flat breads) or *satay* with compressed rice (*ketupat*), commonly from street stalls.
- Dinner: rice with two to three side dishes of soup, meat or fish, and a vegetable dish; fresh fruit.
- Eating out, especially at hawker stalls (as mobile food stalls are called) or small food shops, is very common. These shops specialize in foods that are difficult to make at home because of elaborate ingredients and techniques. Snacks such as noodles or sweet coconut and rice cakes are also available here. Hawker stalls are set up at night in empty parking lots and are open till very late.

Fried Noodles with Seafood
(Char Kuay Teow, *also* Char Kuoi Teow)

This dish is typical of Penang or northern peninsular Malaysia and combines Chinese noodles and sausage with native Malay preference for fiery chilies. *Char kuay teow* has spread throughout the entire country, as well as neighboring Singapore (where it is known as fried *meehon*). The best are usually sold from hawker stalls or small family-owned shops.

Hot chili is not incorporated into the noodles in this recipe, as in the authentic dish. Rather, each diner may add a few drops of belachan and chili sauce at the table, if desired. Any combination of seafood is fine, or use all squid or clams. Serve as a snack, as the main dish for a light meal, or as one of several side dishes for a heavier meal, either lunch or dinner.

1 pound dry flat rice noodles	2 cups fresh squid, cut into rings
2 TBS thick or dark soy sauce	2–3 eggs
3 TBS regular soy sauce	salt and white pepper
2 TBS water	1 cup fresh clams or cockles,
3 TBS peanut oil	shelled
3–4 cloves garlic, minced	3 cups bean sprouts
1 dried Chinese sausage (*lap*	½ cup fresh chives, sliced into
seong), sliced thin, diagonally	1-inch lengths
2 cups fresh medium shrimp,	chili sauce (Tabasco or similar),
shelled	to add at the table

Put the noodles into a large bowl. Pour boiling water to cover and leave to reconstitute for 3–5 minutes; they should still be firm as they will be cooked further. Drain and set aside.

Prepare garlic and belachan sauce (recipe follows), and set aside.

Mix the two types of soy sauce with water; set aside.

In a large wok or skillet, heat oil over medium heat.

Stir-fry garlic until fragrant. Add sausage; stir-fry for 1 minute.

Add shrimp and squid; stir-fry until just opaque, no longer.

Add noodles and increase heat, mixing noodles and seafood well, for about 2–3 minutes.

Add 3–4 tablespoons of soy sauce mixture; stir-fry for another 3 minutes.

Clear a space in the center of the wok, pushing noodles and seafood to the sides.

Pour in 2 tablespoons oil to heat.

Break eggs into oil; season with salt and pepper, and quickly scramble for 1–2 minutes.

Add clams, then more soy sauce mixture. Mix thoroughly.

Increase heat as high as possible to allow noodles to get crisp, stir-frying for 5 minutes.

Add bean sprouts and chives; stir-fry for 2 more minutes, just enough to heat vegetables.

Remove from heat. Divide into 4 plates.

Pass belachan and chili sauce for diners to add as desired.

Belachan and Chili Sauce

2 TBS peanut oil	1 tsp sugar
3 cloves garlic, minced	2 TBS water
1 TBS *belachan*, fish sauce,	chili sauce (optional)
or anchovy sauce	

Heat oil over medium heat in a skillet.

Stir in garlic and fry until fragrant.

Add *belachan* and sugar, stirring until sugar dissolves.

Stir in water; simmer for another 5 minutes.

Remove from heat, and stir in chili sauce to taste, if desired.

HOT AND COLD FOODS

A common belief about foods, particularly prominent in Southeast and south Asia, asserts that foods have an inherent spiritual heat. In order to keep ourselves healthy, these foods must be balanced. Hot foods such as chilies or meat must be balanced with cold foods such as mangoes or certain types of greens. This underlying belief sometimes dictates the choices of menus. It is particularly adhered to with people who are considered vulnerable to health problems: pregnant women, the ill, young children, and the elderly. Rice, in this system, is always healthy, as it is completely neutral.

Mixed Fruit Salad (Rojak Buah)

The fruits and vegetables used in this salad can vary depending on what is in season. Use under-ripe fruit: pears, peaches, and plums are fine substitutes for papaya and star fruit. This is a dish that is also prepared in Indonesia and Singapore. In Malaysia, an Indian variation of *rojak* is made with fritters and soy bean curd, served with the same sweet-spicy sauce. Serve as a side dish. (See box "Hot and Cold Foods.")

1 unripe mango, peeled, diced
1 grapefruit, pomelo or 2 large
   oranges, segmented and sliced
1 cucumber, peeled, diced
1 jicama, peeled, diced
1 star fruit, thinly sliced crosswise

1 small medium-ripe papaya,
   peeled, diced
2 tart apples, peeled, cored, and
   diced, squeezed with 2 TBS
   lemon juice to deter
   browning

Place all prepared ingredients into a serving bowl. Cover and refrigerate. Pour dressing over the salad. Mix well before serving.

Spicy Dressing

1 TBS *trasi* or shrimp paste
   (wrapped in foil and grilled
   under a hot grill for 1–2 minutes
   until aromatic)
1 tsp fish sauce or anchovy sauce
   (alternatively, omit *trasi* and use
   altogether 2 TBS fish sauce)
2 TBS brown sugar

$\frac{1}{2}$ cup roasted peanuts, chopped
   coarsely (or substitute crunchy
   peanut butter)
1 TBS tamarind pulp mixed into
   2 TBS water (or 2 TBS lemon
   juice)
a few drops chili sauce (Tabasco or
   similar)

Prepare dressing by blending together all the ingredients until smooth.

Red-Cooked Chicken (Ayam Masak Merah)

The name of this dish comes from its thick red gravy, authentically made with many fresh red chilies, here substituted by sweet peppers. This is eaten with plain rice or flat Indian-style bread, called *roti*, for lunch or dinner.

4 TBS oil
2-inch cinnamon stick
4 whole cloves
1 star anise
2 onions, quartered
2 large potatoes, scraped and
    cubed
½ cup tomato paste
2 large tomatoes, quartered

4 large chicken portions, quarters
    or whole legs
1 cup water
3 red bell peppers, seeded and
    chopped fine
salt
sugar (optional)

Heat oil in a saucepan over medium heat.
Stir-fry spice mixture (recipe follows) until fragrant.
Add cinnamon, cloves, and star anise; stir-fry for 2 minutes.
Stir in onions, potatoes, tomato paste, and tomatoes; stir-fry for 3–5 minutes.
Add chicken, mixing well; add water. Cover and bring to a boil.
Reduce heat to simmer for 1 hour until chicken is tender and sauce is very
    thick.
Stir occasionally and add a bit (no more than ¼ cup at a time) of water if the
    sauce gets too thick.
Ten minutes before the chicken is done, stir in bell peppers.
Taste and season with salt (and sugar if desired).
Serve hot.

Spice Mixture

10 shallots
4 cloves garlic
1 red chili, cored, seeded
    (optional)

2-inch piece ginger, peeled and
    sliced
2 TBS coriander
1 tsp cumin

Process all the ingredients in a food processor until smooth.

Meat Pastries (Murtabak, Murtaba, *also* Martaba)

These fried meat pastries are common in Malaysia and are sold at *mamak* (Muslim Indian) shops specializing in *roti* (flat bread). The pastries are also common in neighboring Singapore, Indonesia, and even Thailand. Originally Indian but adapted to Malay taste, these pastries are made with flair on large iron griddles in street stalls. The ideal *murtabak* has a crisp pastry, which is chewy and tender inside, enclosing spicy fillings of egg, chicken, or beef. These pastries are eaten as a snack or appetizer, or as a quick lunch. Variations of this are also eaten throughout India and the Middle East.

1 pound flour
¾ tsp salt
½ tsp pepper

¼ tsp baking powder
4 eggs, beaten
1½ cups water

4 TBS ghee (clarified butter)

1 egg, lightly beaten

4 or more TBS oil or ghee
   for frying

4 TBS cilantro for garnish

2–3 fresh chilies, seeded and
   sliced into rings (optional)

Sift flour into a bowl with salt, pepper, and baking powder.

Mix in eggs and add water to make dough.

Knead in bowl for 5 minutes, then on a floured surface for 10 minutes until
   smooth and elastic.

Form into a ball, brush with oil, and leave in a bowl, covered with a damp
   towel, overnight.

Divide dough into four equal portions.

Roll out very thinly on an oiled surface.

Spread each liberally with ghee. Fold over into compact balls.

Cover balls with a damp cloth. Set aside for $\frac{1}{2}$ hour.

Roll out each ball into a thin rectangle.

Place filling evenly in the center of each piece. Pat lightly beaten egg over meat.

Quickly bring corners of dough over, sides first, then top and bottom, to seal
   into a square.

Heat 2 tablespoons oil in a skillet over medium-high heat.

Panfry pastry one at a time till light brown on both sides.

Serve hot, garnished with cilantro and chilies (if using).

Filling

2 TBS oil

1 pound ground meat (mutton
   or beef)

$\frac{1}{2}$ tsp turmeric powder

$\frac{3}{4}$ tsp salt

2 onions, minced

Heat 1 tablespoon oil in a wok.

Stir in meat, $\frac{1}{4}$ teaspoon turmeric, and $\frac{1}{2}$ teaspoon salt, frying until brown.

Remove and set aside.

Add the remaining oil to the wok. Sauté onions until golden. Add the remaining salt and turmeric powder.

Remove from heat; add to meat mixture.

Mix spice mixture (recipe follows) thoroughly into the meat and onion
   mixture.

Spice Mixture

seeds of 20 cardamom pods

2 TBS coriander seeds

1 TBS aniseed

In a skillet, dry fry the spices for 3–5 minutes over medium heat, until
   fragrant.

Process spices in a food processor or blender until fine.

Sweet Coconut Rice Balls (Onde Onde)

Most desserts and snacks in Malaysia, as in all of Southeast Asia, are made of coconut and glutinous rice, usually flavored with the sweet scent of pandan (screwpine) leaf, which also imparts its green color, being a natural food dye. The brown sugar filling melts into a syrup during cooking, and "explodes" in the mouth as the diner bites into the *onde onde*.

1½ cups glutinous rice flour
½ cup coconut milk
¼ cup lukewarm water
pandan or screwpine leaf flavoring
   (available from Asian stores;
   omit food coloring if using)
2–3 drops green food coloring

8 tsp dark brown sugar
1 cup fresh grated coconut (or
   substitute equivalent dry grated
   coconut moistened with ¼ cup
   coconut milk), mixed with ¼ tsp
   salt, steamed over boiling water
   for 5 minutes

Mix rice flour with coconut milk, water, and pandan flavoring (or food coloring) into a firm but elastic dough.

Shape rice dough into 1-inch balls (you should get about thirty).

Push a thumb into the center of each ball and fill the cavity with ¼ tsp brown sugar.

Seal, and roll back into shape with the palms of your hands.

Bring a large pot of water to a boil.

Slip balls into water, only a few at a time. Do not crowd the pan. Keep water at a steady simmer.

When balls float to the surface, continue to let them cook for at least 2 more minutes (to make sure the sugar filling melts), then remove with a slotted spoon and roll in grated coconut.

Serve warm or at room temperature as a snack or dessert.

MALDIVES

The Maldives comprises over 1,000 low-lying islands in the Indian Ocean. From the sixteenth to the nineteenth centuries, the islands came under Portuguese, Dutch, and British control, eventually becoming independent in 1965. With a flat terrain and scarce land for cultivation, locally produced food consists of fish, seafood, coconuts, and some fruits and vegetables; most food is imported.

The Maldivian population originates from South India, Sri Lanka, and Arabia, and are predominantly Muslim. The cuisine is very similar to those of South India and Sri Lanka, centering on fish and seafood, flavored with curry spices and coconut milk. There are elaborate dishes dating to a long-reigning royal (sultanate) court.

Foodstuffs

- Staples: rice, fish.
- Fish and seafood of all kinds: yellow fin tuna, lobster, crab, shrimps.
- Beef (not pork, because it is not allowed for Muslims), chicken eaten on special occasions; eggs.
- Okra, eggplant, gourds, cassava, potato, tomato.
- Coconut, mango, papaya.
- Seasonings: chili pepper, coconut, range of curry spices (fennel, cumin, coriander), curry leaf (*Murraya koenigii*), pandan leaf (screwpine); *sambol* and *mallung* are hot, spicy mixtures of fresh herbs, chilies, and coconut table relishes.

Typical Dishes

- Fish dishes: deep-fried tuna and coconut balls (*gula*), fish curry, fish soup.
- Beef curry.
- Rice-based dishes (*biriyanee*).
- Sweets: coconut and rice-based sweets.

CURRY LEAF

- Drinks: fresh coconut milk, fresh fruit juices (mango, papaya, pineapple), coconut toddy (*raa*), milky drinks (*kiri sarbat*).
- After-dinner chew: areca (betel) nut with pepper leaf, cloves, and lime.

Styles of Eating

- Three main meals and snacks daily.
- Breakfast: rice pancakes (*appa*), sometimes with egg in the center; stringhoppers (rice pancake batter forced out as noodles and steamed); tea.
- Lunch: hoppers with lentil curry and spicy sauce (*sambol*). Fresh fruit for dessert.
- Dinner: rice, fish dish, vegetable curry. Fresh mango or papaya for dessert.
- Snacks: savory or sweet hoppers (*miti kiri appa*) made with coconut milk and brown palm sugar (*jaggery*).

Gourd Relish (Chichandaa Satani)

This fresh relish, using a common Maldivian vegetable, may be served as a salad or as an accompaniment to fried fish (see the next recipe) for a midday or evening meal. Excellent substitutes are zucchini or cucumber.

1 medium onion, finely chopped	or 1 zucchini, peeled, sliced
1 green chili pepper, minced	very fine
(optional)	juice of 1 lime
½ cup coconut milk	salt to taste
½ pound baby snake gourd	
(available from Asian stores),	

In a bowl, mix onion, chili, lime juice, and salt.
Stir in coconut milk.
Add gourd, mixing thoroughly.
Adjust seasoning, and let stand for at least 30 minutes before serving.

Deep-Fried Fish (Theluli Mas)

The original recipe uses fresh tuna. Substitute any sea fish in season, such as mackerel, or a fresh-water fish such as trout. This is served with rice and a fresh vegetable relish for a midday or evening meal.

1 medium dried chili, cored and seeded, soaked 20 minutes in warm water, then drained (optional)	2 curry leaves (*Murraya koenigii*, optional)
	2 tsp whole black peppercorns
1 onion, chopped	salt to taste
5 garlic cloves, minced	1½ pounds fresh fish fillet
1 tsp cumin	oil for deep-frying

In a blender or food processor, blend the chili, onion, garlic, cumin, curry
    leaves, peppercorns, and salt to a smooth paste.
Spread fish with the spice paste.
Keep refrigerated in a covered dish for 30 minutes.
In a frying pan, heat oil until hot.
Deep-fry fish until crisp and golden brown on both sides.
Drain on paper towels.
Serve hot.

Onion Flat Bread (Fiyaa Roshi)

This flat bread is similar to those made all over India, but has a distinctive
flavoring ingredient incorporated into the dough. This is best eaten as soon as
made, as it does not keep well.

1 medium onion, finely sliced	salt to taste
1¼ cups warm (not hot) water	½ cup coconut oil
2 cups strong (bread) flour	flour for dusting

In a blender or food processor bowl, soak sliced onion in water for half an
    hour.
Blend onion till finely chopped. Drain, reserve the onion water, and keep
    solids aside.
Sift flour and salt into a bowl.
Add oil, a third of the onion water, and onion solids to make a dough, adding
    more water as required.
On a floured surface, knead thoroughly for a smooth and elastic dough.
Divide dough into twenty pieces; shape into balls.
Flour the work surface and roll each ball out to between ¼- and ⅛-inch
    thick. Cover rolled out bread with a moist towel to prevent drying out.
Over medium heat, warm a heavy nonstick skillet or frying pan until hot.
Cook the flat bread until lightly browned on both sides. Keep warm in the
    oven while making the rest.
Serve hot with a fish curry, stew, or soup.

Flavored Rice (Kaliyaa Birinjee)

This dish is eaten during Ramadan (Muslim month of daylight fasting) for
breakfast. Traditionally, this dish was an offering sent to the rajah's (king's) court
by island chiefs (see box "Ghee, Making and Use").

2 onions, sliced thin	4 cloves garlic, sliced thin
2-inch piece fresh ginger, grated	3 ounces ghee (clarified butter)

(continued)

2 sticks cinnamon, soaked in
    1 TBS hot water
5 cardamoms, soaked in 1 TBS hot
    water
1 tsp fennel seed, soaked in 1 TBS
    hot water
2 cups long-grain rice, rinsed and
    drained

2 cups coconut milk, diluted with
    2 cups warm water
2 curry leaves (*Murraya koenigii*,
    optional)
salt to taste

In a blender or food processor, blend to a paste the onions, ginger, and half the garlic. Set aside.

In a heavy saucepan, melt ghee over medium heat. Add water from soaking cinnamon, cardamom, and fennel seed. Increase heat and briskly stir until all the water has evaporated.

Stir in onion mixture, frying over high heat until onions are translucent.

Stir in cinnamon, cardamom, and the remaining garlic.

Add rice and stir-fry until rice is well coated with spices.

Stir in coconut milk, curry leaves, and salt to taste; bring to a boil.

Cover the pan, reduce heat to lowest and let simmer until rice is done, for about 20–25 minutes.

Remove from heat. Allow to rest for 10 minutes, then stir up rice to serve.

GHEE, MAKING AND USE

Clarified butter—ghee—is used as a cooking medium and flavoring agent throughout the Indian subcontinent and the Middle East. After butter is churned, the milk solids within the fat go bad fairly quickly. They also burn at low temperatures, making butter a poor cooking oil. Ghee was developed to counter these issues. It is made by heating butter from cow's milk over a low fire. Once the butter melts, heat is raised gradually until the water boils off. The butter is then allowed to cool. The semifluid, clear butterfat is poured off and stored as ghee. In the Middle East it is poured over rice as a flavoring; in parts of India it is the major cooking oil.

Beef Curry (Geri Riha)

Beef is an imported item, usually served for a special occasion, such as a family gathering. This is a mild curry that is served with rice, onion flat bread, and vegetable relish for an evening meal.

2 TBS coconut oil
1 onion, sliced fine
3 cloves garlic, sliced fine
2 curry leaves (*Murraya koenigii*,
    available from Indian stores)

1 chili pepper, cored, seeded,
    and halved (optional)
2 pieces *rampe* (pandanus) leaf (or
    substitute 3 drops pandanus

flavoring; both available from Asian stores)
1 pound beef, cubed
3 TBS coriander powder

$\frac{1}{2}$ cup coconut milk diluted with $\frac{1}{2}$ cup warm water
salt to taste
$\frac{1}{2}$ cup coconut milk

In a saucepan over medium heat, heat oil. Sauté onion until translucent, then add garlic, curry leaves, chili and *rampe* leaf, continuing to fry until onions are golden brown.

Add beef, coriander, diluted coconut milk, and salt to taste.

Simmer until the meat is tender, for about 45–60 minutes.

Add coconut milk, adjust seasoning, and remove from heat.

Potato Curry (Kukulhu Bis Riha)

This curry is a popular and easy to make main dish.

2 TBS coconut oil
$\frac{3}{4}$ cup onions, sliced fine
3 garlic cloves, sliced fine
3 curry leaves (*Murraya koenigii*, available from Indian stores) (optional)
1 chili pepper, cored, seeded, and halved (optional)
2 pieces *rampe* (pandanus) leaf (or substitute 3 drops pandanus

flavoring; both available from Asian stores)
4 medium potatoes, peeled and quartered
$\frac{1}{2}$ cup coconut milk diluted with $\frac{1}{2}$ cup warm water
3 TBS curry powder
salt to taste
4 eggs, hard-boiled and shelled
$\frac{1}{4}$ cup coconut milk

Heat oil. Sauté onions until translucent; add garlic, curry leaves, chili, and *rampe* leaf, continuing to fry until onions are golden brown.

Add potatoes and brown lightly.

Add diluted coconut milk, curry powder, and salt to taste.

Simmer until potatoes are tender.

Add eggs and cook until sauce has thickened.

Add coconut milk, adjust seasoning, and remove from heat.

Serve hot with rice.

Fish and Potato Croquettes (Cutlus)

These are a British-influenced dish, served as a side dish with vegetables and rice.

2 onions, sliced
1 garlic clove, crushed

2 small chili peppers, sliced (optional)

(*continued*)

salt to taste	1 tsp black pepper
juice of 2 limes	2 eggs, beaten
1 cup mashed potatoes	1 cup bread crumbs
2 cans tuna flakes, drained	oil for deep-frying

In a food processor or blender, finely chop onion, garlic, and chili with salt.
Add lime juice and mix well. Add mashed potato, tuna, and pepper.
Add sufficient egg to make a stiff mass.
Mix ingredients thoroughly.
Divide mixture into $\frac{1}{2}$-inch balls; roll in bread crumbs.
In a frying pan over medium heat, heat oil. Deep-fry fish balls until golden brown.
Drain on paper towels.
Serve hot.

Custard Cream Sweet (Bis Haluvaa)

This is a rich creamy sweet, popular as dessert or snack, usually accompanied by tea.

6 eggs	$\frac{1}{2}$ cup ghee (clarified butter)
1 8-ounce can sweetened condensed milk	

Butter an 8 × 10-inch baking dish.
Beat eggs with condensed milk.
Pour into the top half of a double boiler and cook, stirring frequently, over simmering water.
When thickened, add ghee, stirring continuously until the mixture starts to separate from the sides of the pot.
Transfer the mixture to the prepared dish, and smooth the top.
When thoroughly cool, cut into rectangles or lozenges (diamond shapes).
Refrigerate and serve cold.

MALI

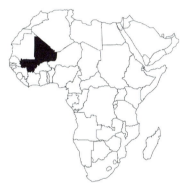

A large landlocked country in central Africa, Mali was a center of Islamic learning for several centuries and famed for gold trading in the fourteenth century. It is the location of the fabled city of Timbuktu. A French colony from 1883, it became independent in 1960.

The terrain is rolling arid plains and rugged mountains, 40 percent of which is the Sahelian desert. In the subtropical and fertile south, rice, peanuts, and other crops are grown; fish is harvested from the Niger River.

There are several ethnic groups; predominant are the Bambara, Mandinka, Songhay, and Touareg. Most Malians are Muslim. Malian cuisine shows influences from Islamic, French, North African, and neighboring Senegalese cooking.

Foodstuffs

- Staples: millet, corn, rice, sorghum, couscous (depending on region).
- Beef, goat, sheep, chicken, fresh or preserved fish.
- Dairy products: yogurt, milk, butter (for Touareg ethnic group).
- Potato (white and sweet), yams, onion, cassava, beans, peas, tomato, eggplant, okra, green leaves (baobab, sweet potato, bean).
- Banana, orange, watermelon, papaya, tamarind, shea nut.
- Seasonings: garlic, onion, black pepper, ground peanut powder; Songhay ethnic group also uses anise, cinnamon, and bay leaves.

Typical Dishes

- Millet or other grain porridge (*to*) or couscous with sauces of peanuts, okra, or green vegetables and meat.
- Stews of vegetables (eggplant, onion, potato) with chicken or meat.
- Meat dishes: grilled goat or lamb, lamb in herb sauce (*fakoye*), meat and baobab leaves in peanut sauce (*naboulou*).
- Senegalese-influenced chicken dishes: chicken and vegetable stew (*kedjennou*), chicken with onions (*yassa*).
- Fish dishes: Nile perch with hot chili sauce, smoked fish in peanut sauce.

Styles of Eating

- One to three meals (depending on availability and affordability) a day.
- Food is eaten with the fingers of the right hand.
- Breakfast: thin porridge of fermented staple grain (cornmeal, millet, or sorghum) with or without peanut powder, with or without sugar.
- Lunch and dinner: staple paste (*to*) with or without vegetable sauce.
- Drinks: slightly fermented staple soaking water (*maheu*) with sugar; red hibiscus juice (*bissap*); watermelon juice; ginger drink; sweet tea (served Arabic style in tiny cups after meals); local millet beer (*dolo*) (see box "African Teas").

Rice and Black-Eyed Peas (Mo Dunguri)

This is adapted from a Songhay dish for an evening meal. Some Asian (East Indian) stores carry packets of ready-fried onions: these are a convenient substitute for frying the onion yourself. If using these, use only 2 tablespoons oil.

$\frac{1}{4}$ cup oil	1 chicken bouillon cube
3 onions, chopped (or 2 cups ready-fried)	$\frac{1}{2}$ cup smooth peanut butter
3 cloves garlic, minced	1 dried red chili pepper, cored and seeded (optional)
2 15-ounce cans black-eyed peas, drained	$1\frac{1}{2}$ cups water
	2 cups hot cooked rice

In a saucepan, heat oil over medium heat.
Fry onions until golden brown. Set aside to drain on paper towels.
In the same oil, fry garlic until fragrant.
Add peas, bouillon, peanut butter, chili pepper, and water.
Cover the pan, bring to a boil, incorporating the peanut butter well into the liquid.
Reduce heat and simmer for 15–20 minutes, stirring to ensure the peanut sauce does not burn. Add up to $\frac{1}{4}$ cup water if needed.
Place $\frac{1}{2}$ cup hot rice into each individual plate.
Sprinkle over a quarter of the fried onions.
Spoon some bean sauce alongside.
Serve hot.

Porridge (To) *with Two Sauces*

Lunch and dinner are built around a staple cereal—cornmeal, millet, sorghum, rice, or couscous—and served with a vegetable sauce, such as given below, or black-eyed pea sauce (see the previous recipe). If affordable, another sauce with meat, fish, or poultry is served alongside. The sauce is usually thickened with okra (also called ladies' fingers), for which cornstarch is substituted here. Although the cereal is conventionally called porridge, its consistency is more of a thick paste.

Vegetable Sauce

1 pound frozen spinach, defrosted and pureed in blender	1 chicken bouillon cube
2 medium onions, chopped coarsely	2 cups water
	1 TBS cornstarch dissolved in 4 TBS water

Combine spinach, onions, bouillon, and water in a saucepan.
Cover and bring to a boil.
Reduce heat; simmer for 10–15 minutes.
Stir in cornstarch slurry 5 minutes before end of cooking.
Mix thoroughly. If too thick, add $\frac{1}{4}$ cup water and continue cooking for 1–2 more minutes.
Serve hot.

Meat Sauce

2 TBS oil	pepper
1 pound beef, turkey, or chicken, diced	water
1 onion, chopped	2 cups okra, chopped
3 level TBS tomato paste	2 cups water
$\frac{1}{2}$ level tsp salt	a pinch of baking soda

In a saucepan, heat oil and fry meat for 2–3 minutes until it changes color.
Stir in onion; fry until softened.
Stir in tomato paste, salt, pepper, and water to cover.
Cover and bring to a boil.
Reduce heat; simmer for 20–30 minutes, or until tender.
In a separate pan, bring to a boil the okra, water, and baking soda.
Reduce heat and simmer for 3–5 minutes until thick.
Stir into meat stew and simmer for another 2–3 minutes.
Serve hot.

Cornmeal Porridge

$1\frac{1}{2}$ pints simmering water	$\frac{1}{2}$ tsp bicarbonate of soda
$\frac{2}{3}$ cup cornmeal (white, preferably)	$\frac{1}{2}$ level tsp salt

Into a pan of simmering water, slowly trickle the cornmeal and soda.
Add salt and cook until the mixture is thick, stirring constantly.
Reduce heat and simmer gently for 20 minutes, stirring occasionally until very thick.

Assembly

Place a portion of the porridge into each individual bowl.
Spoon vegetable sauce and meat sauce next to porridge, keeping them apart.
Alternatively, serve sauces in communal bowls for diners to help themselves.

Hibiscus Juice or Tea (Bissap)

This is a juice commonly drunk cold or hot as tea. Dried hibiscus flowers can be found in natural food stores. Another substitute is red hibiscus tea bags.

1 cup dark red, dried hibiscus
    flowers (or 4 hibiscus tea bags)
4 cups boiling water

½ cup (or more) sugar
4 sprigs fresh mint leaves
1 tsp vanilla

Into a heat-resistant pitcher or teapot, put flowers or tea bags.
Pour boiling water over and let steep for 10 minutes, covered.
Discard flowers or bags, pressing down on them well.
Stir in sugar, adjusting it to personal taste.
Serve hot as tea.
To serve as a cold drink, let cool to room temperature, then chill.
Just before serving, stir in vanilla.
Pour over ice cubes in tall glasses. Garnish with mint.

Fish Stew (Lakh-Lalo)

Dried salted fish are an important market item for communities along the Niger River in the south of Mali. This stew is eaten as a side dish with millet, cornmeal, or other staple grain for a midday or evening meal.

1 pound dried, salted small fish
    (substitute dried anchovies
    available in Oriental
    stores)
water to cover
3 TBS vegetable oil
3 large onions, minced fine

1 fresh red chili pepper, cored,
    seeded, and minced
4 tomatoes, diced
15 okra pods, trimmed, cooked
    until soft in salted water
    for 7–10 minutes, then
    drained

Soak fish for 30 minutes in warm water to cover; drain.
In a saucepan over medium heat, heat the oil.
Fry half the onions until golden. Set aside.
Fry chili and tomatoes for 2 minutes.
Stir in 1 cup water; add fish and simmer gently for about 15 minutes.
In a food processor or blender, puree okra and the remaining onions; stir into
    pan.
Simmer for about 15 minutes or until the fish is tender and the sauce
    thickened.
Stir in the reserved onions.
Serve with boiled potatoes or paste from cornmeal, millet, or other grain.

AFRICAN TEAS

Variously known as *jus de bissap*; *tsobo* (Nigeria); *kare-kare* (Sudan); *Guinea sorrel, l'oseille de Guinée* (Guinea); *karkadé, karkaday* (North Africa and Egypt); and *karkanji* (Chad).

This is an immensely popular drink throughout western and central Africa and Egypt. It is a tea made from the dried red flowers of *Hibiscus sabdariffa*. The dried flowers are available in most markets and the tea is sold by vendors. It is the main ingredient in herbal hibiscus tea bags. In Guinea, parts of Sudan, and Egypt, it is considered the national drink. The taste is pleasantly tart, somewhat like mild cranberry juice. The tea itself is sometimes enhanced by adding other flavorings. It can be drunk hot or cold. (It is also drunk in the Caribbean and there it is known as sorrel.)

   2–3 cups dried hibiscus flowers (available from African, Caribbean, and health food stores)
      or hibiscus tea bags
   2 quarts water
   1–2 cups sugar

Optional Flavorings

Use any of the following:

   sprig of mint
   ½ tsp vanilla extract
   ½ tsp grated fresh ginger root
   1 tsp orange-blossom water
   2–3 cinnamon sticks

   Briefly rinse the dried flowers in water.
   Boil water.
   As soon as the water begins to boil, pour it over a kettle or teapot with the hibiscus
      flowers.
   Let the flowers steep for 10 minutes.
   Pour the water through a fine strainer.
   Stir in sugar to taste.
   Add any one or a combination of flavorings (if desired).
   Serve hot, or allow to chill and serve over ice.

Cardamom Tea

This is popular in eastern Africa.

   4 cups water
   5 tsp tea leaves
   1 tsp ground cardamom or 4 cardamom pods
   sugar or honey to taste
   1 cup milk

(continued)

Heat the water to a near boil.

Place leaves in a teapot and add water. Steep as normal.

Pour the tea into cups and add to each cup a pinch of ground cardamom, sugar or honey, and milk to taste.

East African Milk Tea (Chai)

Chai is the word for tea throughout the Middle East, western Asia, and in Swahili-speaking eastern Africa. There are many variants of serving tea. This one is common throughout eastern Africa.

2 cups water
2 cups milk
5 tsp tea leaves
4 cardamom seeds
1 tsp dried ginger powder
sugar to taste

Combine all ingredients in a saucepan and bring to a boil.

Simmer for a few minutes.

Pour the tea through a strainer into a teapot and serve immediately.

Moroccan Mint Tea (Chai bi'Naana)

In Morocco and throughout the Moroccan diaspora, hot mint tea is served as a refreshment at any hour of the day. It is always served in glass tumblers.

a full handful fresh mint
2 TBS black or green tea leaves
5 cups boiling water
6 ounces sugar

Place mint and tea into a long-spouted teapot.

Pour in about $\frac{1}{2}$ cup boiling water, rapidly swirl around to wash leaves, then discard water.

Add sugar.

Add 2 cups boiling water.

Allow to steep for 5–6 minutes.

Pour into small thick-walled glasses (shot glasses are ideal).

Add another cup boiling water and more sugar for a second serving.

Add another cup boiling water, more sugar, and more mint if necessary for a third serving.

The tea should be sweet and very minty.

Songhay Date and Meat Stew with Dumplings

Famed horsemen, the Songhay live in the southern and eastern parts of Mali. Their usual meal, often eaten twice a day, is a hard ball of pounded millet placed in a bowl, softened with water (or milk with a bit of sugar if available).

This dish is for a celebratory meal. For special occasions or when guests arrive, a goat is slaughtered and cooked in this North African–influenced stew perfumed with spices. Beef has been substituted in this recipe for goat or lamb.

2 pounds frozen bread roll dough,   water for 20 minutes
   defrosted   and finely chopped
3 TBS oil   5 cloves garlic, minced
2 pounds beef, cubed   1 TBS anise seed
6 onions, chopped   1 tsp cumin
1 cup tomato paste   1 stick cinnamon
8 large tomatoes, peeled, seeded,   2 bay leaves
   and chopped (or 2 16-ounce   ½ tsp salt
   cans tomatoes)   ¼ tsp pepper
10 dried dates, pitted,
   soaked in 1 cup warm

With floured hands, tear off bits of dough to make golf-ball-sized dumplings.
Place dumplings well apart on a greased tray and cover with a moist cloth; let
   rest for 1 hour.
In a thick-bottomed 5-quart saucepan, heat oil over medium heat.
Brown the meat, a few pieces at a time; remove and set aside.
Fry onions until softened.
Add tomato paste, tomatoes, and dates, including soaking water.
Stir in and mix well the garlic, anise, cumin, cinnamon, bay leaves, salt, and
   pepper.
Cook covered over medium heat for approximately 15 minutes.
Add 12 cups of water and continue to simmer for about 30 minutes.
Drop some dumplings into the simmering stew, leaving room for them to
   expand. Do not stir them in.
Cover and cook for approximately 30 more minutes.
Take out the cooked dumplings and keep warm.
Continue to cook the remaining dumplings.
If stew becomes too thick, add more water, tomatoes, spices, and dates.
When all the dumplings are done, adjust the seasoning as necessary.
Put three or more dumplings in a plate. Spoon sauce and meat
   on the side.

Sweet Millet Fritters (Maasa)

This sweet dish originates from the south of the country, where millet and cassava are both staples. These are commonly sold in the market or in the street stalls freshly made, for snacks.

6 TBS milk   1 TBS sugar
6 TBS cold water   2 tsp active dry yeast

(continued)

2 cups millet flour (available
from health food stores)
2 cups brown rice flour (available
from health food stores)

1 TBS baking powder
vegetable oil for frying
confectioners' sugar for
dusting

Combine milk and water in a pan.
Gently heat to body heat; transfer into a mixing bowl and stir in sugar until
dissolved.
Add yeast, keeping mixture in a warm place until yeast is frothy.
In a large bowl, blend together both flours and baking powder.
Stir in yeast mixture; cover with damp towel and leave in warm draft-free
place to rise for 30–40 minutes.
Gently stir mixture to the consistency of thick pancake batter.
In a large, heavy-bottomed skillet, heat about $\frac{1}{8}$ inch of oil over low to
medium heat.
Fry a few spoonfuls of the mixture at a time to golden brown.
Drain on paper towels; sprinkle with confectioners' sugar.
Serve at once.

Peanut Biscuits (Kulikuli)

Peanuts are a ubiquitous food item, made into snacks and savory sauces. Like
these biscuits, sugared peanuts are a common snack sold in the streets.

$3\frac{1}{2}$ cups smooth natural peanut
butter
$\frac{1}{2}$ cup warm water

peanut oil for deep-frying
salt to taste

Put peanut butter in a bowl.
Knead and squeeze to extract excess oil.
Add small amounts of warm water occasionally to help extract the oil.
Continue kneading and squeezing until most of the oil is extracted and
the result is a smooth paste.
Add extracted oil to frying oil.
Taste the peanut paste, and add salt, if desired (most peanut butter is salted).
With floured hands, mold the paste into small, flat patties.
In a thick-bottomed skillet over low heat, heat $\frac{1}{8}$ inch of peanut oil. Fry the
patties to a golden brown.
Remove from heat; drain and cool.
These can be stored for about a week in an airtight container at room
temperature.

MALTA

The smallest country in the European Union, Malta is an archipelago with only three inhabited islands. Its strategic location has made it occupied by Phoenicians, Greeks, Romans, Arabs, and French. In 1800 it became an English protectorate, becoming independent in 1964, but is still part of the British Commonwealth.

The climate is Mediterranean: mild, rainy winters with hot, dry summers. The terrain consists of low hills and cliffs with thin and rocky soil; some valleys are terraced and farmed for wheat, fruits, vegetables, and livestock, but these constitute only 20 percent of the country's food. The sea is another important food source, but the rest is imported. Maltese cuisine is influenced by nearby Sicily (Italy) and North Africa.

Foodstuffs

- Staples: bread, pasta.
- Rabbit (preferred), pork, chicken, lamb, goat, horse, eggs, cheese (locally made from goat's and sheep's milk).
- Potato, tomato, zucchini, eggplant, cabbage, cauliflower, pumpkin, squash, spinach.
- Cantaloupe, watermelon, grape, peach, nectarine, apricot, pomegranate, medlar, plum, citrus (grapefruit, tangerine, and orange).
- Seasonings: marjoram, mint, parsley, basil, garlic, pepper, tomato, olive oil.

Typical Dishes

- Oven-baked dishes: rice or pasta with meat and tomato sauce.
- Rabbit dishes: rabbit stewed in wine (*fenkata*), fried rabbit.
- Pasta dishes: meat- or cheese-filled hand-made ravioli (*ravjul*).
- Pastry-enclosed dishes: cauliflower with sheep or goat cheese; fish pie (*lampuki*); pasta and meat sauce covered with pastry (*timpana*).
- Stewed dishes: stuffed octopus, squid, and cuttlefish in spicy tomato sauce; stuffed roast chicken.
- Soups: fish (*aljotta*), young broad bean (*kusksu*), baby zucchini (*qarabali*).
- Vegetable dishes: stuffed eggplants, tomatoes, peppers, and other vegetables; mixed simmered vegetables (*kapunata*).

Styles of Eating

- Three meals and snacks daily.
- Breakfast: bread, goat or sheep cheese, olives, tomatoes, cooked egg, coffee or tea.
- Lunch: crusty slices of bread rubbed with ripe tomatoes and olive oil (*hobz biz-zejt*), topped with capers, olives, tuna or anchovies or goat or sheep cheese; or baked pasta dish.
- Dinner: first course of mixed or single vegetable soup (*minestra*) with crusty bread (*hobz*); main course of rabbit stewed in wine (*fenkata*) or stuffed eggplant served with fried potatoes and vegetable salad; dessert of fresh fruit; coffee with sugared almonds.
- Snacks (to eat with coffee or tea at mid-morning or mid-afternoon): boat-shaped pastries filled with cheese or peas (*pastizzi*); date-filled pastries (*imqaret*); treacle rings (*qaghaq tal-ghasel*).
- Drinks: orange, lemon, and other fruit juices, local and imported wine, local and international beer, international bottled soft drinks.
- Many types of eating places serve international food in the cities.

Spicy Bean Mash (Bigilla)

This is a Turkish-influenced dip for the crusty rolls called *hobz* that accompany most meals. It can be served for a snack or as a first course.

1 pound dried broad or navy beans (or 1 16-ounce can)	1 chili pepper, cored, seeded, finely minced (optional)
salt to taste	1 TBS mixed fresh marjoram and mint, finely chopped
2 TBS olive oil	1 TBS lemon juice
2 sprigs parsley, finely minced	Garnishes: 1 TBS olive oil, 2 TBS fresh parsley, minced
2–3 cloves garlic, peeled and crushed	

Soak beans overnight (or, if using canned beans, drain, and skip first three steps).

Put beans in a pot with water to cover.

Bring to a boil and simmer until beans are soft, for about 45 minutes to 1 hour.

In a food processor or blender, puree beans with the remaining ingredients.

Place in a serving bowl.

Make a depression in the center of the bean mash; drizzle in olive oil and sprinkle with parsley.

Serve with bread.

Fish Soup (Aljotta)

Many Maltese meals include fish in one form or another. Fish soup is a common way of preparing any medium-sized fish. This can be served with rice as a main meal for lunch or as a first course for dinner.

2 TBS olive oil
2 onions, chopped
5 garlic cloves, minced
2 TBS fresh marjoram
4 peppercorns
1 tsp tomato paste
1 pound tomatoes, peeled and
   chopped roughly

4 cups fish stock (or 2 stock
   cubes in 4 cups boiling water)
1 pound white fish fillets (any
   type), sliced into bite-sized pieces
salt, pepper to taste
1 TBS fresh mint, 1 TBS fresh
   marjoram, finely chopped, for
   garnish

In a saucepan, heat oil over medium heat.
Stir in onions and fry until soft.
Stir in garlic, marjoram, peppercorns, and tomato paste; cook for 2 minutes.
Stir in tomatoes and fish stock; bring to a boil.
Add fish fillets, and return to a boil. Add seasoning.
Reduce heat; simmer for about 10 minutes, or until fish are done.
Ladle into soup bowls; sprinkle with herbs and serve hot.

Stuffed Eggplant (Bringiel Mimli)

The Turkish influence on Maltese cuisine is evident in this dish. Serve as a main course after fish soup or as a first course for dinner.

2 large eggplants, halved
   lengthwise
1 large pot of boiling water
1 TBS butter
1 onion, finely chopped
1 garlic clove, minced
½ pound ground meat
   (beef, pork, or lamb, or
   a mixture)

1 tsp tomato paste
1 small tomato, chopped
1 TBS parsley, chopped
½ cup bread crumbs
1 egg, beaten
½ cup grated mild yellow
   cheese
salt and pepper to taste

Parboil eggplants in boiling water for 5 minutes; drain.
Scoop out flesh, leaving a ½-inch shell. Reserve flesh.
Heat butter in a saucepan, and fry onion until translucent; stir in garlic and
   meat.
When meat is lightly browned, stir in the eggplant flesh, tomato paste,
   tomato, parsley, and half the bread crumbs.
Cook until meat is done, about 15 minutes, stirring constantly.
Remove from heat.
Stir in the egg, half the cheese, and seasoning; mix well.
Stuff eggplant shells with mixture.
Sprinkle with remaining bread crumbs and cheese.
Bake in 350°F oven for 40–45 minutes or until eggplant shells are soft and
   the tops are nicely browned.

Meat Loaf (Pulpettun)

There are many variations of this popular dish, commonly served with rice or fried potatoes and a salad for a midday or evening meal.

1 large onion, grated
3 ounces soft bread crumbs
½ cup stock
3 TBS chopped parsley
2 eggs, beaten
2 TBS grated hard cheese such as
    Parmesan
1 tsp salt
½ tsp black pepper
2 pounds ground meat (beef or
    mix of pork and beef)

3 hard-boiled eggs, shelled
2 TBS olive oil
2 TBS tomato puree
¾ cup hot water
1 clove garlic, crushed
½ tsp sugar
¼ tsp salt
¼ tsp pepper

Preheat oven to 350°F.
In a large bowl, combine onion, bread crumbs, half the stock, parsley, beaten
    eggs, cheese, salt, and pepper.
Add beef and mix thoroughly.
Lightly oil a large loaf pan.
Press half of the meat mixture in an even layer.
Lay hard-boiled eggs in a row in the middle of the meat mixture.
Cover eggs with the remaining beef mixture.
Smooth the surface of the meat; brush with olive oil.
Bake for 20 minutes.
Meanwhile, combine remaining stock, tomato puree, hot water, garlic,
    sugar, salt, and pepper; pour over the meat loaf.
Bake for 40 minutes more until cooked through.
Baste occasionally with the tomato stock, adding a little hot water if the
    sauce begins to scorch.
Leave meat loaf in pan to cool slightly, for about 10 minutes; pour off sauce
    into a bowl or gravy dish.
Unmold meat loaf onto a platter and slice crosswise.
Spoon sauce over meat and serve.

Easter Cookies (Figolli)

The *figolla* (singular) is the equivalent of a chocolate Easter bunny or egg. It is a cookie sandwich with an almond filling traditionally eaten during Easter. *Figolli* were traditionally made into symbolic shapes, but now they can be of any shape.

1 pound flour
½ pound sugar
1 cup butter, diced
juice and grated rind of 1 lemon
vanilla extract
2 eggs, beaten well
water

½ cup milk (for assembly)
For Decoration:
    pastel colored small icing tubes
    (pink, yellow, green, white,
    etc.); candied almonds;
    miniature Easter eggs
    (candies)

In a food processor, prepare a soft dough with all the ingredients except the milk.

Remove the dough and knead for 5 minutes on a floured surface until glossy.

Roll the dough into a ball.

Wrap in plastic film and refrigerate for at least 2 hours or overnight.

On a floured surface, roll out the pastry dough to about ⅕-inch thick.

Cut out pairs of figures with a cookie cutter (lambs, chickens, eggs, Easter symbols).

Spread some almond paste onto one figure in a pair; leave a margin of about ½ inch all around.

Brush the margin with milk; lay the second figure over, pressing gently to seal.

Brush tops with milk; place onto a lightly greased baking sheet.

Bake for 5 minutes at 400°F.

Lower heat to 325°F and bake for about 10–15 minutes more until lightly golden.

When cool, decorate with piped icing in pastel colors. It is traditional to stick a miniature (candy) Easter egg on the decorated cookie.

Filling

½ pound plain marzipan, diced
½ cup rough chopped almonds
1 tsp orange blossom water

2 TBS lemon juice
2 TBS water

In a food processor, mix marzipan, chopped almonds, orange blossom water, lemon juice, and water to make a soft paste.

Add a bit more water if necessary.

MARSHALL ISLANDS

An archipelago in the Pacific Ocean, comprising over 1,000 coral islands, the Marshall Islands were under Spanish, German, Japanese, and American control until independence in 1986. The climate is tropical but the soil is poor, largely coral sands, and yields breadfruit, pandanus, swamp taro, and coconut. The sea is the main food source.

The population is predominantly Malay-Polynesian, with many mixed Europeans (German, American) and Japanese. Traditional food was based on a few locally available ingredients. Because of fallout from nuclear testing from the 1940s to the 1970s, contamination affects food crops and marine life on some islands. So modern food is mostly canned or frozen, imported from the United States, Australia, New Zealand, Japan, and Taiwan.

Foodstuffs

- Staples: rice, breadfruit, taro.
- Noodles (*ramen*).
- Tuna (yellowfin, albacore, skipjack, bigeye), marlin, mahi-mahi, grouper, many varieties of open sea and coral fish; preserved fish—canned sardines and tuna, tuna jerky; seafood (mangrove crabs, octopus, shrimps, squid, giant clams, lobster); canned meat (Spam, corned beef), chicken, pork, eggs.
- Squash, pumpkin, arrowroot, carrot, peas, cabbage, green leaves (pumpkin, sweet potato), eggplant, beans.
- Banana (unripe and ripe), pandanus fruit, papaya (unripe and ripe), coconut, mango, orange, canned fruit (peaches, pineapple, fruit cocktail), macadamia nut, peanut.

Typical Dishes

- Traditional stews in coconut milk: pumpkin (*banke kalel*), breadfruit (*ma*).
- Traditional dishes with taro: cooked with breadfruit, bananas. or nuts in grated coconut (*wuden*); flavored with coconut, wrapped in taro leaves and baked (*jebwater*); grated and mixed with coconut oil and coconut sap (*totaimon*).
- Traditional dishes with breadfruit: boiled, roasted, steamed, fried, or baked in an underground oven (*um*), made into soup. Also preserved by fermentation.

- American-influenced dishes: potato salad, coleslaw, doughnuts, pancakes, fried chicken.
- Chinese-influenced dishes: fried vegetable roll.
- Japanese-influenced dishes: rice (introduced during World War II); raw tuna (*sashimi*); instant noodles (*ramen*).

Styles of Eating

- Three meals and snacks daily.
- The traditional diet was a boiled or steamed staple (breadfruit, yam, or taro) served with freshly caught fish or seafood, roasted or stewed, or vegetables, usually pumpkin fruit or leaves, flavored with coconut milk. This diet is still observed in some islands far from urban and Western conveniences.
- Everyday meals are based on rice topped with a meat or fish dish (usually with no other accompaniment).
- Breakfast: urban—store-bought doughnuts/pancakes or packaged breakfast cereal, milk, coffee.
- Lunch: rice, corned beef hash.
- Dinner: rice, fried chicken or fried fish.
- Snack: traditional—mashed banana or taro and coconut balls (*jukjuk*), fresh pandanus fruit, banana; contemporary—ice cream, candy, coookies, cheese-burger, pizza, French fries, or hotdog with carbonated bottled drink.
- Drinks: coconut water, coconut toddy (fresh and fermented), bottled soft drinks.
- Celebration meals (e.g., birthday) include *sashimi* served with mayonnaise, vegetable rolls, fried chicken, lobster, shrimps, potato salad, coleslaw, fruit salad, and traditional pumpkin stewed in coconut milk.
- Chinese, Korean, Japanese, Indian/Sri Lankan, and Western fast food (burgers, pizza, pasta) are available in restaurants or cafes in the capital city.

Dried Fish

This Japanese-influenced dish is served for a midday or evening meal over rice.

2 TBS vegetable oil
1 clove garlic, minced
1 pound fish fillet, parboiled, skinned, and flaked (or substitute 2 cans tuna in brine, well drained)

1 packet *furikake* with *nori* (a Japanese seaweed-based seasoning sold in packets in Oriental food stores)

Heat oil over low heat in a wok or frying pan.
Add garlic and stir-fry until fragrant (about 1 minute).
Add fish; raise heat to medium-high. Stir constantly to dry the fish, for about 15–20 minutes.
When the fish is dry, remove from heat.
Add 2 TBS *furikake* and mix.
Serve over rice.

Crab and Potato Cakes

The original recipe calls for coconut crab and breadfruit, which would be difficult to obtain outside the country. The substitutes are regular or imitation crab and potatoes. Grated coconut is added to replicate the distinctive flavor of the coconut crab's flesh, from its diet of coconuts. Serve with coleslaw and rice for dinner.

$\frac{1}{4}$ cup bacon, diced
$\frac{2}{3}$ pound imitation or real
   crabmeat (fresh or canned),
   diced
1 onion, finely chopped
2 cloves garlic, minced
1 green bell pepper, cored, seeded,
   chopped
$\frac{2}{3}$ cup boiled potatoes, diced

3 stalks green onions, chopped
2 tsp mustard
salt, pepper to taste
$\frac{1}{4}$ cup mayonnaise
$2\frac{1}{4}$ cups bread crumbs
$\frac{1}{4}$ cup grated coconut
4 eggs, beaten
1 cup flour
oil for frying

In a skillet, cook bacon over medium heat until it starts to brown.
Drain off the fat, leaving just a film.
Stir in crab, onion, garlic, and bell pepper; fry until vegetables are softened.
Transfer mixture to a large bowl.
Let cool slightly; add potatoes, green onions, mustard, salt, and pepper.
Mix well; stir in mayonnaise, $\frac{1}{4}$ cup bread crumbs, and coconut.
Chill for 1 hour or more.
Divide mixture into eight; shape into patties.
Dip into the beaten eggs, then into flour, into the eggs again, and finally cover with the remaining bread crumbs.
Fry in medium-hot oil until golden brown on both sides. Drain on paper towels.
Keep fried cakes hot in a medium oven (350°F).

Macadamia Nut Pie

Macadamia nuts are not native to the Marshall Islands but are popularly made into confections for special occasions, such as a birthday.

4 TBS butter, melted
$\frac{2}{3}$ cup grated coconut
frozen readymade pastry for a 10-
   inch single crust pie, defrosted
4 large eggs
$\frac{1}{2}$ cup light corn syrup
$\frac{1}{2}$ cup white sugar

1 tsp vanilla extract
a pinch of salt
$2\frac{1}{2}$ cups macadamia nuts,
   coarsely chopped
1 cup whipping cream
5 TBS coconut milk

Mix butter and coconut well and press onto the bottom and sides of the unbaked crust.

In a large bowl, mix well the eggs, corn syrup, sugar, vanilla, and salt.

Stir in macadamia nuts; pour into pie shell.

Bake in a preheated 350°F oven for 15 minutes.

Reduce temperature to 325°F; continue baking for about 30 minutes, or until top is golden brown and filling tests set. (Stick a toothpick or skewer in the middle; if it comes out clean, the pie is done.)

Take pie out of oven, and set aside on a rack to cool.

For coconut-milk topping: in a well-chilled bowl, whip cream to soft peaks.

Pour in coconut milk a little at a time; stop whipping when all the coconut milk has been mixed.

Slice pie into wedges. Pass coconut milk for diners to help themselves.

MAURITANIA

Mauritania is a large country in Northwest Africa, most of which is the barren Sahara desert. Historically part of a vast Arab Berber empire that stretched toward Spain and Portugal from the eleventh century, Mauritania became a French colony in 1814 and gained independence in 1960.

The terrain is mostly flat; its climate hot, dry, and dusty. The southern region, where most Mauritanians live, is watered by the Senegal River. Coastal fishing is a major resource of food (though heavily depleted by foreign fishing). Livestock (tended by the mostly nomadic population), dates, and cereal grains (sorghum, millet) are raised.

Mauritanians are divided between Arab Berbers to the north and black Africans to the south. The cuisine is influenced by neighboring North African (Algeria, Morocco) and sub-Saharan African (Senegalese) elements.

Foodstuffs

- Staples: couscous, rice.
- Camel, lamb, goat, beef, sea fish, chicken, eggs, dairy products (camel, goat, sheep milk, yogurt, cheese).
- Potato, carrot, parsnip, sweet pepper, beans, cowpeas, chickpeas, lettuce.
- Dates, figs, watermelon, cantaloupe.
- Seasonings: cumin, coriander, pepper, mint.

Typical Dishes

- Stewed camel meat over rice, couscous, or spaghetti.
- Breads: French-style baguette and rolls, flat bread.
- Grilled and dried fish.
- Senegalese-style dishes: rice and fish stew (*tieboudienne*, also spelled *ceebujenn*); fish balls; chicken *yassa* (stew with onions).
- Salads of seasonal vegetables, usually tomatoes and cucumbers.
- French fried potatoes served with most dishes, including sandwiches.

Styles of Eating

- One to three meals a day and snacks (food shortages are common).
- Before eating, hands are washed with water from a pitcher and soap. At home, food is eaten from a common dish set on the floor on a cloth, using the right hand only. Men and women generally eat separately.
- Breakfast: baguette or roll, coffee or tea.
- Lunch: rice and fish (*ceebujenn*), vegetable salad, fried potatoes.
- Dinner: pasta with camel meat, vegetable salad, fried potatoes, watermelon or other seasonal fruit, sweet mint tea.
- Snacks: sweet fritters, grilled skewered meat, nuts.
- Drinks: camel's milk (*zrig*), sweet mint tea, yogurt, and fruit shake (*chakri*). Alcoholic drinks are frowned upon by Muslims.
- Western-style fast foods (pizza, hamburger) and Mexican, Chinese, and Senegalese food are available in restaurants in the capital.

Stuffed Leg of Lamb (Mechoui)

Next to camel, the most common meat eaten in Mauritania is lamb. The Moroccan original *mechoui* is roast lamb flavored with paprika; this Mauritanian version includes a stuffing of assorted dried fruits. This would be served for a celebration.

1 leg of lamb, boned, about
    4 pounds

Stuffing

2 ounces raisins
2 ounces pitted dates, chopped
2 ounces dried figs, chopped
1 small onion, chopped
1 cup uncooked rice
1 tsp salt

$\frac{1}{4}$ tsp coriander powder
$\frac{1}{8}$ tsp pepper
3 cups stock or bouillon
    (or $1\frac{1}{2}$ bouillon cubes dissolved
    in 3 cups warm water)

In a saucepan, combine all the stuffing ingredients with 2 cups stock and
    bring to a boil.
Cover and allow to simmer for 15 minutes, or until the rice is almost done.
Remove from heat and allow to cool.
Meanwhile preheat the oven to 325°F.
Put the stuffing into the cavity in the lamb. Secure firmly with skewers or
    kitchen string.
(Any remaining stuffing can be placed in a greased baking pan, covered with
    foil, and baked at the same time in a lower shelf in the oven.)
Place the stuffed leg on a rack in a shallow roasting pan; put remaining stock
    into the pan.
Roast the lamb for $2\frac{1}{2}$–3 hours in the center of the oven. This results in a
    slightly pink center. Calculate roasting time per pound of meat and

(*continued*)

stuffing at 25 minutes, plus an extra 25 minutes for medium done. (For well done, roast at 30 minutes per pound, plus an extra 30 minutes.)

Baste the lamb occasionally with the remaining stock and meat juices while roasting.

Let rest for 10 minutes before carving to let the meat settle. Serve surrounded with the rice stuffing.

Pepper Steak

This is common in the south of the country as a luxury dish.

$\frac{1}{4}$ cup vegetable oil
1 tsp salt
$\frac{1}{2}$ tsp black pepper
2 cloves garlic, minced fine
   (or 1 tsp garlic powder)
$\frac{1}{4}$ tsp chili or cayenne powder
2 green bell peppers, cored,
   seeded, cut in strips

4 beef steaks, cut in strips
1 cube beef stock, crushed
$\frac{1}{2}$ cup coconut milk
$\frac{1}{4}$ cup water
2 TBS cornstarch, dissolved in
   3 TBS water

Heat oil in a frying pan and add salt, pepper, garlic, and chili.

Sauté the green peppers for 2 minutes.

Add strips of steak and sauté for 2 minutes.

Add crushed stock cube.

Remove the meat and bell peppers from the pan and keep warm.

Mix the coconut milk and water. Add to the gravy remaining in the pan and bring to a boil.

Stir in the cornstarch slurry, and simmer over low heat until smooth and thickened.

Return the steak and peppers to the pan briefly to heat through.

Serve at once with rice.

Chicken and Chickpeas (Chaj)

Chickpeas and other legumes are commonly eaten, made into stews, for a midday or evening meal.

$\frac{1}{4}$ cup butter
4 large portions chicken, legs or
   quarters
2 large onions, sliced into rings

1 8-ounce can chickpeas
salt and pepper to taste
$\frac{1}{2}$ cup water

Heat the butter in a saucepan.

Stir in chicken and onions, frying until chicken is browned and onions soft.

Add chickpeas, salt, and pepper.
Cook on high heat for 10 minutes, stirring constantly.
Add water, cover; reduce heat and simmer for 25–30 minutes, stirring occasionally.
Serve with flat bread (*pita*) and fried potatoes.

Nomad-Style Lamb

Grilled skewers of lamb are a common snack food.

2 TBS oil	1 eggplant, cut into 2-inch cubes
2 TBS mustard	2 green bell peppers, cored and seeded, cut into 2-inch cubes
1 chili pepper, cored, seeded, and shredded	2 large semi-ripe tomatoes, cut into eighths
1 tsp salt	2 large onions, cut into eighths
1 bunch thyme	salt and cayenne pepper to taste
1 pound lamb (or turkey, chicken, beef) cut into bite-sized cubes	

Mix a marinade of oil, mustard, chili, salt, and thyme.
Marinate the meat for 1 hour or more.
Thread meat and vegetables alternately onto four skewers.
Grill over hot coals or under a broiler, until meat is done but still pink in the middle (if using turkey, it must be thoroughly cooked in the middle, but still moist).
Sprinkle with some cayenne powder and additional salt to taste.
Serve with flat bread (*pita*).

Couscous

Couscous is eaten all over North Africa. This is a festive dish, with Mauritanian characteristic fruit additions.

Stew

2–3 TBS vegetable oil	3 carrots, peeled and sliced
2 pounds boneless stewing lamb (chicken, beef, or turkey), cut into 1-inch cubes	3 small potatoes, quartered
	1 cup cabbage, chopped coarsely
2 onions, chopped	1 cup pumpkin, chopped
3 cloves garlic, thinly sliced	2 medium tomatoes, chopped
3 turnips, peeled and chopped	salt, pepper to taste

(continued)

In a large, deep, covered saucepan, heat the oil over medium heat, and quickly brown the meat.

Push the meat to one side, reduce heat and sauté the onions and garlic until golden.

Add vegetables, stirring for 2–3 minutes.

Add seasoning and enough water to cover vegetables, and simmer, covered, until the vegetables are tender and the meat is cooked, about 45–60 minutes.

Couscous

2 cups couscous	1 cup cooked chickpeas
1 cup dates, pitted and chopped	$\frac{1}{4}$ cup butter, melted
$\frac{1}{2}$ cup raisins	

Prepare the couscous by sprinkling with about 1 cup of cold water to moisten.

Work the water into the couscous with the fingers so that lumps do not form.

Mix in the dates, raisins, and chickpeas, place in a colander and steam for 30 minutes over the simmering stew or over boiling water in a separate pan (see Algeria for the box "Couscous").

Transfer the couscous to a large bowl. Sprinkle with 1 cup of cold water and work into the couscous as before, breaking apart any lumps.

Stir in the butter and mix into the couscous.

Return couscous to the colander and steam for another 30 minutes.

To serve: place a mound of couscous on individual plates, and surround with the stew, ensuring that everyone gets an equal share of meat and a variety of vegetables.

MAURITIUS

A small island in the Indian Ocean noted for being the home of the now extinct dodo bird, Mauritius was a Dutch, French, then British colony until independence in 1968 and still remains part of the British Commonwealth. The terrain consists of a coastal plain and central plateau, with a warm subtropical climate tempered by trade winds, ideal for a wide range of tropical crops such as sugarcane (a major export).

The multicultural Mauritians are mostly of Indian descent (whose forebears were brought in for the colonial plantations), with minorities of African, European, Chinese, and mixed Creoles. The cuisine reflects this multiethnic mix. Though many of the islanders are Hindus, meat is eaten by most.

Foodstuffs

- Staples: rice, French baguette, Indian flat breads.
- Chicken, beef (not for Hindus), pork (not for Muslims), fish, seafood (giant prawns), wild game (boar, venison).
- Potato, maize, tomato, cucumber, pumpkin, gourds, carrot, lettuce, eggplant, cabbage.
- Banana, pineapple, coconut, mango.
- Seasonings: tomato, ginger, garlic, chilies, curry spices, Chinese cooking spices, French cooking herbs/spices, olive oil.

Typical Dishes

- Creole *rougaille* (spicy tomato sauce).
- Indian-style dishes: curries of meat, lentils; pickled vegetable relish (*achard*).
- Chinese-style dishes: roast pork, sweet-sour vegetable stir-fry, noodles, spring roll.
- English-style dishes: bacon and eggs.
- French-style dishes: bean casserole (*cassoulet*), braised meat (*daube*), cream-based desserts, confectionery.

Styles of Eating

- Three meals a day and snacks.
- Normal urban table settings are European standard (with knife, fork, spoon); in rural villages people eat with spoon and fork on individual plates, or with the fingers of the right hand.
- Breakfast: French pastries or baguette with butter, jam, coffee, or tropical fruits.
- Lunch: Indian-style curry with rice, French-style custard for dessert.
- Dinner: Chinese-style red braised pork with rice.
- Snacks/mid-afternoon tea (holdover from British rule): lentil-stuffed pastry (*dholl* with *puri*) eaten with Creole tomato sauce; vegetable-filled pastries (*samossa*); fruits; sweet French pastries; peanuts.
- Drinks: tamarind, mango and other fruit juices, yogurt-based drinks, *alooda* (milk drink), coffee, tea.
- Fast food (fried chicken, pizza, burger) outlets can be found in the capital.

Choko Salad (Salade Chou Chou)

Choko, *chou chou*, or chayote is a member of the gourd family and can be eaten fresh or cooked. Serve this as side dish with any main dish for the midday or evening meal.

3 *chokos* (chayote, available from Asian and Hispanic groceries)	1 medium onion, sliced finely
¼ tsp salt	1 green chili, cored, seeded, and shredded (optional)
water, as needed	
1 TBS white vinegar	salt and freshly ground black pepper to taste
3 TBS extra virgin olive oil	
1 TBS garlic, freshly crushed	

Place the *chokos* into salted boiling water.
Boil for about 5–7 minutes, until just crisp-tender.
Remove and immediately place into cold water to cool.
Peel and halve the *chokos*.
Slice lengthwise.
The soft seeds may be included, if desired, or separated and eaten on their own, lightly salted.
Mix a dressing with vinegar, oil, garlic, onion, chili, salt, and pepper.
Pour the dressing over the *choko* slices.
Mix together just before serving.

Chili Cakes (Gateaux Piments)

These Indian-style fritters are common snacks, eaten with hot bread and butter or on their own.

1 cup split peas

1–2 green or red chilies, cored, seeded, and shredded

2 TBS cilantro, chopped

2 TBS spring onions, chopped finely

salt to taste

½ tsp whole cumin seeds, lightly crushed

oil for deep-frying

Rinse peas, soak in water to cover overnight, and drain.

Take half the peas and grind very fine in a blender.

Grind the second batch roughly.

Mix thoroughly remaining ingredients with the ground peas.

Add a little bit of water, if needed, for a stiff mixture.

Shape mixture into large marbles.

Heat oil and deep-fry a few at a time until golden.

Drain on paper towels.

Serve hot with fresh bread or on their own as a snack.

Chicken Stew (Daube de Poulet)

This stew is a blend of Indian and French influences. Serve with *faratas* (flaky flat bread) or rice, with a side dish of lentils for midday or evening.

3 TBS oil

2 onions, chopped

1 TBS garlic, minced

1 tsp fresh ginger, grated

2 pounds chicken, cut into serving-size pieces

3 cloves

1 cinnamon stick

1 TBS thyme

¼ tsp salt

¼ tsp pepper

1 16-ounce can chopped tomatoes

1 TBS cilantro, minced fine

1 TBS cilantro, chopped, for garnish

Heat oil in a deep, thick-bottomed saucepan over medium heat.

Stir in onions, garlic, and ginger; fry until the onions are soft.

Add chicken, cloves, cinnamon, thyme, salt, and pepper; cook for 5–8 minutes, stirring well.

Stir in tomatoes and cilantro; reduce heat and let simmer for 1 hour or until chicken is tender.

Adjust seasoning.

Serve hot, garnished with cilantro.

Pancakes (Faratas)

These flaky flat breads are widely made and eaten with grilled meats. The flakiness is achieved by brushing melted butter several times into the folded dough, similar to making flaky pastry.

2 cups sifted white flour
1 tsp salt
½ cup + 2 TBS water

3 TBS (or more) ghee or melted butter

In a bowl, mix flour with salt and half the water into a dough.

Knead well for 20 minutes, adding the remaining water a little at a time to get a smooth, elastic dough.

Sprinkle with 1–2 tablespoons water; cover with a moist towel. Set aside for 20–30 minutes.

Divide dough evenly into six balls.

On a lightly floured surface, roll out each ball into a 6-inch disk.

Lightly brush a little ghee or melted butter on each disk; fold over into a semicircle.

Brush more ghee over the top; fold again.

Lightly and gently roll out again to make a disk but do not roll out to the edges to keep the air in, and not as thin as previously. Brush with more ghee.

Heat an iron griddle slowly until very hot.

Place *farata* on hot griddle to cook for 2–3 seconds.

Turn over and brush the cooked side with melted butter.

Cook for a further 2–3 seconds or until *farata* is light golden on both sides.

Keep warm while making the remainder.

Serve hot with grilled meats.

Cold Jelly Drink (Alooda Glacée)

Cold drinks are very welcome in a hot and humid climate. This is a popular drink. An alternative to the agar agar strips is firmly set gelatin of any fruit flavor, diced. Canned sweet basil drinks can be found in Asian food stores. These can be substituted for the syrup and seeds called for in the recipe.

2 TBS sweet basil seeds (available at Thai food stores; optional)
1 cup agar agar strips chopped into ½-inch pieces (agar agar or seaweed gelatin strips are available from Asian shops)
3 cups water
4 TBS sugar

1 quart very cold milk
1 tsp vanilla or almond extract
food color, red or green (optional)
4 tall drinking glasses, chilled in the refrigerator about 20 minutes before serving
2 cups crushed ice

Soak basil seeds and chopped agar-agar strips in water to cover overnight.

Make a light syrup by combining water and sugar over low heat until sugar is dissolved; cool.

Mix thoroughly syrup, milk, vanilla or almond extract, and a drop of chosen food color (for a very pale tint); chill thoroughly for at least 30 minutes.

Into each chilled glass, place 3–4 tablespoons of basil seeds and softened agar
    agar strips.
Pour over chilled milk mixture.
Top with crushed ice and serve.

Raspberry Cakes (Napolitaines)

These French-influenced tiny cakes filled with raspberry jam and covered in
pink icing are popular and served with coffee or tea.

⅔ cup butter   ½ cup confectioners' sugar
1 cup sifted white flour   2 drops red food color
¼ cup good quality raspberry jam

Rub butter into flour to make a soft dough. (Add a little more butter if
    needed to achieve this.)
On a lightly floured surface, roll out dough to about ¼-inch thick.
Cut out 2-inch diameter rounds.
Reroll trimmings and repeat.
Place dough rounds on a lightly greased baking sheet.
Bake in a preheated oven at 325°F until done, but not brown, for about
    10–15 minutes.
When cool, spread jam over half of the biscuit rounds; cover with remaining
    half.
Mix confectioners' sugar, food color, and about 3 tablespoons warm water to
    make a glaze of flowing consistency. (Add a bit more water if needed.)
Set sandwiched cakes on a grid placed over waxed paper to catch drips.
Spoon glaze over cakes to coat evenly.
Set aside to cool.

MEXICO

Directly south of the United States, Mexico covers a wide area, almost three times that of Texas. With cold mountain ranges and high plateaus, but warm coastal lowlands, Mexico has a varied climate suited to both temperate and tropical crops: coffee, sugar, corn, citrus fruits.

For 300 years a Spanish colony, Mexico became independent in 1810. The Spanish legacy is still evident in the predominantly mixed (*mestizo*) Spanish-Amerindian population, Catholicism, language, culture, and food.

Mexican cooking displays a rich mix of native Amerindian (Maya), Spanish, and French elements (from a brief period of French rule in the 1860s).

Foodstuffs

- Staples: corn, beans, wheat, rice.
- Wheat tortilla in the north; corn tortilla elsewhere.
- Pork, beef, chicken, turkey, beef, fish and shellfish, red snapper, turtle, game, edible insects.
- Vegetables and fruits: chili peppers, tomato, cactus "leaves" (*nopal*), *jicama* (a sweet, crisp tuber eaten raw), avocado, sweet pepper, pumpkin, squash, chayote, melon, grapes, citrus fruits, nuts.
- Seasonings: combined use of many types of fresh and dried chilies (not all hot) in the same dish, for example, *ancho* (large, wide, brown); *tepin* (small cranberry-like, hot); *serrano* (small, green, hot); spice and herb mixes (cilantro, *epazote* [goosefoot], and *hierba santa* [root-beer flavored leaf]); *achiote* paste (herb/spice mix colored with red seeds of *achiote* plant, *Bixa orellana*); dark chocolate in savory stews; cinnamon; cumin; oregano; cloves; vanilla.

Typical Dishes

- Spanish-style stews of meat, vegetables, and fruit (*mancha manteles, caldillo*).
- *Mole*, the national dish: rich, spicy, herby stew with nuts or pumpkin/sesame seeds (many regional variants). *Mole* sauce can be green, red, black (with chocolate), or yellow.
- Spit-roasted meat (*barbacoa*—the original barbecue, *asado*): goat, lamb, venison, suckling pig.
- Steamed leaf-wrapped dumplings (*tamales*) of corn, meat and vegetables.

- Stuffed fried chili peppers with nuts (*chiles en nogada*).
- Sweets: Spanish-style egg-rich custards and flans; cakes of fruits, nuts, coconut; fruit pastes (quince, guava).
- Drinks: *aguas frescas* (fruit juices, often with flowers and edible seeds, such as *chia*—the gelatinous seed of a sage relative), chocolate, coffee, locally brewed beer, tequila (distilled spirit from maguey cactus).

Styles of Eating

- Three meals a day and snacks.
- Breakfast: between 8 and 9 a.m., hot chocolate or coffee with refried beans, porridge. Tortilla or crusty roll, eggs (omelet, fried or scrambled). Around 11 a.m., for upper class; brunch-like meal.
- Lunch (*comida*): between 2 and 4 p.m. Many offices close for lunch. This is the heaviest meal, with as many as five to seven courses, featuring soup, main course, salad, and sweet. Rice, pasta dishes are considered a "dry soup" course and are served separately. Families eat together.

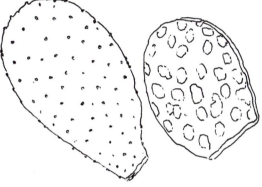

- A late afternoon snack or early evening meal, *merienda*, eaten between 6 and 7 p.m., consists of a savory dish or hot sandwich or sweet breads with coffee.
- Supper is eaten between 8 and 10 p.m., usually a light entrée or dessert with coffee or tea.

CACTUS LEAF

- Snacks: tortillas stuffed with cheese, bean, or meat fillings (*tacos, quesadillas, burritos, carnitas*); hot sandwiches (*pambazos*); *nanches* (yellow, tart, plum-sized fruit) eaten with chili sauce, salt, and lime; steamed green chickpeas in the pod; shaved ice and fruit syrup (*raspado*); crisp pork skin (*chicharron*); ripe plantains with condensed milk. Recently sweet cakes, biscuits, and candy are increasingly eaten by young children.
- *Comida corrida* (lunch on the run) is a multicourse meal complete with fresh fruit drink served at all eating places during lunch for office workers. Street stalls and vendors sell various snacks in see-through plastic cups.

Hot Sandwiches (Pambazos)

Pambazos—bread rolls filled with chicken or cheese and served with a hot sauce—are a common street food in Puebla and Veracruz, in central-eastern Mexico. This can be served as a snack or, with a salad or soup, as a light meal.

4 bread rolls
3 cups cooked chicken meat, shredded
1 onion (slice ½ onion thinly into rings and

reserve the other half for sauce)
1 avocado, sliced lengthwise

(continued)

Split the rolls and distribute the chicken evenly among them.
Spoon the hot sauce over the chicken.
Garnish with avocado and onion slices.

Sauce

2 TBS oil	¼ tsp cumin
2 cloves garlic, minced	a pinch of cloves
½ onion, minced	a pinch of allspice
2 large ripe tomatoes, finely chopped	⅛ tsp cinnamon
	¼ tsp oregano
1 *guajillo* chili pepper, seeded (optional, available from Hispanic groceries, or substitute red chili pepper)	salt to taste
	¼ cup water

In a saucepan, heat oil over medium heat, add the garlic and onion, and cook until soft.
Stir in the tomatoes, chili pepper, spices and herbs, and water; cover and simmer until thick for 10–15 minutes. Add salt to taste.
Pass through a sieve before using.

Avocado, Orange, and Radish Salad
(Ensalada de Aguacate con Naranja y Rábanos)

Avocados and oranges are often used in both sweet and savory dishes. The radishes add a brilliant contrasting color.

1 large or 3 small avocados, cubed (sprinkle with lime juice to prevent browning)	juice of two limes (use some for avocados)
2 oranges, peeled, segmented, and white membranes removed	juice of one orange
	¼ cup olive oil
5–6 radishes, sliced into circles	¼ cup chopped fresh cilantro
½ medium red onion, sliced thinly	salt and pepper to taste

Place the prepared vegetable in a bowl.
Mix the citrus juices, olive oil, cilantro, salt, and pepper.
Pour over the vegetables.
Chill for 30 minutes and serve.

Oaxacan-Style Lentils (Lentejas Oaxaqueñas)

In Oaxaca, southern Mexico, this dish is traditional during Lent as it contains no meat. The deft use of fruit is typical of cooking in this part of Mexico.

2 cups lentils
5 cups water
1 head garlic (about 10 cloves),
  minced
1 large onion, chopped
2 TBS oil
2 unripe plantains, cubed

1 small fresh pineapple, peeled,
  cubed
2 tomatoes, chopped
$\frac{1}{2}$ tsp cloves
1 tsp allspice
salt to taste

Bring the lentils, water, half the garlic, and half the onion to a boil.
Cover and simmer for 20–30 minutes, until lentils are tender but still firm.
Add salt to taste. Set aside.
Heat oil over medium heat in a saucepan and sauté the remaining onion and
  garlic until soft.
Stir in plantains, pineapple, and tomatoes, and cook until the plantains are
  soft, for about 10–15 minutes.
Stir in the spices, lentils, and about half of the liquid in which the lentils were
  cooked.
Continue cooking until thick, adding more liquid as necessary.
Serve with fried slices of plantain if desired.

Beef Roullades with Green Mole
(Bistec Relleno con Mole Verde)

The idea of this dish is to use the bacon and vegetables as a colorful stuffing for
the beef rolls. Serve this as a main course for lunch, with plenty of soft tortillas to
mop up the flavorful sauce, and a salad (see box "Mole Sauces").

Beef Roullades

$1\frac{1}{2}$ pounds thinly sliced beef
$\frac{1}{4}$ pound raw smoked bacon or
  ham, or a mix of both, sliced
  into thin strips

1 potato, cut into thin strips
$\frac{1}{4}$ pound string beans, cut
  lengthwise into thin strips
salt and pepper

Spread each piece of beef and sprinkle with salt and pepper.
Lay strips of bacon, ham, potatoes, and green beans in a line along the edge
  of the meat closest to you.
Taking hold of the edge of the meat, fold it over the stuffing to enclose it,
  continuing to roll tightly until all the stuffing is covered. Secure ends of
  the meat with toothpicks. Set aside.

Mole

$\frac{1}{4}$ cup roasted green pumpkin
  seeds
$\frac{1}{3}$ cup roasted sesame seeds

1 serrano chili (optional)
4–5 tomatillos (substitute green
  tomatoes)

(continued)

5 sprigs cilantro
3 sprigs epazote (substitute oregano or thyme)
3 green onions, chopped
¼ onion, chopped

2 garlic cloves, chopped
½ tsp powdered cumin
3 cups chicken stock
1–2 TBS olive oil
salt to taste

In a food processor, blend the seeds, chili, tomatillos, spices, and herbs with ½ cup chicken stock until smooth. Set aside.

In a saucepan, heat olive oil and add the blended ingredients. Add salt to taste.

Stir in the rest of the chicken stock.

Put the beef rolls into the sauce and cover, simmering for 30–45 minutes or until the vegetables in the stuffing are tender.

Banana and Nut Dessert (Torta de Plátanos y Nueces)

This rich dessert showcases fruits and nuts in season. Mangoes, plums, or apples can be used instead of the bananas. Serve with cream, whipped or poured, if desired.

½ cup sugar
½ cup water
juice of 1 lime or lemon
⅓ cup butter
2 eggs, beaten

6 bananas, sliced, divided into three portions
2 cups chopped walnuts, almonds, or pecans, divided into three portions

In a small saucepan, make a light syrup by boiling sugar, water, and lime or lemon juice until the sugar dissolves. Set aside.

In a bowl, cream the butter until light.

Beat in eggs one at a time, incorporating well after each.

Pour in the still-warm syrup slowly over the butter mixture, mixing well.

In a buttered 8-inch square baking dish, place a layer of bananas.

Sprinkle with one portion of the nuts and pour a third of the butter syrup over.

Continue with the remaining bananas, nuts, and syrup.

Bake at 350°F for 15–20 minutes or until done.

MOLE SAUCES

Among the sauces originating in Mexico, the most commonly known is *mole poblano* (mole from Puebla), which features bitter chocolate and smoked chili peppers. Many pre-Columbian Mexican dishes were, apparently, prepared with mole sauces. The current form of *mole poblano* was refined by nuns in the seventeenth century, though its origins are much earlier. A popular dish, *mole poblano de guajolote* (turkey in mole), originates in a Mayan codex, according to one source.

MICRONESIA, FEDERATED STATES OF

Sometimes simply called Micronesia or FSM, this country comprises four Pacific island groups: Chuuk, Kosrae, Pohnpei, and Yap. (The shorter name Micronesia is confusing as it also refers to a wider geographical region that includes four other independent countries and 3 U.S. territories; see "Pacific Islands: Micronesia" entry.) With a tropical climate year round but variable terrain (some islands are volcanic, others are coral atolls with thin soil cover), only a few food crops can grow: breadfruit, taro, coconut. The sea and recent food imports are major food sources.

Traditional cuisine was based on local ingredients. Modern cuisine is influenced by food from the United States, Japan, other Asian countries (China, Thailand, Korea), and nearby islands, especially Guam and Hawaii.

Foodstuffs

- Staples: breadfruit, taro, sweet potato, cassava, yam (*Dioscorea sp.*). Pounded breadfruit (*kon*), preserved breadfruit, pounded taro, sweet taro, banana, and tapioca. Contemporary: rice, bread, potatoes.
- Fish (tuna, grouper, snapper—reef and open sea fish), shellfish (clam, octopus, crayfish, shrimp), dried salted fish, sea cucumber.
- Meat: pork, beef, goat, chicken, duck, eggs. Contemporary: canned meat (corned beef, Spam), canned fish (tuna, mackerel, sardines), frozen turkey, lamb, other meats, tuna jerky; macadamia nuts.
- Plantain, green vegetables (leaves of taro, sweet potato, pumpkin), pumpkin, tomato, eggplant. Contemporary: lettuce, potato.
- Coconut, mango, papaya, banana, citrus, cacao (source of chocolate), guava, local nuts. Contemporary: canned fruits (peach, cocktail), orange.
- Seasonings: black pepper (locally grown), onion, garlic, ginger, lime/lemon, coconut milk.

Typical Dishes

- Fried fresh-water eel (in Kosrae).
- Fermented breadfruit (*furoh*).
- Mashed boiled taro topped with syrup or coconut milk (*fafa*).
- Fried bananas (*tempura* style) with coconut.

DIOSCOREA YAM

BREADFRUIT

- Grated tapioca and mashed ripe banana baked overnight (*pihlohlo*).
- Vegetables stewed with coconut milk.
- Starchy staples (taro, banana, breadfruit, yams) cooked with sweetened coconut milk (*ainpat*).
- Baked vegetables with coconut milk wrapped in taro leaves.
- Baked pork (in underground oven).
- Corned beef and Spam dishes with or without vegetables.
- American-style fast food (burger, pizza, spaghetti, macaroni).
- Japanese-style dishes: raw tuna (*sashimi*), *sushi*.
- Canned tuna or mackerel with or without vegetables.
- Chinese-style dishes: spring roll, fried noodles with vegetables.
- American-style baked goods (cakes, cookies, doughnuts).

Styles of Eating

- Three meals and snacks daily.
- Rural families eat more traditional type menu of local staple and locally caught fish or raised chicken/meat. Urban families eat more canned and Western-type processed food.
- Breakfast: bread, cereal, rice, egg, canned meat, juice.
- Lunch: U.S.-style fast food (sandwich, pizza, pasta); rice, canned or fresh fried or grilled fish.
- Dinner: rice, corned beef with cabbage, fresh fruit.
- Snacks: U.S.-style snacks of cookies, candy; traditional fritters.

Barbecued Chicken

Chickens are commonly raised in backyards in rural areas. There are many variations of this dish, typically eaten with rice or other boiled staple (breadfruit, taro, or sweet potato). A potato or macaroni salad may accompany it for guests.

4 chicken quarters or other large portions (bones and skin intact)	1 cup coconut milk
	½ cup soy sauce
	1 onion, finely chopped
juice of 3 lemons	2 garlic cloves, minced

Marinate chicken in lemon juice for 15 minutes.
Combine coconut milk, soy sauce, onion, and garlic; stir into marinating chicken.
Cover and refrigerate for 5 hours or overnight.
Grill chicken over hot charcoal or under electric grill for about 40 minutes, turning frequently to avoid burning.

Brush chicken several times with the marinade during cooking.
Serve at once.

Sweet Potato Tops Salad

This is a dish from Pohnpei. Serve this as a side dish to go with rice and
chicken, meat, or fish for a midday or evening meal.

2 pounds sweet potato tops
   (young leaves), trimmed and
   washed (or substitute young
   spinach or watercress)

juice of 1 lemon
1 tsp salt
$\frac{1}{4}$ cup mayonnaise

Blanch greens for 1–2 minutes in plenty of boiling water.
Drop into cold water to arrest cooking; drain well.
Mix lemon juice, salt, and mayonnaise.
Stir into greens; chill for 20–30 minutes.

Vegetable Curry with Mackerel

This is a dish from Chuuk. Serve as a main dish with rice for a midday meal, or
as a side dish to go with a meat or chicken main dish for dinner.

2 TBS oil
1 onion, chopped
2 TBS curry powder
2 cups water
1 can mackerel (in oil or
   brine)
3 cups eggplant, cubed

1 red chili pepper, cored,
   seeded, and minced
   (optional)
3 cups frozen sliced green beans,
   defrosted

In a saucepan, heat oil over medium heat.
Stir in onion and fry until soft.
Stir in curry powder.
Add water and mackerel; bring to a boil.
Stir in eggplant and chili pepper.
Cook for 5 minutes; add green beans.
Cook for 3 minutes more, or until beans are done but still green.

Tropical Fruit Salad

This salad from Yap is served for dessert or as a snack. Feel free to use just a few
from the list or substitute any fruit in season.

2 ripe mangoes, diced
1 small ripe papaya, diced
1 small ripe pineapple, diced
juice of 1 lime or lemon
2 ripe bananas, diced
2 passion fruits, seeds and juice

1 orange, segmented
1 cup fresh or frozen grated coconut
2 cups watermelon or cantaloupe,
 cut into 1-inch cubes

Mix all fruits in a bowl.
Chill well for about 30 minutes or longer.

Mango and Passion Fruit Milk Shake

This is a cool drink from Yap served as a snack.

3 cups ripe mango puree
15 passion fruits, seeds and juice
 (or substitute 1 cup passion fruit
 juice)

4 cups water
2 cups milk
1 tsp vanilla

Blend all the ingredients. Chill for 30 minutes or more.

MOLDOVA

Moldova is a small landlocked country in Eastern Europe that was once part of the Ottoman-Turkish Empire and Romania, and annexed by the Soviet Union in 1945 until independence in 1991. Its fertile soil between two rivers and temperate climate of warm summers and mild winters make it a supplier of fruits, vegetables, and meat to its neighbors.

Moldovans are the majority, with minority groups of Ukrainians, Russians, Romanians, and Bulgarians. Moldovan cuisine reflects the meld of these groups as well as Greek, Jewish, Turkish, and German elements, and is noted for its preference for sour cream and sour soups.

Foodstuffs

- Staple: cornmeal (*mamaliga*) cooked in various consistencies—from porridge to a stiffer mixture—cut into wedges and eaten like bread.
- Pork, mutton, beef, poultry, sheep's cheese, smoked preserved meat or goose (*pastrama*).
- Eggplant, zucchini, sweet pepper, tomato, green beans, cabbage.
- Apple, quince, plum, grape, apricot, cherry, walnuts.
- Wine is very important, sometimes as substitute for drinking water.

Typical Dishes

- Sour soups (*ciorba*) are considered the national favorite.
- Greek-influenced sweet and savory pastries with a variety of fillings (*placinte*, *vertuta*).
- Turkish-influenced preference for mutton.
- Grilled meat dishes: fennel-flavored grilled beef rolls (*mititei*); meat patties (*parjoale*).
- Hard, white cheese made from ewe's milk (*brinza*).
- Meat stews: *tocana* (pork stew) served with fruit relishes.
- Chicken dishes: jellied chicken.
- Vegetable dishes: Turkish-influenced stuffed cabbage (*sarmale*); stewed mixed vegetables with meat (*ghiveci*); assorted pickles.
- Soups: *cutia* (a wheat soup with honey).

ELDERFLOWER

- Turkish-influenced rich sweets of honey, nuts: halvah (*alvitsa*), nougat.
- Preserved fruits in syrup: quince, apricot, plum, cherries, green walnuts.

Styles of Eating

- *Brinza* cheese and *mamaliga* (flat cake from cornmeal) are common center-pieces on a table.
- Meat is often served with fruit relishes.
- Breakfast: bread or cornmeal mush (*mamaliga*), sheep's cheese, egg, coffee.
- Lunch: chicken sour soup, cheese, milk, cream, corn mush.
- Dinner: chicken in jelly, baked fish, *mamaliga*, wine.
- Drinks: elderflower cordial (*socata*), wine (over 100 local varieties), fruit brandies, fruit juices, bottled carbonated drinks.
- There are plenty of small restaurants and coffee shops, as well as international fast food outlets in towns and in the capital.

Jellied Chicken

This dish is considered a delicacy, and is often served at home or during celebrations, as a first course or as a cold main dish after soup.

1 chicken cut into serving pieces	5 cloves of garlic (3 left whole,
water to cover	2 finely minced)
1 onion, quartered	5 black peppercorns
1 carrot, cut into chunks	⅔ tsp salt
2 bay leaves	1 packet unflavored gelatin

Put chicken to simmer in a pot with just enough water to cover.
Skim foam as the water boils.
Add vegetables, bay leaves, whole garlic cloves, peppercorns, and
    salt.
Gently simmer for 1 hour until chicken is tender but not falling apart.
Take out chicken; set aside to allow to cool.
Discard vegetables and strain broth through a fine sieve or cheesecloth.
Dissolve gelatin in 1 cup warm broth; stir into remaining broth.
Debone chicken and discard skin, keeping the flesh in large chunks.
Arrange chicken pieces in a glass casserole dish.
Stir in minced garlic to the broth, and heighten seasoning to compensate for
    a slight loss of flavor when chilled.
Pour broth over chicken.
Cover with plastic film and refrigerate overnight to gel.

Moldavian Burgers
(Parjoale Moldovenesti)

These, like *mititei*, are commonly eaten for dinner. Popular accompaniments are mashed potatoes, a fried pepper salad, and pickled cucumbers or peppers.

1 TBS lard
3 onions, finely chopped
1 pound ground meat (mixed beef
   and pork)
1 egg, beaten
2 slices white bread, torn and
   soaked in $\frac{1}{4}$ cup milk for 20
   minutes

3 TBS each parsley and dill,
   chopped
salt, pepper
$\frac{1}{2}$ cup bread crumbs
lard or oil for frying

In a skillet, melt lard over medium heat; fry $\frac{2}{3}$ of the chopped onions until
   softened.
Remove from heat and stir into ground meat with egg, bread, herbs, salt,
   pepper, and the remaining raw onion. Mix thoroughly.
With moistened hands, shape into burger-sized patties.
Coat patties with bread crumbs; chill for 20–30 minutes.
Fry in shallow fat until golden brown on both sides.
Serve hot.

Fried Pepper Salad
(Salata de Ardei Prajiti)

This is a favorite salad to accompany meat or chicken dishes.

3 TBS oil
6 red bell peppers, cored, seeded,
   and cut in long, narrow
   ($\frac{1}{8}$-inch) strips

3 onions, chopped
1 large tomato, chopped
$\frac{1}{4}$ cup tomato paste
salt, pepper to taste

Heat oil in a frying pan over medium heat; sauté peppers until soft. Set
   aside.
Fry onions until softened in the remaining oil, adding more oil if
   needed.
Stir in chopped tomato, tomato paste, salt, and pepper; simmer until thick,
   for about 15 minutes.
Mix peppers with onion and tomato mixture.
Serve cold.

New Potatoes (Cartofi Noi)

Serve this as a side dish with meat or vegetable dishes for lunch or dinner.

1 onion, finely chopped	salt to taste
2 TBS oil	1¾ pounds golf-ball-sized new
½ tsp flour	potatoes, peeled, left whole
1 pound tomatoes, peeled, seeded,	1 tsp fresh parsley, chopped
and diced	1 tsp fresh dill, chopped
1 TBS tomato paste	

Fry chopped onion until softened in oil over medium heat.
Sprinkle with flour and blend thoroughly.
Add tomatoes, tomato paste, and salt; stir well.
Add potatoes, parsley, and dill; simmer, covered, over low heat until tender, about 20–25 minutes.
Serve hot.

Cheese Crepes (Placinte Poale'n Brau, Placinte cu Poale in Briu)

These are popularly eaten as dessert and also as snacks to go with coffee or tea. For good results, all ingredients for the dough must be at room temperature.

1 ounce yeast	2 TBS oil
1 TBS sugar	1 TBS melted butter
1 cup milk	½ tsp salt
2 pounds flour	confectioners' sugar
3 eggs, beaten	

Mix yeast with sugar, 2 tablespoons warm milk, and 2 tablespoons flour in a large bowl.
Cover and let rise in a warm, draft-free place for about 10 minutes.
Add eggs, remaining milk, oil, butter, and salt to the risen starter.
Blend in flour to make a soft dough.
Cover and let rise until doubled in size in a warm place.
When the dough has risen, roll out to ¼-inch thick.
Cut out pastry squares measuring 8–10 inches.
Place spoonfuls of filling in the center.
Fold over the pastry corners over the filling, envelope style.
Press edges firmly to seal in filling.
Place on a lightly greased and floured baking sheet, 1–2 inches apart.
Let rise for 15–20 minutes; brush with egg wash and bake at 350°F for 25–35 minutes or until lightly golden.
Sprinkle generously with confectioners' sugar.
Serve warm.

Filling

1½ cups cottage cheese   2 TBS sugar
1½ cups sour cream   a pinch of salt
3 eggs

In a food processor, mix all ingredients until smooth.

MONACO

A Mediterranean constitutional monarchy and city-state, Monaco is roughly the size of New York's Central Park and is the world's second smallest independent country. Monaco has been under Saracen (Arab), Spanish, and Italian rule over the centuries, and since 1951 has had a special alliance with France.

Native Monegasques are a minority in their own country, together with Italians and other nationalities; the French make up half of Monaco's population. Monaco's cuisine reflects its history and its place in the Mediterranean: it has a lot in common with robust Italian and neighboring Nicoise cooking.

Foodstuffs

- Staples: wheat, potato.
- Lamb (preferred), fish (bass, sole, snapper), seafood (scallop, shrimp, crayfish, mussel), beef, chicken, dairy products (sheep's and goat's cheese), dried salted codfish.
- Chard, tomatoes, eggplant, bell peppers, lettuce, carrots, potatoes, mushrooms, cabbage, zucchini, artichokes, asparagus, preserved olives.
- Apricot, cherry, grape, melon, berries, fig, date, lemon, orange, pear, and apple.
- Seasonings: garlic, onion, fennel, olive oil, anchovy paste, herbs (thyme, sage, basil, marjoram, rosemary), saffron.
- Table sauces: chili and garlic mayonnaise (*rouille*); *aioli* (garlic mayonnaise).

Typical Dishes

- Breads: *fougasse* (herb-flavored roll), baguette, crusty rolls.
- Potatoes, fried or boiled, are served with most dishes.
- Vegetable dishes: Swiss chard (*blette*) features often in vegetable pies (*tourta de blea*); stuffings for pasta (*cannelloni de blette*); and fried ravioli (*barbagiuan*).
- Chickpea flour pancakes and patties (*socca*).
- Dried salted cod dishes: *estocaficada* (also called *stocafi*); codfish in tomato sauce.
- Sweet pastries flavored with orange blossom water, nuts, and honey.

Styles of Eating

- Three meals and snacks daily.
- European table settings.

- Breakfast: bread, jam, butter, milky coffee, juice.
- Lunch is the main meal, usually two or three courses—first course of soup or vegetable appetizer eaten with bread and butter; second course of fish or lamb or poultry accompanied by potatoes or rice, a vegetable side dish; pastry or other sweet.
- The evening meal is usually light: bread with eggs, cheese, or preserved meats, salad.
- There are many restaurants, bars, and cafes providing all types of international and local food.

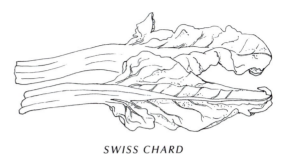

SWISS CHARD

Fried Dumplings (Barbaguian, Barba-juan)

The name of these fried stuffed dumplings means "Uncle Jean" in Monegasque. They are usually made in the mountains beyond Monaco and Nice and are also called *borsoutou*, depending on the type of filling. This recipe is for the Monegasque version using Swiss chard (*blette*), a very popular green vegetable. Other fillings, such as pumpkin, are also used. For convenience, use round wonton wrappers or fresh lasagna sheets. These can be served as a first course or a main course for a light meal.

Wrappers

2 cups flour	$\frac{1}{2}$ cup olive oil
$\frac{1}{2}$ tsp salt	1 egg
$\frac{3}{4}$ to 1 cup water	

In a food processor, combine all the wrapper ingredients to make a dough.
On a floured surface, knead well for 20–30 minutes.
Let rest for 30 minutes to 1 hour covered with a moist towel.
Roll out to $\frac{1}{8}$-inch thick and cut out 3-inch diameter circles.
Cover wrappers with moist towel until ready to use.
Put a spoonful of filling in the center, cover with another wrapper.
Moisten edges with water and seal firmly.
Deep-fry dumplings in medium-hot oil until golden brown on each side.
Drain on paper towels.
Serve hot.

Filling

2 TBS olive oil	$\frac{1}{4}$ cup cooked rice
2 cups finely chopped leek, white part only	$\frac{1}{2}$ cup Parmesan cheese, grated
4 salted anchovies in oil, finely chopped	2 eggs, beaten
3 cups squeezed, parboiled Swiss chard or spinach, chopped fine	pepper, salt

(continued)

Heat oil in a big frying pan; fry leeks, covered, over low heat, until very soft, for about 10 minutes.

Add anchovies, crushing them into the oil and leeks.

Stir in chard or spinach, raise heat to medium, and fry for another 3–5 minutes.

Off the heat add rice, cheese, eggs, and pepper.

The anchovies and cheese are quite salty, so taste first to see if salt is needed.

Stuffed Vegetables with Tuna and Sardines
(Petits Farcis Thon et Sardines)

This vegetable dish can be a first course for a meal or a light dish for lunch.

2 quarts water
1 TBS salt
12 small red (sweet) onions
3 zucchini, each about 8 inches long, cut into 2-inch sections
12 plum tomatoes, roughly same size as onions
2 TBS olive oil
1 small can tuna, drained

3 TBS lemon juice
2 cans sardines, drained
⅓ cup sour cream
1 small jar pickled red bell peppers, drained, finely chopped
2 cups rocket (arugula), washed and drained

Boil water and salt.

Parboil onions and zucchini for 5 minutes. Drain and set aside to cool.

Cut a thin slice off the tops of the tomatoes; hollow out and reserve pulp.

Take out inner rings from onions; reserve.

Take out center flesh from zucchini sections, leaving one end intact and a ¼-inch wall; reserve flesh.

Stuff vegetables with the fillings.

Place on baking dish; drizzle with remaining olive oil and put under hot grill for 5–8 minutes, or until heated through.

Arrange vegetables on a bed of rocket on individual plates.

Serve at once.

Tuna filling: finely chop the reserved pulp and flesh of the tomatoes, onions, and zucchini. Mix thoroughly with flaked tuna, half of the olive oil, and lemon juice.

Sardine filling: mash sardines, mix with sour cream and bell peppers.

Chickpea Cakes (Socca)

Socca are savory cakes sold all around the markets of Monaco and neighboring Nice, freshly made and eaten piping hot as afternoon snacks.

2 cups water
2 tsp salt
2¼ cups chickpea flour (available

from Middle Eastern and
Indian stores)
¼ cup + 2 TBS olive oil

Preheat oven to 425°F. Preheat broiler.
Place water and salt in a large bowl. Dribble in chickpea flour, whisking
  constantly until well mixed.
Stir in olive oil; let mixture stand for about 30 minutes.
Grease a heavy skillet with 2 TBS olive oil; pour in batter. Place under broiler
  for 2–4 minutes, until the batter is slightly blistered.
Remove and place in the oven; bake for 2–5 minutes, until cake is firm.
Remove from oven; cut into squares or wedges.
Serve with finely chopped tomatoes, or a salad, and fresh bread.

Olive Oil-Caper Paste
(Tapenade)

Olives grow all over the southern Mediterranean coast of Europe, and the wild
caper bush, with its magnificent blooms, can be found there as well. The paste is
served with fresh bread as a snack or appetizer.

2 cans pitted black olives, drained
  and chopped fine
2 TBS capers, drained, minced fine
3 small dill pickles, minced fine

olive oil from 1 tin of anchovies
3 tins anchovies (in olive oil),
  chopped fine
2 TBS lemon juice

Mix olives, capers, and pickles well. Add olive oil and mix well.
Add anchovies.
Add lemon juice and blend well with all other ingredients.
Cover and leave at room temperature for several hours prior to serving.
Store any remainders in a covered container in the refrigerator; topped with
  1 or 2 tablespoons of oil to keep out the air, this spread will keep for a
  month.
Serve on toasted or fresh French bread.

Almond and Melon Pie
(Galapian)

This Monegasque almond pie is originally made with candied melon slices and
glazed with lavender flower honey. Serve as dessert or with coffee or tea as a
snack.

Pastry

½ cup butter, diced	⅔ cup flour
¼ cup + 1 TBS confectioners' sugar	1 tsp orange blossom water or
⅓ cup grated almonds	orange rind
¼ tsp salt	1 egg

In a food processor, process all ingredients just until they come together.

Take out and smooth the pastry into a ball, patting with lightly floured fingers for 1–2 minutes.

Place in a plastic bag and let rest in the refrigerator for 2 hours.

On a floured surface, roll out pastry to fit a 10-inch pie plate or tart pan.

If using pie plate, crimp edges decoratively; for tart pan, smooth top edge of pastry.

Prick pastry, setting a sheet of foil and some baking weights to keep pastry from puffing up.

Bake at 375°F for 10 minutes; remove foil and weights.

Lower heat to 350°F and bake for another 5–8 minutes or until golden. Let cool slightly.

Place fruit evenly on pastry.

Spread almond filling over, and decorate with "flowers" made of candied cherry slices.

Bake at 375°F for 12–15 minutes or until golden brown.

Brush honey glaze over pie while still warm.

Almond Filling

4 egg whites	¾ cup finely ground almonds
3 TBS sugar	¼ cup sugar

Beat the egg whites to soft peaks.

Add sugar gradually and beat till stiff.

Blend together ground almonds and sugar; fold gently into egg whites.

Fruit Filling and Decoration

1½ cups fresh cantaloupe, sliced into ¼ × 2-inch pieces	5–7 candied cherries, sliced

Honey Glaze

3–4 TBS boiling water	2 TBS honey

Stir boiling water into honey to enable it to be brushed for a glaze.

MONGOLIA

Landlocked Mongolia is the sixth largest country in Asia and the eighteenth largest in the world. In the thirteenth century the most famous Mongol ruler, Genghis Khan, founded an empire that spanned central Europe and East Asia. Mongolia later came under Chinese and Russian satellite control, becoming self-governing in 1990.

Mongolia comprises vast open grasslands, inhospitable mountain ranges, and desert, with about 10 percent forest. Long, very cold winters and short, very hot summers; the seasonal nomadic lifestyle; and water and soil conditions deter large-scale agriculture.

Besides the majority Mongol ethnic group, there are Kazakhs, Uighur, Tibetans, and other minorities. Most are nomads or semi-settled, herding goats, sheep, horses, camels, and cattle. A minority are Muslim, but most are polytheistic Buddhists.

Wheat and a limited range of fruit and vegetables are grown in some regions. A few semi-settled Mongolians grow carrots, potatoes, or onions for home use. Mongolians who live near lakes supplement their mostly dairy diet with fish, but the majority of Mongolians do not eat fish as a rule.

Although influenced by Russia and China, Mongolian cooking is typical of other nomadic-style cooking, being simple and based predominantly on dairy products and rice, flat bread, or noodles, supplemented rarely by dried strips of meat. Among the rural Mongolians with herds, animals are only slaughtered for fresh meat on special occasions.

Traditional families live in *gers* (round felt-wrapped yurts), and cooking methods are those possible within the *ger*, or, when the family is on the move, on outdoor fires. Mongolians practice nomadic hospitality and offer unexpected guests shelter and meals.

Foodstuffs

- Staples: fresh and dried meat (goat, sheep, camel); dairy products—fresh milk, clotted cream (*urum*), fermented milk products such as yogurt, cottage cheese (*aarts*), dry curd cheese (*aaruulth*, also spelled *aaruul*); rice, fried dough fritters.
- Homemade wheat noodles, commercial (imported) pasta.
- Fresh and dried meat of camel, yak, reindeer, wild horse, other wild animals. Russian cans of meat, salmon, and crabmeat available in capital markets.

- Vegetables not widely eaten, and limited to onion, potato, carrot; in capital city and towns also beets, cabbage, cucumber, tomato, cauliflower, usually imported from China; commercial pickled vegetables (Korean-, Chinese-, or Japanese-style, imported).
- Canned, usually imported, fruit; in capital city tangerine, banana, plum, peach can be bought fresh.
- Seasonings: salt, pepper, garlic; rarely, wild chives.

Typical Dishes

- Roasted or baked meats: barbecue or shish kebab (*shorlog*), baked mutton (*khorkhog*).
- Soup: mutton soup with noodles (*guriltai shul*); Russian-style borscht in the capital.
- Fried meat pastries (*khoorshoor*).
- Russian-influenced salads of carrots or beets with cabbage, seasoned with garlic and mayonnaise or oil and vinegar, served with restaurant meals in the capital.
- Steamed dumplings with mutton or beef (*buuz*).
- Drinks: tea (made from hard-pressed blocks of Russian or Chinese tea leaves and stems) with milk and salt, drunk during meals and all other times; vodka; fermented horse milk (*airag*); local bottled citrus drinks; carbonated drinks (international brands); Western beer.

Styles of Eating

- Three meals and snacks daily.
- Breakfast: wheat noodles; wheat bread with yogurt or cheese, often stirred into salty milk tea.

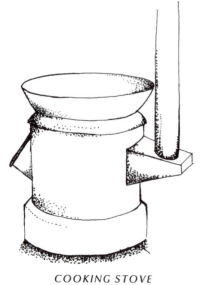

- Lunch: dairy products such as dry curd cheese (*aaruulth*) and other hard cheeses; flat bread for summer and autumn; salty milk tea; in winter and spring, meat soup with noodles, potatoes, or carrots. No dessert.
- Dinner: similar to lunch; no dessert.
- Snacks: deep-fried dough fritters or, occasionally, store-bought biscuits with salty milk tea.
- In the capital city Ulaanbaatar, Italian, Japanese, Korean, and Western-style restaurants offer pizza, chicken, and fish, mainly for tourists, which Mongolians (those who can afford them) are able to sample.

COOKING STOVE

Fried Meat Pies (Khoorshoor, *also* Huurshuur)

These fried pastries, like the large meat-filled dumplings called *buuz*, are made for special occasions. They are also sold as snacks at open-air food stalls during the summer festival of *naadam*.

2 cups flour
¼ tsp salt

½ cup water to mix
oil for deep-frying

Mix ingredients together in a bowl and knead into a dough (add more water or flour as necessary to achieve a smooth consistency). Remove onto floured board and knead for 10 minutes until smooth and elastic.

Divide into 16 pieces and roll each into a ball.

Make each ball into a circle 4 inches wide, thicker in the middle than at the edges. Place 2 tablespoons of filling onto one half of each circle, leaving the margin clear of filling.

Fold the other half over to form a crescent. Seal edges tightly with a fork or crimp into a "braided" edge.

Repeat with the rest of filling and dough.

Heat enough oil, about 4 inches deep, in a wok for deep-frying, making sure oil is well below rim.

Fry 3 or 4 pies at a time, each side for 2 minutes, until they are golden and the meat is cooked. Eat dipped in soy sauce.

Filling

1 pound fat minced meat (mutton preferred; or substitute beef, chicken, or turkey)
1½ tsp salt

½ onion, chopped
1 clove garlic, crushed
1 TBS water

In a food processor, mix the filling ingredients together into a firm paste.

Mutton Soup (Guriltai Shul)

This is a festive dish eaten by nomadic and semi-settled families in the Gobi desert, who live in traditional round yurts called *ger*. Noodles are always made from freshly kneaded dough, stretched into very thin, tortilla-like pancakes to be toasted briefly on a metal sheet over the *ger* cooking stove. Once cooked, the pancakes are chopped into the desired sizes and dropped into the soup. For convenience, commercially prepared noodles are used in this recipe.

2 TBS mutton fat (or substitute vegetable oil)
1 pound fat mutton, goat, or beef, cut into thin strips
2 large potatoes, peeled and diced
3 turnips, peeled and diced

2 onions, chopped
2 carrots, peeled and diced
8 cups stock (or 2 bouillon cubes dissolved in 8 cups hot water)
1 packet flat egg noodles
salt to taste

Heat the fat in a large wok and quickly brown the meat.
Add stock and simmer, covered, until meat is almost tender, about 20 minutes.

(continued)

Add vegetables and simmer until almost done, about 20 minutes.

Add noodles and salt and continue simmering until noodles are ready, about 10 minutes.

Serve in individual bowls.

Steamed Meat-Filled Dumplings (Buuz)

These steamed savory dumplings are made for special occasions. *Buuz* are similar to meat-filled dumplings (*bao* or *pao*) commonly eaten in northern China, and these are most likely to have originated in Mongolia. Smaller dumplings are called *bansh*, which are also steamed, or fried or boiled in soups.

½ cup white flour

½ cup whole wheat flour

½ cup water

10 ounces minced meat (fat mutton preferred, substitute turkey, chicken, or beef)

⅓ cup onion, minced fine

4 TBS ghee (clarified butter)

1 TBS ginger, grated

1 tsp salt

Mix flours. Add water a little at a time to make a dough. Knead well to make a shiny, elastic dough.

Roll out dough on a floured surface to ⅛-inch thick.

Cut dough into 4-inch disks. Cover disks with a moist cloth to prevent drying out.

Mix meat, onions, ghee, ginger, and salt.

Place a disk of dough on your left palm (if you are right-handed). Place 1 tablespoon of filling in the middle.

Bring the fingers on your left hand together to cup the disk; pleat the dough edges to enclose the filling, but do not seal completely so that steam can escape.

Steam over water in a steamer (about 20 minutes) until done.

Eat with mutton soup or on its own, washed down with salted buttered tea.

Baked Lamb (Khorkhog, *also* Horhog)

Sheep or lamb are slaughtered to mark the arrival of a guest. Traditionally, this dish was made with a whole sheep or lamb chopped up, and with no seasoning except salt and onions. The following recipe has been adjusted to smaller servings and a modern kitchen.

2 pounds lamb on the bone, cut in serving pieces

1 pound onions, chopped coarsely

2–3 garlic cloves, or to taste, minced

1 inch or more fresh ginger root, or to taste, grated

salt to taste

dried chili to taste, cored, seeded, and minced

1 thick ovenproof casserole with a tight-fitting lid

several handfuls smooth pebbles, about 2–3 inches in diameter, washed thoroughly

Mix meat, onions, garlic, and ginger; season with salt and chili.

Heat oven to maximum, and place pebbles inside. Heat for $\frac{1}{2}$ hour.

Place a layer of the meat mixture in the bottom of the casserole.

Using tongs, carefully transfer hot pebbles in a layer over the meat.

Repeat with a layer of meat, then pebbles, until meat is all used up. Be very careful while transferring the hot pebbles not to touch or drop them.

Cover casserole and seal tightly with foil.

Leave for 3 hours inside turned-off oven.

Unwrap casserole and discard pebbles. Serve meat and broth over rice.

Deep-Fried Fritters (Boortsog)

Boortsog are eaten instead of bread for most meals, as they keep well for almost a month. They are popular as snacks with salted milky tea and are taken along during long trips. The frying oil normally used is leftover fat from cooking meat, giving *boortsog* a distinctive aroma much appreciated by Mongolians. Substitute any vegetable oil.

a pinch of salt

$\frac{2}{3}$ cup sugar

$\frac{1}{2}$ cup butter

warm water

2 cups flour

oil for deep-frying

powdered sugar

Dissolve salt, sugar, and butter in warm water.

Mix in flour and knead well and thoroughly into a smooth, soft, and elastic dough.

The kneading process is very important: the dough must be kneaded until no air remains.

Cut the dough to check if the dough is sufficiently kneaded: it must be smooth and soft throughout, with no holes or air bubbles.

Let the dough rest, covered with a moist cloth, after kneading for about 15–20 minutes.

Roll out on a floured surface to $\frac{1}{4}$-inch thick.

Cut dough into strips 2 inches wide.

Cut out into 2-inch squares or small triangles with a sharp knife.

In the middle of each piece, make two shallow cuts. This is to let any remaining air out, as well as for decor.

Heat oil over medium heat. Fry *boortsog* in small batches until golden brown.

Drain on paper towels or a rack until cool.

Dust with powdered sugar for a snack, or leave plain, to be eaten with jam, butter, or cheese.

MONTENEGRO

A relatively new country in the Balkans on the Adriatic Sea coast, Montenegro was part of the former Yugoslav Republic and was federated with Serbia until June 2006. The country has a largely mountainous terrain with a temperate climate.

The cuisine is strongly influenced by the Turks who controlled the area for centuries.

Foodstuffs

- Staples are a mix of potatoes and flour dishes. People eat a variety of breads (bread is almost always on the table), noodles, and rice.
- Pork and lamb are favorite meats.
- Fish and seafood are great favorites along the coast.
- Fruit, particularly soft fruit such as plums, apricots, and grapes, are eaten and go to making wine and liquors.
- Various forms of cooked vegetables are prepared for stews, relishes, and pickles, which accompany most meals. Vegetables include carrots, eggplant, cabbage, tomatoes, peppers, onions, garlic, beans.

Typical Dishes

- Pancakes with both savory and sweet fillings.
- Vegetable dishes, including spreads (*pindzur*) and stews (*gyvetch*).
- Sweet pepper or eggplant relishes.
- Roast meats, particularly pork and mutton.

Styles of Eating

- Three meals a day plus snacks are usually eaten.
- Place settings are European standard.
- Breakfast: bread and jam with coffee, or dumplings.
- Lunch: the heaviest meal of the day, usually with several courses, including a salad, soup, main dish of meat or fish, and a sweet, very often washed down by wine for all.
- Dinner: a light meal of pancakes, bread with vegetable dips; or similar to breakfast.
- Snacks, sweet or savory, are served with coffee.

Vegetable Spread (Pindzur)

Pindzur has many variations and is popular as a salad all over the Balkans.

1 pound large red bell peppers
   (or preferably sweet paprika
   peppers)
½ pound unripe tomatoes

½ pound eggplants
½ cup oil
salt to taste
3 cloves garlic, finely minced

Dry-fry the peppers until well blistered in a heavy skillet over medium
   heat.
Bake the tomatoes and eggplants in a moderate oven for about 45 minutes,
   or until soft.
Peel the peppers and tomatoes. Slit the eggplants and remove the pulp.
Chop all the vegetables fine by hand or in a blender or food processor.
Heat 2 tablespoons oil in the skillet.
Add vegetables, then pour in remaining oil gradually, stirring all the time.
Cook until all oil is absorbed.
Add garlic; mix and season to taste.
Place into a serving bowl and cool well before serving.
Serve with grilled meat or warm corn bread.

Pashtrovic-Style Macaroni (Pashtrovski Makaruli)

This is a simple peasant dish that blends Italian and Greek influences.

1 pound whole-wheat macaroni
¼ cup olive oil
salt and pepper to taste

½ cup salty ewe's cheese (*brinza* or
   feta), cut into small cubes

Boil noodles in salted water till tender but still firm, about 8 minutes.
Strain and discard water.
Toss the noodles with olive oil, seasoning, and cheese.
Serve hot or cold.

Balchic-Style Baked Meat (Balshica Tava)

Balchic is a small town famous for its veal.

2 pounds boneless veal (or
   substitute pork, chicken, or
   turkey), cut into stewing pieces

¼ pound carrots
¼ pound onions
½ cup parsley, finely minced

(continued)

1 bay leaf	pinch of salt
salt to taste	1 cup sour cream
2 TBS butter	2 cups milk
3 eggs	3 TBS parsley for garnish

Simmer the meat with the carrots, onions, parsley, bay leaf, and salt for 20–30 minutes, or until the meat is tender.

Grease a heavy ovenproof pan or casserole dish with butter, and place the meat mixture in it.

Preheat the oven to 350°F.

Meanwhile make the topping: beat together the eggs, pinch of salt, cream, and milk.

Pour evenly over the meat mixture and bake until golden brown, about 15 minutes.

Remove from oven, and serve in bowls garnished with fresh parsley.

Potato Porridge
(Mocani Kacamak)

Kacamak derives from the term *kajmak* (clotted cream), which in Montenegro became the term for a porridgy dish.

2 pounds potatoes, peeled and cubed	4 TBS heavy cream
water to cover	$\frac{1}{4}$ pound crumbled (not grated) semi-hard cheese
salt to taste	1 cup yogurt for serving
4 TBS cornmeal	

Boil potatoes in salted water until almost done, about 15 minutes.

Sprinkle with cornmeal, reduce heat, and simmer for about 20 minutes, stirring constantly.

Pour off any remaining water.

Remove pot from heat and mash the potato and cornmeal mixture until smooth.

In another pot heat the cream and cheese until hot but not completely melted.

Pour the cream and cheese mixture over the mashed mixture; stir thoroughly.

Serve hot, topped with yogurt.

Stuffed Kale (Japraci)

Stuffed dishes are common throughout the Levant and the Balkans and are often eaten as the main dish.

2 pounds large kale (or collards, Savoy or Chinese cabbage), tough ribs trimmed flat
2–3 TBS oil
1 large onion, chopped
1 pound ground beef, veal, turkey, or chicken

3 ounces uncooked rice, rinsed and well drained
salt and pepper to taste
2 TBS parsley, finely minced
juice of 1 lemon
yogurt for serving

Blanch the leaves in boiling salted water to soften for a couple of minutes. (If using cabbage, blanch the entire head and detach the leaves as they soften.)

Remove leaves and plunge into cold water to arrest cooking. Drain and set aside until needed.

Meanwhile prepare the stuffing. In a frying pan, heat oil and sauté onions until golden.

Add meat and sauté for about 10 minutes, or until the meat has changed color.

Stir in the rice and fry for 5 minutes. Season with salt, pepper, and parsley, and mix thoroughly.

Remove from heat and let the stuffing cool.

Sort through the leaves and reserve the best ones for stuffing. Set aside any imperfect ones for lining the cooking pan.

To wrap the rolls: lay a whole leaf face up on a large plate or chopping board (the base closest to you and the top away from you).

Place about 1–2 tablespoons of the filling (depending on the size of the leaf and number of leaves) on the base of the leaf. Roll the base of the leaf over and away from you to enclose the filling once.

Then bring the left side of the leaf snugly across the filling; then the right.

Proceed to roll tightly from the base until the leaf completely encloses the filling. Fasten the ends with a toothpick, if needed.

Line the bottom of a heavy-bottomed saucepan with a layer of spare leaves.

Pack the rolls, open side down, neatly and tightly in one layer. Lay another layer on top, until all the rolls are in.

Gently (to avoid dislodging the rolls) pour lightly salted hot water mixed with lemon juice, just slightly below the topmost rolls.

Lay more leaves on top, and place a small plate face down to keep the rolls from floating.

Gently simmer at very low heat for 2 hours.

Allow to cool down in the pan for at least 30 minutes before serving. These also taste good, if not better, the day after, when they have mellowed.

Refrigerate once they have cooled down to room temperature.

Serve topped with yogurt.

Fried Dumplings (Malisorske Priganice)

These are served for dessert or as a snack, and, like most fried sweets, are best eaten freshly made.

1 pound flour	hot water and 1 tsp salt, as needed
pinch of salt	4 TBS butter mixed with 3 TBS
2 tsp baking powder	olive oil
2 TBS butter, diced	½ cup honey
1 cup water	

Combine flour, salt, and baking powder. Rub in the diced butter until the
   mixture is like coarse meal.
Stir in water to make a dough.
Knead for 10 minutes or more until smooth and elastic.
Divide into eight portions, and shape into balls.
In a large pot, bring salted water to a simmer. Drop the balls in, one at a time.
   Allow them to cook for an additional 10 to 15 minutes, from the time they
   start to float.
Remove the balls, drain, and pat dry with paper towels.
Heat the butter and oil in a frying pan.
Place a few balls to fry gently. Press on the balls lightly to flatten them so that
   they fry evenly. When brown underneath, turn and cook until brown.
   Drain on a rack and keep warm while frying the rest.
Serve at once with honey.

MOROCCO

Morocco is a North African country at the extreme northwest of the continent, opposite Spain. Wide coastal plains and craggy mountains with temperate to hot climate are ideal for Mediterranean-type fruits and vegetables, and for raising sheep.

The population comprises Muslim Arabs and Berbers. The former relations with Arab Andalusia in Spain (many refugees of the Reconquista settled in Morocco), extensive trade ties with the Muslim Mediterranean, Turkey, and sub-Saharan Africa, and French colonial influence have combined to create a unique and sophisticated cuisine. The existence of a royal court for many centuries has also contributed greatly to the variety and sophistication of the cuisine.

Foodstuffs

- Staples are rice, flat bread traditionally baked in a common village or neighborhood oven, and wheat couscous (steamed semolina; see Algeria for the box "Couscous").
- Lamb is the preferred meat. Fish, chicken, pigeon, and beef are also used extensively. Eggs are a common dish for all classes.
- Vegetables: hot and sweet peppers, carrots, onions, garlic, cucumbers, tomatoes, eggplant, olives, beans.
- Fruits: grapes, figs, pomegranates, dates, plums.
- Moroccan cuisine uses many spices subtly. Flavorings include ginger, cinnamon (for both savory and sweet dishes), saffron, cumin, turmeric, and fresh mint.

Typical Dishes

- *Chakchouka* (eggs cooked in a vegetable stew).
- *Tajine*, a slow, simmered stew with meat or chicken and vegetables, comes in many forms.
- Couscous and stew flavored with saffron.
- Charcoal-grilled or fried fish; shad is a popular fish.
- Chicken dishes: stewed with olives; with chickpeas; with almonds and saffron (*tajine t'faia*); in a sweet-savory pie (*bastilla*, also *bisteeya*).

TAJINE POT

- Skewered grilled meats (kebabs, also called *brochettes*).
- Vegetables (peppers, grape leaves, eggplants) stuffed with rice, or a mixture of rice and meat.
- Eggplant dishes: as a salad after roasting, fried, baked, stewed.
- Lentils, beans, and chickpea dishes, especially in *harira,* a soup eaten in the evening during the Ramadan fast.
- Rich honey-drenched sweets with nuts.

Styles of Eating

- Three meals a day and extensive snacks.
- Food is generally eaten from a central dish or tray on a carpet on the floor, with diners helping themselves by hand or with a spoon. Families eat together, but when entertaining, males and females generally eat separately.
- Lunch is the main meal, consisting of numerous courses: hot and cold salads to start; then a *tajine* or stew; a main dish of meat or poultry; followed by couscous with its accompanying meat and vegetables; sweetened mint tea to finish.
- The evening meal (except during the fasting month of Ramadan when it becomes the only and main meal) is less elaborate and based largely on vegetables or eggs.
- Formal meals often end with some form of sweet, usually sweetened with honey or syrup and often containing dates or other fruit.
- The favorite and most common drink is tea. This is heavily sweetened and strongly laced with fresh mint. Tea is drunk at all hours of the day and serves to close many meals. Coffee is also drunk extensively, usually very sweet and black.

Tomatoes and Eggs (Chakchouka)

This is a popular dish for any meal, especially breakfast and supper.

3 TBS oil	1 TBS vinegar
3 large onions, sliced	1 tsp salt
3 large tomatoes, peeled and sliced	4 eggs
2 large green bell peppers, chopped	1 green bell pepper, grilled, skinned, and cut into thin strips
1 small chili pepper, cored, seeded, and minced	

Heat oil and cook onions in a 10-inch frying pan until golden brown.

Add all the ingredients except the eggs and pepper strips. Simmer until the vegetables are reduced to pulp, about 20 minutes.

Make four indentations in the vegetables and carefully break an egg into each one.

Cover the frying pan and cook over low heat until eggs are well set (some people scramble the eggs lightly in the vegetables).

Garnish each serving with strips of green pepper.

Braised Chicken with Olives (Tajine)

Long-simmering stews are a feature of Moroccan cuisine, and are served with either bread, with which the stew is scooped up, or couscous. This is a typically Moroccan delicacy.

$1\frac{1}{2}$ ounces butter

1 chicken, cut into serving pieces (or about 2 pounds turkey pieces with bone)

$\frac{1}{2}$ pint water

2 medium onions, chopped

$\frac{1}{2}$ tsp ground ginger

$\frac{1}{8}$ tsp paprika

$\frac{1}{4}$ tsp powdered chili pepper

2 heaped TBS parsley, minced

6 ounces pitted whole green olives

2 TBS lemon juice or $\frac{1}{4}$ cup thin slices of pickled lemon (available in Middle Eastern groceries)

2 level TBS flour mixed with 2 TBS water

Heat butter until frothing subsides, in a large saucepan. Quickly brown the chicken.

Add water, onions, ginger, paprika, chili pepper, and parsley to browned meat. Mix well.

Cover and simmer gently for 45 minutes.

Add olives shortly before removing from heat.

Place chicken with olives on a heated serving dish and sprinkle with lemon juice.

Thicken pan juices with flour and water paste (add water, if necessary, to make up to 1 cup gravy).

Cook for 3 minutes over low heat, stirring constantly, or until the flour has lost its raw taste.

Pour sauce over chicken and olives.

Couscous Marrakech

Couscous is the Moroccan national dish and is almost always made there of semolina flour. This version is from the ancient imperial city of Marrakech.

Couscous

(or see Algeria for the box "Couscous" for general couscous instructions)

2 cups couscous (available from Asian sections of

most supermarkets)

1 cup cold water

pinch of salt

1–2 TBS olive oil

(continued)

Moisten couscous by sprinkling with a little water in a large bowl.

Stir well with a fork or fingers, breaking up all lumps. Allow to stand for 10 minutes to swell.

Place couscous in a cheesecloth-lined colander or the top portion of a couscousier.

Place the colander over the stew pan, and steam for 30 minutes, uncovered.

Break up the mass every 10 minutes with a fork.

Remove the couscous and transfer to a large bowl.

Sprinkle more water over the couscous, salt, and olive oil.

Stir thoroughly with a fork or fingers. Return couscous to the colander and steam for another 30 minutes, or until tender.

Stew

¼ cup olive oil	freshly ground pepper to taste
2 cups onions, chopped coarsely	2 quarts water
2½ pounds boneless lamb (or beef) cut in 1-inch cubes	1 pound fresh tomatoes, quartered
1 chicken, cut into small pieces	1 tsp chili flakes or cayenne
1 pound carrots, peeled and cut in 1-inch chunks (or half carrots, half turnips)	1 pound yellow squash, peeled and cut in 2-inch slices
½ tsp (20 threads) saffron or powdered ginger	12 ounces string beans
	14 ounces canned chickpeas (*garbanzos*), drained
1 tsp salt	½ pound black seedless raisins

Heat oil in the bottom of a couscousier or saucepan and sauté onions until soft.

Add the meat, chicken, carrots, saffron, salt, pepper, and water, and simmer for 45 minutes.

Fit the top pan of the couscousier (or the colander) with the couscous grain over the stew; allow stew to simmer gently for 30 minutes.

Add all remaining ingredients to stew, and correct seasoning.

Cook for about 20–25 minutes or until vegetables are soft but still separate and not mushy.

To serve: mound the couscous on a large, round serving platter.

Make a large crater in the center.

Arrange meat and vegetables in the center. Pour some of the sauce over all, placing the remaining sauce on the table for diners to add if they so wish.

Garnish with minced parsley.

This is traditionally served to follow the main meat dish.

Chicken with Chickpeas (Gdra)

Chickpeas are a favorite legume and are often combined with meat or poultry for main meals.

3 TBS butter

20 threads saffron or $\frac{1}{2}$ tsp
  powdered ginger

1 tsp salt

1 tsp ground pepper

3 medium onions, finely chopped

4–6 serving pieces of chicken

1 14-ounce can chickpeas
  (*garbanzos*)

water to cover

1 pound uncooked rice, rinsed
  and drained

$\frac{1}{4}$ cup cilantro

1 large bunch parsley

juice of 1 lemon

Melt butter in a saucepan.

Stir in the saffron, salt, pepper, and 1 onion.

Add chicken and chickpeas. Cover with water and simmer for 30 minutes.

Place rice in a clean muslin bag. Tie the bag securely and add to the pan. The rice should be completely immersed in the cooking liquid.

Remove the bag of rice after 15–20 minutes and keep warm in a low oven.

To the saucepan, add cilantro, parsley, and the remaining onions.

Continue cooking until chicken is tender, another 20–25 minutes.

Serve chicken in the center of a large dish; surround with the rice and chickpeas. Pour some sauce over the chicken, and put the rest in a sauce boat or bowl to be placed at the table for diners to help themselves.

Drizzle lemon juice over the entire dish.

Almond Croissants (Kab el Ghzal)

These pastries are shaped like gazelle horns, hence their Moroccan name. Marzipan was invented by the Moors of Andalusia, and when they were expelled from Spain in the fifteenth century, they brought the art with them to add to Moroccan cuisine.

1 pound flour

about 5 ounces butter, melted

water

$\frac{1}{4}$ tsp orange blossom water or
  rosewater

$\frac{1}{2}$ pound marzipan, diced

Heat oven to 325°F.

In a food processor, blend flour, 2 ounces melted butter, and water just until the mixture forms a ball.

Remove dough and knead on a floured surface for 10–15 minutes until elastic. Put the dough into a covered container and allow to rest for 30 minutes in the refrigerator.

Meanwhile prepare the almond filling: in the food processor, blend the marzipan, orange blossom water, and butter until well mixed and marzipan is softened. Set aside until needed.

Divide the dough into 3 portions. Roll out on a lightly floured surface $\frac{1}{8}$-inch thick.

(continued)

Cut into 6-inch-wide strips with a sharp knife.

Cut the strips on the diagonal, creating triangles about 3 inches wide at the base.

While working, cover the pastries with a moist cloth to prevent drying.

To assemble the pastries:

Brush melted butter on the pastry triangle.

Take about 1 tablespoon of almond filling, press lightly but quickly to flatten, and lay on the base of the triangle.

Roll up the pastry and filling together, starting from the base of the triangle, and ending at the apex.

Pinch the two ends up to form the gazelle's horns.

Prick the pastry in several places with a pin to avoid bubbling while baking.

Cover rolled up horns with a moist towel and continue with remaining pastry and filling.

Place horns on a buttered baking sheet; bake for about 15 minutes, or just until very faintly colored.

Serve with coffee or mint tea.

MOZAMBIQUE

Mozambique is a Southeast African country along the Indian Ocean opposite Madagascar. It has a 2,000-mile-long coastline, making fish and seafood very popular. The coastal plain is wide and tropical, drier in the south and well watered to the north. The northwest of the country on the border with Zimbabwe is mountainous and cooler.

A former colony of Portugal (until 1975), Mozambique suffered a devastating 20-year civil war after independence. Some agricultural areas are still mined, making life difficult for the population, most of whom are subsistence farmers.

The population is composed of many local groups who speak different languages. The common language is Portuguese. About half the population are Christians, less than one-fourth Muslims, and the rest belong to indigenous religions.

The Portuguese influence on cooking is very palpable, particularly in the large cities along the coast. Inland, the food is more like the rest of southern and eastern Africa.

Foodstuffs

- Staples: maize and cassava millet in the form of stiff porridge. In the cities, wheat breads are popular. Rice for those who can afford it.
- Meat: chicken is the most common meat. Beef, goat, pork.
- Fish: a variety of coastal fish. In inland areas, riverine fish, both fresh and dried. Seafood, including *camarao* (prawns) and *lulas* (squid).
- Vegetables: onions, carrots, cabbage, pumpkin and squashes, peppers, beans.
- Fruits: coconuts, bananas, mangoes, papaya, tree-tomato, a variety of non-domesticated forest fruit.

Typical Dishes

- Soups (*sopa*) of meat and vegetables.
- Rice cooked with seafood.
- Grilled meats; freshly caught, grilled fish are very popular.

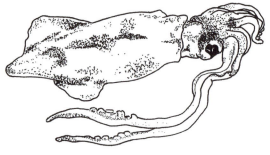

SQUID

Styles of Eating

- Three meals a day and snacks preferred.
- Families generally eat together. Traditional rural families sit on a mat around a common pot, and urban families eat European style with European place settings. Dishes are served together on the table, for diners to help themselves.
- Breakfast: bread, rolls, or toast with milky coffee.
- Lunch: three dishes, including an appetizer, a main dish of meat fowl or fish, and a dessert such as an egg custard (*pudin*).
- Supper: usually eaten fairly late. Several dishes, which might include a soup, fish or seafood, meat, rice, and a dessert.
- Coffee and tea, and many kinds of fruit drinks are popular.

Green Bean Soup (Sopa de Feijao Verde)

This dish is served as a starter.

3 cups water
2 large potatoes, peeled and cubed
1 medium tomato, chopped
1 large onion, chopped
salt and pepper to taste

2 cups fresh string or French beans, cut diagonally in thin slices (or one pack cleaned, finely sliced green beans)

Bring water to a boil in a large pot.
Add potatoes, tomato, onion, salt, and pepper.
Simmer for 30 minutes or until vegetables are tender.
Puree in food mill or blender. Add water if necessary to make a thin puree.
Return to pot and add string beans.
Simmer for about 10 minutes until beans are tender.
Correct the seasoning.
Serve hot.

Clam and Peanut Stew (Matata)

Mozambique's long coastline has made seafood a major source of protein for the country's population. The clams in this recipe can be replaced by any shellfish.

½ cup onions, chopped fine
1 TBS vegetable oil
2 cups fresh or canned clams, chopped

¾ cup peanuts, ground fine (or ½ cup natural peanut butter)
1 tomato, chopped fine

1 tsp salt
½ tsp black pepper
1 tsp red chili flakes

1 pound fresh, young pumpkin
leaves (or substitute spinach
leaves)

Sauté onions in oil until translucent.
Add clams, peanuts, tomato, salt, pepper, and chili flakes.
Simmer gently for 30 minutes.
Add greens.
Cover tightly and serve as soon as leaves have wilted (about 2–3 minutes).
Serve over rice.

Hot Pepper Sauce, Mozambique Version (Piri-Piri)

The long period of Portuguese occupation was interfertile for both Portugal and its colonies in terms of food. This is the Mozambican version of a common Afro-Portuguese sauce. The sauce is placed on the table in every restaurant and virtually every home.

4 TBS lemon juice
4 TBS olive oil
4 TBS coarsely ground red pepper
  or chili flakes

1 TBS salt
1 tsp crushed garlic or garlic
  powder

Combine all ingredients in a small glass bowl.
Serve over meat, fish, and vegetable dishes.

Chicken Zambezia (Galinha à Zambeziana)

Zambezia province in the country's northeast provides Mozambique's most luscious recipes, often flavored with coconut milk.

4–6 serving portions of chicken
½ cup piri-piri sauce

1 cup butter, melted

Marinate the chicken pieces in piri-piri sauce in the refrigerator for at least
    3 hours.
Add butter to the marinade before cooking, and turn chicken pieces to
    thoroughly coat them with the marinade.
Broil the chicken, or grill over charcoal fire.
Cook for 10–15 minutes on each side, over medium coals, basting several
    times with the sauce.
Serve with rice.

Papaya and Egg Pudding (Ovos Moles de Papaia)

Huge papayas are sold from barrows throughout the large cities, and many households in the city and in the countryside have a papaya tree.

1 medium-sized ripe papaya	4 cloves, whole
½ cup lime juice (from about 3–4 limes, or substitute 3 lemons), strained	1 medium cinnamon stick
	5 egg yolks
	½ tsp grated rind from limes
½ cup water	1 tsp powdered cinnamon for garnish
2 cups sugar	

Peel, seed, and coarsely chop the papaya.

Puree papaya, lime juice, water, and sugar in a blender or food processor until smooth.

Place puree in a stainless steel (not aluminum) pan.

Add cloves and cinnamon.

Bring to a quick boil, stirring constantly.

Cook until the mixture reaches thread stage (about 230–234°F).

Remove the pan from heat and discard the cloves and cinnamon.

Beat the egg yolks vigorously in a deep heat-proof bowl until lemon yellow in color.

Pour the hot mixture into the egg yolks in a thin, steady stream, while continuing to beat constantly (or use a hand mixer).

Continue beating the mixture until it is smooth and thickened.

Place mixture into four dessert bowls and cool.

Chill and serve, dusted with lime rind and cinnamon, if desired.

MYANMAR (BURMA)

Myanmar was a part of Britain's Indian empire until independence in 1948. The climate is tropical, with the Irrawady River drainage forming a huge, well-watered plain ideal for growing rice. The highlands are lush, covered by tropical vegetation. Tropical lowlands produce rice, corn, fruits, and vegetables; the highlands produce tea.

The country is peopled by over a hundred ethnic groups, predominantly Burmans; endogenous Shan, Karen, Naga, and other minorities; and Chinese and Indian immigrants.

Food in Myanmar is influenced by its neighbors India and China and tends to include spicy hot curries; the Burmese pride themselves on their ability to eat hot foods.

Foodstuffs

- Staple: rice, vegetables, fish.
- Sea and fresh-water (from Irrawady River and tributaries) fish, seafood (oyster, shrimp, clam).
- Chicken, duck, goat, pork, wild game (quail, squirrel, deer), soybean products (*tofu*).
- Core (heart) of the banana plant, bamboo shoot, beans, potato, cabbage, corn, green vegetables (such as roselle leaves), wild mushrooms.
- Pineapple, papaya, mango, melon, banana, orange, mangosteen, avocado, highland strawberries, peanuts, sesame, sugarcane, coconut.
- Seasonings: curry spices, cilantro and other herbs, pressed shrimp and fish paste (*ngapi*).

Typical Dishes

- Indian-influenced curries: very spicy, well-reduced stews of goat, pork, beef, duck, chicken, and fish or seafood.
- Chinese-influenced noodles: rice noodles in fish soup (*mohingar*), wheat noodles in coconut chicken soup (*ohn-no-kauk-swey*).
- Soups: sour soup (of fish or seafood, flavored with citrus juice, tamarind, or roselle leaves with bamboo shoots), sweet soup with mushrooms.

PREPARING BANANA, TARO, OR CABBAGE LEAVES AS WRAPPERS

Warm the leaves for half a minute in a pot of boiling water. This makes them easier to manipulate for folding.

Cut off the center rib of each banana leaf, and use the two large sheets thus produced to cut into smaller sheets as needed. Cabbage, taro, and lotus leaves also have their tough ribs removed, except they need not be cut further.

Keep in mind that some of the wrappers (taro leaf and cabbage) are edible, whereas others (banana leaf and lotus leaf) are not, and must be discarded.

In a pinch, you can substitute 10 × 10-inch (or larger) sheets of aluminum foil for the inedible leaves, though you ought to keep in mind that the leaves not only provide a container but also add specific flavors to the dish, which aluminum foil will not. Line the foil with one or two lettuce or cabbage leaves, if desired, to evoke an approximate flavor.

- Vegetable dishes: green tea leaf salad (*let phet thoke*), ginger salad (*gin thoke*), fried gourd or banana, stir-fried bean sprouts with bean curd.
- Sweets: steamed or fried confections of rice, semolina, or sago with coconut and palm sugar, often wrapped in banana leaves, such as the cone-shaped *monpetok* (Hidden Treasure) (see box "Preparing Banana, Taro, or Cabbage Leaves as Wrappers").
- Drinks: strong sugary tea with milk; sugarcane juice.

Styles of Eating

- Three main meals and snacks daily.
- Breakfast: rice noodles in fish soup (*mohingar*, also spelled *moat hin har*); fried rice and peas; steamed sticky rice with deep-fried vegetables; sweet and savory rice cakes; *nan pya* (Indian-style flat bread); plain green tea, sweet, milky tea, or coffee. Many have breakfast at cafes.
- Lunch and dinner are very similar: rice, curried meat, fish, or poultry, stir-fried vegetables or parboiled vegetables, sour soup of fish or vegetables, and fish or shrimp paste relish. Or, for a light lunch, noodles in soup. Meals often end with savory offerings, such as a salad of green tea leaf or ginger, or *sui gi mok*, a cream of wheat cake with poppy seeds. A traditional after-meal treat is an astringent betel nut chew, made of ground betel palm nut mixed with lime powder, tobacco, or mint, wrapped in pepper leaf and chewed like gum. Betel chewers end up with orange-reddish teeth.
- Snacks: batter-fried gourd (*boothee-kyaw*), sweet and savory steamed or fried rice cakes, vegetable salads, noodles in soup.

Ginger Salad (Gin Thoke)

This is one of two typical salads served after a meal or eaten at any time as a snack. The other is pickled green tea leaf salad. Both are similarly flavored with peanuts, chilies, dried shrimp, and other condiments. These two salads are eaten throughout the country and served everywhere—at street stalls, markets, and restaurants.

2 cloves garlic, sliced

¼ cup cooked lentils, broad beans, or chickpeas

1 banana, sliced into rings

¼ cup green bell pepper, sliced

¼ cup peanuts, shelled

1 green chili pepper, seeded and sliced into rings

¼ cup dried ground shrimp (available in Asian and specialty markets)

¼ cup toasted sesame seeds

½ cup sliced pickled ginger (sushi relish, available in Japanese stores)

corn or other oil for frying

Fry garlic over low heat in 1 TBS of corn oil until just golden brown. Set aside.

Fry separately lentils, banana, green pepper, and peanuts in 1–2 TBS oil at medium to high heat for about 2–3 minutes. Set aside.

Assemble salad in individual bowls: arrange the fried lentils, banana, green pepper, and peanuts next to each other.

Sprinkle with garlic, chili, shrimp, sesame seeds, and ginger.

Each diner adds dressing at the table, and mixes (or not, as desired) everything before eating.

Dressing

3 TBS fish sauce (available in Asian and specialty markets)

4 tsp fresh lemon or lime juice

4 TBS corn oil

Whisk sauce ingredients; drizzle over vegetables.

Wheat Noodles in Coconut Chicken Soup (Ohn-no-kauk-swey)

This dish is second only to rice noodles in fish soup (*mohingar*) as the most typical dish for eating at any time: breakfast, snack, or as an accompaniment to lunch or dinner. *Mohingar* is often claimed to be the national dish. Both are served everywhere, from cafes and street stalls to restaurants, and of course made at home. Slices of onion, fried rice crackers, fresh lemon juice, roasted chili powder, and all sorts of garnishes are added at the table.

4 large portions chicken, quarters or legs

8 cups water

5 TBS fish sauce (*nuoc mam* or *patis*)

3 TBS vegetable oil

1 tsp salt

1 TBS or less chili flakes (optional)

¼ cup thick coconut milk

1 or 2 chicken stock cubes (optional)

2 onions, quartered

3 pounds fresh Chinese egg noodles (or dried, soaked 10 minutes in cold water, then simmered for 2 minutes in boiling water, and drained)

Garnishes

3 hard-boiled eggs, shelled and sliced

1 onion, sliced fine

chili flakes

cilantro, chopped

(continued)

Simmer chicken in water and fish sauce for 15–20 minutes.

Remove chicken, reserving stock. Let chicken cool. Shred meat and discard bones. Set aside.

Heat 1 TBS oil and salt. Add chili flakes and fry for 1 minute on low heat.

Add coconut milk and reserved chicken stock, mixing well.

Add chicken stock cubes if necessary to make a well-flavored stock.

Add quartered onions and simmer for 30 minutes or more, until needed.

To assemble: just before serving, heat 2 tablespoons oil in a wok. Stir-fry noodles for about 5–8 minutes.

Distribute noodles into four soup bowls.

Add the shredded chicken meat to the simmering soup and allow to heat through.

Ladle hot soup into the bowls, making sure each diner gets some shredded chicken.

Place garnishes in separate small bowls.

Each diner takes garnishes to add as desired.

Gourd Fritters (Boothee Kyaw)

This is a common accompaniment to rice or wheat noodle soups and can also be made with bananas. Zucchini substitutes for the original gourd. The fritters are dipped into a hot and sour shrimp paste relish (see the next recipe). These are also commonly served after meals as a savory dessert.

3 TBS rice flour

1 TBS sticky rice flour (also called glutinous rice flour, and packets are sometimes labelled "*mochikō*" in Japanese and Oriental food stores)

2 TBS or less water

2–3 TBS cornstarch

4 zucchini or firm, semi-ripe banana, quartered lengthwise and sliced into 3- to 4-inch pieces, wiped dry

oil for deep-frying

Mix the two flours with enough water to make a thick batter.

Dust the zucchini pieces with cornstarch. (A fast, easy way to do this is to put cornstarch in a paper or plastic bag with the zucchini and shake thoroughly.)

Heat enough oil for deep-frying to about 350°F in a thick-bottomed pan or wok.

Dip zucchini into batter and fry a few at a time so as not to lower the oil temperature.

Drain on paper towels. Serve warm with wheat noodle soup (see the previous recipe) with a dollop of shrimp paste relish.

Shrimp Paste Relish (Balachaung, Ngapi Kyaw)

No meal in Myanmar is complete without some form of fish sauce. The simplest is a mix of fish sauce, fresh citrus juice, and slices of chili. The dish given here is a more elaborate version, consisting of fried shrimp paste with pounded dried shrimps, crushed garlic and onions, and chilies. This relish is also eaten with bread as a sandwich. Another variation is roasted shrimp paste with sesame oil and a squeeze of lime, frequently eaten with leftover rice or at regular meals. These sauces or relishes are also used to flavor quickly boiled green vegetables served as a salad accompaniment to main meals. Although only 1 chili is used in this recipe, most relishes would use 10 or more for a really fiery sauce.

2 TBS oil	3 cloves garlic, minced
4 TBS shrimp paste in block form (also available as *belachan* or *blachan*, from Indonesian or Malaysian stores), diced	1 medium onion, chopped fine
	1 green chili, seeded, minced (or add more, as desired)
	1 tsp sesame oil
2 TBS dried shrimps	2 TBS fresh lime or lemon juice

In a wok or frying pan, heat oil at medium heat.
Add shrimp paste, stirring frequently and mashing the cubes into the oil.
Stir in shrimps, garlic, onions, and chili.
Fry until the onions and garlic are aromatic. Turn off heat.
Mix in sesame oil and citrus juice.
Adjust seasoning, adding more lime or lemon juice as desired.
Kept in a covered jar and topped with a covering of hot oil, this will keep for a
     week refrigerated.

Coconut Milk with Sago
(Moh Let Saung)

Dessert is typically fresh fruit, or a sweet drink such as this. This is made of ingredients commonly available throughout the country: coconut milk, sago (the starch granules from palm trunks), and palm sugar.

1 cup sago pearls	chopped; or unrefined brown sugar
4 cups water	
$\frac{1}{2}$ cup palm sugar (jaggery available from Asian stores),	12 or more ice cubes, crushed roughly

Wash sago and soak for approximately 1 hour.
Drain and put in pot with 3 cups water.
Bring to a boil, reduce heat, and gently simmer until sago pearls are transparent (there may still be a white bit at the center, but this should disappear upon cooling).

(continued)

Allow to come to room temperature in the pot. When cold, drain and chill in
the refrigerator.

Meanwhile, make the syrup. Place palm sugar in a small saucepan with
remaining water and heat gently until dissolved.

Cool and strain.

For each serving, place 4 tablespoons of chilled sago into a tall glass. Add
3 tablespoons syrup (or according to taste) and mix well.

Add 2–3 ice cubes and fill glass with coconut milk.

Stir and serve immediately.

INDEX

animals, **1:**47, 131, 161, 216, 221; **2:**68, 102, 112, 124, 128, 191; **3:**16, 32, 86, 197; **4:**44; **5:**51, 141, 142, 154

animism, **1:**181; **2:**202

anise, **1:**1, 76, 120, 121, 153, 199, 200; **2:**57, 171; **3:**23, 109, 138, 142, 151, 157; **4:**97, 102, 167, 177, 178; **5:**50, 52, 99, 183; anise-flavored, **2:**16, 73; **3:**92; **4:**92; **5:**39

aniseed, **1:**212; **2:**15, 18; **3:**143

anisette, **5:**99

Ankole, **5:**118

annatto, **1:**102; **2:**1; **4:**30, 92, 97; **5:**177

anoush, **1:**42

ansam, **1:**155

antelope, **4:**144

Antigua, **1:**30, 31, 33

ants, **1:**130

aoili, **3:**192

Apennines, **4:**137

aperitif, **1:**42, 43

appa, **3:**146

appam, **4:**176, 177

appas, **5:**1

appelation controlé, **2:**103

appetite, **1:**211; **3:**18, 19

apple-filled, **4:**183

applesauce, **1:**55, 99; **5:**35

apricot, **1:**1, 21, 41, 60, 65, 124, 140, 192; **2:**11, 25, 29, 56, 122, 141, 146, 155, 179, 184, 192, 209; **3:**45, 49, 65, 66, 78, 128, 159, 187, 188, 202; **4:**76, 107, 118, 119, 159, 182, 201, 203, 204, 207; **5:**33, 34, 35, 37, 39, 43, 57, 59, 77, 101, 104, 109, 115, 127, 130, 131, 146, 166, 167, 170, 171; apricot-stuffed dumplings, **1:**55

Apulian cuisine, **3:**16

Arab(s), **1:**11, 21, 41, 76, 181; **2:**55, 74, 157, 190, 200, 209; **3:**1, 38, 91, 105, 159, 168, 192, 207; **4:**35, 70, 114, 195, 196, 213; **5:**10, 11, 38, 39, 57, 63, 66, 98, 104, 122, 137, 190, 201, 202

Arab-style, **5:**202

Arabia, **1:**152; **2:**55; **3:**70, 145; **4:**144, 196; **5:**139

Arabian cuisine, **1:**60; **2:**116

Arabian influences, **1:**151; **2:**27; **5:**102

Arabic, **2:**57, 159; **3:**5, 18, 152; **4:**195; **5:**122

arabica (coffee), **2:**74

aragi, **5:**11

Aragon, **4:**207

arak (aniseed-flavored liquor), **3:**92; **5:**1

araw, **4:**153, 156

archaeology, **1:**207; **5:**169

Arctic, **1:**165; **2:**95

areca nut. *See* betel nut

arepa, **1:**211; **5:**178

arequipe, **1:**39

arisia, **4:**50

aristocrats, **2:**102; **5:**83

armadillo, **2:**147

aroma, **1:**24, 61; **2:**74, 207; **3:**201; **4:**98; **5:**48, 61, 106

arreglados, **2:**2

arrowroot, **3:**164; **4:**59; **5:**6

arthropods, **1:**47, 129

artichoke, **2:**102, 103; **3:**12, 13, 17, 18, 192; **4:**137, 207; **5:**98

arugula, **1:**122; **3:**17, 194; **4:**137, 191

asado, **1:**35, 192; **2:**47, 63; **3:**180; **4:**88

asafetida, **1:**1; **4:**6

asam aur-aur, **1:**40

ashes, **1:**48, 51

Asir province, **4:**144

asma-yaprak, **1:**42

asopao, **2:**47; **5:**179

asparagus, **2:**30, 103, 128, 129, 132, 179; **3:**118, 192; **4:**25, 45, 46, 153, 207, 214; **5:**33, 137, 142

aspen, **1:**48

aspic, **1:**96; **3:**118; **4:**104

Assyrians, **3:**1

astringent, **3:**80, 218

Athabascan, **4:**123

Atlantic Ocean, **1:**22, 85, 131, 165, 171; **2:**68, 101, 102, 112, 147, 154, 163; **3:**6, 100; **4:**108, 171

attiéké, **2:**7, 8

aur-aur, **1:**135

aush, **1:**2

Austro-Hungarian, **1:**54; **2:**11, 25, 179, 180; **3:**110; **4:**159; **5:**115

Austronesian, **4:**55, 58; **5:**50

aviyal, **2:**198

avocado, **1:**111, 119, 192, 194, 212, 213, 214; **2:**1, 6, 7, 15, 17, 40, 43, 46, 48, 51, 148, 150, 152, 156, 160, 163, 166, 167, 208; **3:**10, 23, 178, 179, 180, 217; **4:**37, 80, 94, 130, 152, 165; **5:**25, 45, 63, 64, 89, 118, 177, 178, 179, 180, 181

awarra, **5:**17

baba ganouj, **3:**92

baba ghanoush, **4:**70, 71

bacalhau (also *bacalau, bakalar*), **1:**20, 220; **2:**42; **4:**108, 109, 112, 188, 208

backhendle, **1:**54

bacon, **1:**19, 20, 32, 50, 54, 55, 56, 67, 68, 82, 83, 86, 93, 95, 103, 111, 112, 134, 166, 169, 170, 174, 175, 170; **2:**13, 17, 31, 103, 129, 131, 132, 148, 161, 179, 180, 182, 183; **3:**6, 7, 16, 19, 87, 88, 89, 102, 113, 115, 119, 120, 121, 126, 166, 173, 181; **4:**13, 26, 92, 93, 104, 105, 121, 182, 183, 184, 186, 188, 189, 190, 202, 204, 214, 215; **5:**6, 28, 35, 36, 53, 115, 116, 132, 142, 148, 153, 154, 161, 164

Baganda, **5:**118

bagoong, **4:**97

baguette, **1:**57, 154, 155; **2:**112, 115; **3:**80, 81, 128, 129, 168, 173, 174, 194; **5:**44, 84, 99, 172, 184

baharat, **1:**73; **2:**198; **5:**38

bakeapple, **1:**165

bakery, **1:**26, 36, 55, 61; **2:**55, 103; **3:**17, 37; **4:**141, 152, 189

baking soda (bicarbonate of soda), **1:**9, 70, 99, 161, 189, 190, 212, 224, 225; **2:**45, 54, 58, 59, 73, 74, 116, 129, 177, 189; **3:**103, 153; **4:**85, 95, 104, 122; **5:**1, 69, 85, 90, 99, 119, 132, 138, 143, 151, 155, 156, 160, 179, 197, 199, 200

baklava, **1:**42, 125; **3:**11, 123, 124; **4:**118, 160; **5:**11, 39, 42, 99, 104, 105

baleadas, **2:**174

Balearic islands, **4:**209

Bali, **2:**202, 208

Balkans, **1:**6, 8, 47, 140, 142; **2:**11, 56; **3:**123, 202, 203, 204; **4:**159, 161, 188, 192; **5:**104

balm, Vietnamese, **5:**183, 185

Baltic Sea, **2:**30, 95, 96; **3:**86, 112, 114, 117; **4:**103, 123; **5:**29

Baluch, **1:**1; **4:**65

baluck plaid, **1:**42

balut, **4:**98

bambam, **1:**101

Bambara ground nut, **1:**180; **3:**128, 151; **4:**173

bamboo, **1:**154, 155, 197, 200, 203; **2:**172; **3:**29, 30, 36, 47, 79, 81, 84, 217; **4:**4, 20, 179; **5:**50, 77, 81, 88, 183

bamee goreng, **5:**73

bammies, **3:**24

bobolo, **1:**25
bocaditos, **2:**16
bodi, **5:**94
Boer, **4:**200, 201, 203
boerewors, **4:**201
bogobe, **1:**129
Bogotá, **1:**211, 212, 215
bograch, **4:**189
bois bande, **2:**147
bok choy, **1:**117, 198, 202
bokoboko, **1:**152; **5:**67
boletus mushrooms, **5:**33
bolos de bacalau, **4:**108
bombas, **5:**161
bombilla, **4:**89
bonelos aga, **4:**60
bonelos dago, **4:**60
bonelos, **4:**60
bones, **1:**63, 82, 88, 122, 133; **2:**14, 23, 41, 52, 117, 130, 133, 187, 213; **3:**2, 76, 184, 200, 209, 220; **4:**19, 40, 48, 52, 54, 82, 112, 126, 178; **5:**9, 12, 52, 54, 59, 60, 67, 68, 87, 112, 122, 127, 168
bonito, **1:**86; **2:**89; **3:**30; **4:**70, 91, 151, 169, 205; **5:**1, 45
boortsog, **3:**201
boothee, **3:**218
bor-bo, **1:**155
borek, **5:**105
boron, **2:**73
borscht, **1:**90; **3:**198; **4:**104, 124; **5:**131, 132
borsoutou, **3:**193
boshbaz, **1:**61
Boston, **2:**108
botifarra, **1:**18
boughasha, **2:**57
bouiller, **1:**177
bouillon, **1:**8, 28, 45, 50, 92, 106, 109, 161, 173, 184, 218; **2:**9, 33, 113, 117, 118, 119, 120, 124, 133, 144, 181, 213; **3:**76, 77, 119, 128, 152, 153, 169, 199; **4:**11, 40, 47, 51, 126, 173, 186, 210, 212; **5:**18, 86, 87, 192, 198, 199, 204
bourbon, **1:**66
bouyé, **4:**151, 157
bouza, **5:**99
boza, **1:**125; **4:**160; **5:**105
braç de gitano, **1:**19
Brahma, **2:**191
Brahmin, **2:**190, 191

brains, **1:**61, 140; **2:**102; **5:**98
braise, **1:**2, 86, 125, 173, 196, 203; **2:**7, 20, 129, 141; **3:**173, 174; **4:**113, 137, 201; **5:**33, 54, 115, 116, 180, 183
brandy, **1:**6, 19, 42, 43, 125; **2:**101, 103, 122, 150; **3:**188; **4:**119, 160, 183; **5:**181
brass, **2:**192; **3:**42, 154; **4:**166; **5:**195
bratwurst, **2:**130
brazier, **2:**74; **5:**53
Brazzaville, **1:**221
breadbasket, **2:**55
breadcrumbs, **2:**107; **4:**193; **5:**141
breaded, **1:**212; **2:**15, 129; **3:**116
breadfruit, **1:**67, 82, 225, 228; **2:**40, 89, 90, 147, 148, 200; **3:**23, 24, 56, 57, 164, 165, 166, 183, 184; **4:**16, 17, 18, 19, 21, 55, 58, 59, 61, 64, 80, 84, 133, 135, 166; **5:**6, 44, 46, 89, 91, 94, 172, 173, 174, 201
bream, **1:**85; **2:**56, 102; **3:**44; **4:**70
brède mafana, **3:**129
bredie, **4:**201
brem, **2:**201
Breton, **2:**110
Breughel, **4:**11
brewing, **1:**36, 155, 197; **2:**41, 55, 64, 74, 152, 153, 166, 175; **3:**24, 28, 37, 80, 179; **4:**36, 76, 98, 119; **5:**1, 11, 51, 72, 78, 85, 90, 120, 143, 154, 197
brik dough, **3:**105; **5:**99
brine, **2:**21, 173; **3:**33, 107, 112, 165, 185; **4:**105, 186
brinza, **3:**124, 187, 203; **4:**186; **5:**167
brioche, **1:**61, 62; **2:**104
brisket, **3:**7, 45
British-style, **1:**81, 111
Brittany, **2:**101, 103, 110; **4:**192
broccoli, **1:**197, 208; **3:**138; **4:**7, 8, 176; **5:**50, 142, 143, 153, 156
brossat, **1:**19
broth, **1:**31, 41, 45, 62, 68, 102, 122, 133, 151, 152, 193, 213; **2:**3, 41, 56, 57, 60, 147, 154, 155, 201; **3:**8, 41, 42, 45, 71, 76, 107, 111, 188, 201; **4:**7, 8, 31, 32, 39, 67, 73, 77, 89, 100, 109, 142, 143, 146, 173, 174, 178, 190, 211; **5:**12, 13, 40, 52, 53, 54, 78, 128, 148, 163, 179, 203, 204. *See also* bouillon
brownies, **5:**159
brunch, **1:**68, 111; **2:**148
Brussels, **1:**98; **4:**10, 11; **5:**153
bryndzove, **4:**182
buang, **5:**72
bubur, **2:**201

buckwheat, **1:**90, 91, 114, 115, 117; **2:**110; **3:**59, 120; **4:**4, 5, 104, 123, 124, 125, 128, 188, 189, 191, 192; **5:**77, 115, 132
Buddhism, **1:**114, 196, 202; **2:**190, 191; **3:**32, 79, 138, 197; **4:**4, 5; **5:**71, 77, 80, 156
budinca, **4:**119
buffalo, **1:**1, 135; **2:**56, 191; **3:**17, 79, 80; **4:**4, 5, 102; **5:**2, 4, 5
buffet, **1:**2, 170; **2:**31; **4:**99; **5:**28, 145
Buganda, **5:**118, 124
buhobe, **5:**196
bukayo, **4:**60
bulghur, **1:**41, 42, 44, 60, 152; **2:**56, 57; **3:**65, 66, 67, 68, 91, 93; **4:**41, 144, 148; **5:**38, 39, 67, 105, 106, 107, 137
bun, **1:**50, 110, 141, 204; **3:**111; **5:**28, 105, 183
bundia, **1:**77
bundt pan, **5:**158
Bunyoro, **5:**118
burani, **1:**2
burciak, **4:**183
burek, **1:**124, 125; **3:**124; **4:**160
burger, **1:**72, 82; **2:**195; **3:**27, 135, 165, 174, 184, 189; **5:**39, 119, 138
Burmans, **3:**219
burping, **3:**75
burrito, **1:**25, 219; **3:**179
bustard, **4:**144
bustrengo, **4:**137
butcher, **3:**32
butterfat, **3:**148
buttermilk, **1:**41, 54, 64, 187, 189; **2:**30, 45, 72, 96, 128, 191, 192, 193; **3:**89, 105, 112, 113, 116; **4:**5, 31, 50, 51, 114, 115, 153, 200, 201; **5:**77, 132, 138, 155
butternut squash. *See* squash, butternut
buuz, **3:**198
buw. See betel nut
Byzantine, **1:**6; **3:**16

cachaça, **1:**132
cachapa, **1:**171, 174, 175; **5:**178, 179
cactus, **1:**154, 211; **3:**178, 179
café, **1:**36, 125
caffeine, **1:**120, 132; **2:**74; **4:**88
cah-weh, **2:**201
caimite, **5:**94
Cajun, **5:**156
calabash, **1:**150; **4:**165
calalloo (also *calalu*), **1:**105, 106; **2:**40, 147, 148, 168; **3:**23; **5:**17, 94
calamansi, **4:**97, 98, 99
calamari, **4:**188

2:32, 41, 44, 63, 96, 123, 124, 128,
148, 152, 153, 174, 181, 182, 192,
201; **3:**17, 24, 45, 47, 64, 65, 66,
75, 77, 111, 113, 115, 118, 121,
156, 158, 179, 193, 198, 200, 202;
4:4, 7, 30, 32, 33, 35, 36, 45, 48,
71, 76, 86, 87, 98, 103, 104, 182,
183, 186; **5:**7, 8, 17, 23, 50, 51, 58,
60, 78, 80, 94, 95, 104, 110, 115,
116, 126, 127, 128, 131, 135, 167
dunes, **1:**71
durian, **1:**135, 154; **2:**200; **5:**1, 71,
183
durum wheat, **1:**11; **3:**17
duvec, **4:**160
dwaeji, **3:**61
dye, **2:**174; **3:**57, 144; **5:**75
dyed, **2:**210; **3:**57

earth oven, **1:**229; **3:**56, 57; **4:**17, 20,
23, 24, 53, 54, 55, 56, 57, 58, 81,
133, 134; **5:**44, 45, 89, 175
earthenware, **2:**8; **4:**105
ecology, **1:**54; **3:**112, 128; **4:**207;
5:154
economy, **1:**87, 171; **2:**15; **5:**50
eddo (taro), **1:**30, 32; **5:**6, 95
eel, **1:**54, 76, 86, 96, 105, 191; **2:**30,
56, 103; **3:**56, 183; **4:**9, 59, 103,
104, 188
eggfruit, **4:**92
eggroll, **4:**98
eggs benedict, **4:**202
egushi/egusi, **1:**178, 218
Eid-al-Fitr, **2:**36; **4:**144
elderberry, **5:**33, 143
elderflower, **1:**125; **3:**188; **5:**143
elephantipes, **2:**63
elk, **1:**165; **4:**44, 47
elotes, **4:**59
emasi, **5:**22
embotits, **1:**19
embutido, **4:**98
Emmenthal, **2:**110
empanada, **1:**35, 36, 119, 212; **2:**2,
47, 52, 64; **4:**76, 209; **5:**178
encebollado, **2:**63
enchiladas, **2:**2
encurtido, **1:**212; **2:**174
endive, **1:**95; **3:**118; **5:**17
enguitado, **4:**108
entrails, **4:**207; **5:**50. *See also* innards
entrecosto, **4:**109
enyucados, **4:**78
epazote, **1:**102; **3:**180, 184
erkesous, **2:**57
escabeche, **1:**96, 101; **4:**97; **5:**164
escalivada, **1:**19; **4:**208, 212
escudela, **1:**18; **4:**208

Eskimo. *See* Inuit
espresso, **3:**18
estocaficada, **3:**192
estofado, **4:**97
ethnic groups, **1:**1, 22, 30, 54, 60, 90,
101, 105, 124, 131, 144, 145, 154,
160, 196, 211, 216, 221; **2:**6, 36,
68, 83, 112, 116, 135, 156, 160,
165, 200; **3:**1, 11, 29, 44, 51, 79,
134, 138, 151, 197, 217; **4:**1, 4, 35,
38, 65, 80, 91, 97, 118, 130,
151, 159, 182, 201; **5:**10, 11, 17,
18, 33, 38, 50, 57, 71, 77, 84,
118, 119, 131, 141, 172, 183,
196, 207
ethnicity, **1:**47; **5:**208
etiquette, **2:**123; **3:**45; **5:**59
Eton, **5:**152
Etruscans, **3:**16
Euphrates, **3:**1
evaporated milk, **1:**168; **2:**42, 49, 92,
163, 169, 171, 1733; **3:**56; **4:**54, 95
ewe's milk, **1:**6, 41; **2:**39, 141; **3:**189,
205; **4:**35, 44, 70, 114, 186
expatriate, **4:**108, 184

fabada asturiana, **4:**208
fabada, **4:**208
fafa, **3:**183; **5:**44
fafaru, **3:**80; **5:**44
fagioli, **3:**17
faiai, **4:**133
fakhdet kharouf bel furun, **4:**70
fakoye, **3:**151
falafel, **1:**72; **2:**141; **3:**10, 92; **4:**70,
71; **5:**16, 39, 40, 137, 191
famine, **1:**116, 196; **3:**6, 56
Fang, **2:**68, 112
Fante, **2:**137
farata, **3:**177, 178
farik, **2:**56
farina, **4:**53; **5:**198
farka, **5:**99
Faroe isles, **2:**30
farofa, **1:**23, 131; **5:**85
fast food, **1:**68, 72, 91, 102, 192;
2:193; **3:**60, 124, 135, 165, 169,
184, 188; **4:**60, 75, 98, 146, 148;
5:18, 29, 51, 90, 95, 106, 119, 138,
154, 173, 183; Lebanese, **4:**152
fasuliya, **5:** 39, 190
fat, **1:**14, 16, 32, 38, 56, 60, 63, 64,
90, 92, 93, 142, 145, 166, 174,
189; **2:**49, 95, 101, 110, 124, 131,
179, 182, 183, 187; **3:**2, 7, 16, 46,
48, 49, 71, 76, 77, 119, 121, 148,
166, 189, 199, 200, 201; **4:**13, 47,
48, 51, 93, 123, 126, 180, 186,
195, 201; **5:**36, 52, 59, 93, 110,

116, 127, 132, 141, 142, 147, 151,
159, 166, 167, 169, 171, 187
fatayer, **4:**152
fatta, **4:**50; **5:**191
fat-tailed sheep, **3:**75, 76; **5:**166
fava, **2:**58; **3:**40; **5:**41
fechouada, **5:**84
feijoada, **1:**131, 134
fellaheen, **2:**55
fenkata, **3:**159, 160
fennel, **1:**54, 60, 62, 135; **2:**126, 127;
3:45, 50, 145, 148, 187, 192;
4:149; **5:**137, 138
fenugreek, **1:**42, 76; **2:**39, 55, 56, 57,
75, 84, 85, 89, 127; **3:**108; **4:**6,
115; **5:**17, 57, 65, 145, 190, 193
ferakh bel burgul, **2:**57
fermentation, **1:**18, 24, 25, 26, 64,
95, 120, 148, 154, 177, 192, 197,
198, 202, 225, 226; **2:**36, 57, 73,
83, 116, 117, 135, 136, 185, 201,
205; **3:**30, 31, 44, 45, 56, 57, 80,
81, 138, 152, 164, 165, 197, 198;
4:4, 45, 55, 58, 59, 60, 76, 103,
105, 151, 176; **5:**11, 15, 23, 28, 44,
48, 50, 51, 64, 74, 85, 109, 119,
120, 126, 132, 143, 166, 183, 208
fern, **1:**114, 135, 165; **3:**29, 63, 135;
4:80, 81; **5:**77
fessikh, **2:**56
festival, **1:**44, 192, 210, 226; **2:**20,
36, 56, 72, 80, 141, 206; **3:**11, 25,
27, 35, 57, 64, 102, 171, 198, 199;
4:23, 24, 30, 53, 64, 103, 144, 156,
183, 189, 198; **5:**57, 120, 129, 139
feta (cheese), **1:**7, 9, 204, 216; **2:**21,
56, 57, 141, 182, 214; **3:**65, 93,
123, 124, 203; **4:**94, 160, 186;
5:10, 34, 39, 167
fettuccine, **3:**20
fiber, **1:**139; **2:**73; **4:**59; **5:**12
fichi, **5:**110
fig, **1:**6, 11, 30, 60; **2:**42, 52, 56, 141,
147, 152, 209; **3:**1, 17, 38, 56, 65,
109, 168, 169, 192, 207; **4:**70, 92,
107, 137, 139, 193; **5:**57, 59, 95,
126, 166, 167
figolla, **3:**163
fika, **5:**29
filé, **5:**156, 157
fillet, **1:**28, 73, 82, 98, 107, 111, 157,
164, 217, 228; **2:**31, 81, 91, 96, 97,
120, 163, 187, 188; **3:**8, 34, 82,
117, 119, 144, 160, 164; **4:**9, 10,
26, 46, 84, 124, 127, 142, 154,
166, 178, 179, 205, 210; **5:**66, 173,
199
filo dough, **2:**57; **3:**11, 66; **5:**42, 102
finadene, **4:**60, 64

Ilocano, **4:**97
imam, **5:**105
immigrants, **1:**165; **2:**129; **3:**10, 217;
  4:4, 24, 133, 165, 167, 200, 210;
  5:62, 153
impeke, **1:**149, 150
imqaret, **3:**160
Inca, **4:**92
incense, **5:**80
Indiana, **5:**93
Indian-influenced, **2:**41, 196; **3:**129,
  217; **4:**4; **5:**1, 77, 201, 202, 204
Indo-Aryan, **3:**65
Indochina, **1:**154; **2:**203
Indo-Fijian, **2:**93
Ingush, **4:**123
injera, **2:**72, 73, 74, 75, 76, 77, 83,
  84, 86; **4:**196; **5:**10, 11
innards, **1:**18, 60, 140, 186; **2:**122,
  206; **3:**12, 39; **4:**97, 118; **5:**78, 115,
  154. *See also* intestines
insect, **1:**130; **2:**68, 191; **3:**178; **5:**154
insima. See nsima
intestines, **3:**76
Inuit, **1:**165, 167; **2:**30, 185; **4:**123
involtini alla cacciatora, **1:**18
irimshik, **3:**50
irio, **3:**52, 53, 55
Irrawady, **3:**217
Islam, **1:**1, 6; **2:**191, 200; **3:**11, 138;
  5:62; Islamic, **2:**193, 211, 215;
  3:151
Issas, **2:**36
Istrian, **4:**188
ivory, **3:**30; **4:**50; **5:**201
izote, **2:**63

jackfruit, **1:**154, 159; **2:**192, 196,
  200; **3:**23; **4:**4, 97, 165; **5:**46, 71,
  183, 184, 201
jaggery, **3:**146, 221; **4:**57, 116; **5:**5
jagne, **3:**123
Jain, **2:**190, 191
jalapeño, **5:**181
jalebi, **1:**2, 77; **2:**192
jalfrezi, **1:**78
jam, **1:**19, 21, 31, 32, 35, 36, 39, 82,
  89, 94, 96, 111, 125, 141, 192,
  212; **2:**12, 21, 47, 52, 79, 81, 94,
  146, 184, 185, 186, 188; **3:**6, 50,
  56, 124, 129, 174, 177, 193, 201,
  202; **4:**5, 17, 48, 49, 54, 98, 124,
  160, 177, 183, 208; **5:**18, 23, 29,

34, 37, 45, 48, 104, 105, 108, 110,
  146, 155, 161, 162, 164, 165, 167,
  197
jasmine, **5:**75
Java, **2:**200, 207; Javanese, **2:**200,
  204; **5:**17
jelabi. *See jalebi*
jelly, **1:**61, 87, 203, 208; **2:**33, 173,
  184, 214; **3:**24, 36, 93, 188; **5:**23,
  50, 51, 95, 163
jellyfish, **1:**196; **3:**29
jerk seasoning, **2:**196; **3:**23, 25, 26,
  27
jerky, **1:**64, 119, 131; **3:**84, 131, 164,
  183; **4:**200
Jerusalem, **3:**12; **4:**73
Jerusalem artichoke, **2:**102; **3:**13
Jewish: community of Rome, **3:**18,
  19; delis, **2:**81; holidays, **3:**11;
  immigrants, **5:**62; influences,
  3:187; **4:**103; **5:**98; Jerusalem,
  2:12; law, **2:**189; **3:**11; people,
  3:10
jhelli, **3:**118
jhol, **1:**76, 77; **5:**95
jibneh, **2:**74; **3:**153; **5:**10
jicama, **1:**158; **3:**141, 178
Jollof, **2:**156, 158; **3:**100, 101, 102
Judaism, **2:**189
jorbilbil, **5:**39
jujube, **3:**64, 78; **4:**151; **5:**170
jukjuk, **3:**165
juniper, **1:**97, 125; **2:**107, 129;
  4:183, 185; **5:**28, 115
jute, **5:**12. *See also molokhiya*

kabanos, **1:**125
kabubu, **3:**56
kacha, **4:**189
kachuri, **1:**77
kadaif, **1:**42; **3:**11; **4:**71, 73, 74
kaffir lime, **3:**82; **4:**178; **5:**75
kafta, **4:**114, 115
kaipen, **3:**79
kajmak, **3:**204; **4:**160. *See also kaymak*
kakadu plums, **1:**48
kalakukko, **2:**96
kalamai, **4:**60
kale, **1:**106, 131, 132, 134, 161, 174,
  219, 220, 222, 223; **2:**21, 30, 69,
  117, 137, 158, 159; **3:**8, 23, 53,
  102, 135, 205; **4:**40, 72, 109, 110,
  131, 143, 210; **5:**200, 209
Kalimantan, **1:**135; **2:**200
kangaroo, **1:**47; **4:**80
kanya, **4:**171
kaoliang. See sorghum
kapenta fish, **5:**199
kapunata, **3:**159

Karakorum, **4:**123
karaw, **4:**153, 156, 157
kare raisu, **3:**30
kare-kare, **3:**30, 155; **5:**11
karewe, **3:**57; **4:**59
kari, **4:**182; **5:**73
kariya, **3:**65
karkaday. *See* kare-kare
karkanji. *See* kare-kare
Karomojong, **3:**51
Karoo, **4:**200
kasha, **1:**91; **4:**124, 192
Kashmir, **2:**190, 191
kaskan, **3:**48
kaskaval, **2:**180
katsuobushi, **5:**1, 2
kava, **2:**90; **4:**59
kaymak, **1:**1; **4:**162; **5:**109, 166
kaysi, **3:**66
Kazakh, **1:**1; **3:**44, 46, 47, 48, 50,
  197; **5:**126, 127
kazmag, **1:**65
kazy, **3:**44
kchuch, **1:**42
kebab, **1:**2, 42, 63, 64, 72, 77, 124,
  145; **2:**129, 192, 194, 195; **3:**66,
  198, 208; **4:**50, 65, 66, 146, 159;
  5:39, 104, 127, 137, 138, 166, 169,
  170, 191
kecap, **2:**200, 203, 206
kedgeree, **1:**77; **4:**201
kedjenou, **3:**151
keema, **5:**204
kefir, **1:**187, 188
kefta, **4:**70
kelaguen, **4:**60, 63
kemiri. See candlenuts
keshkegh, **1:**41
ketchup, **1:**35, 37, 50, 111, 112, 192;
  2:51, 129, 139, 201; **3:**31, 32, 57;
  4:97, 152, 153, 168; **5:**153, 155,
  156. *See also* ketjap
ketiakh, **4:**152
ketjap, **5:**17
khaladnik, **1:**90
khmeli-suneli, **2:**126, 196
Khmer, **1:**154
Khoisans, **4:**200
kholtmash, **1:**189
kholva, **5:**167. *See also* halvah
khoorshoor, **3:**198
kibbutz, **3:**11
kid, **2:**141, 157; **4:**146
kidney, **1:**1, 83, 103, 132, 149, 150,
  163; **2:**15, 17, 123, 137, 177, 212;
  3:19, 24, 52, 65, 66; **4:**31, 92; **5:**24,
  26, 69, 86, 142, 154
kielbasa, **4:**185
Kiev, **5:**131

mantou, **2:**181; **3:**47; **5:**104. *See also manti, mantu, manty*

mantu, **5:**58, 60. *See also manti, mantou, manty*

manty, **3:**45, 75, 77; **5:**104, 126. *See also manti, mantou, mantu*

maple syrup, **1:**165, 167; **5:**94, 154, 155

margarine, **1:**89, 92, 166; **2:**44, 45, 134; **4:**79, 88, 136; **5:**9, 23

marinade, **1:**27, 28, 173, 174, 205, 206, 207, 218; **2:**3, 18, 65, 115; **3:**21, 34, 36, 55, 116, 171, 185, 215; **4:**33, 46, 60, 93, 101, 112, 126, 155, 204, 205; **5:**47, 48, 96, 145, 181, 187

marjoram, **1:**168; **2:**13, 79, 179, 182; **3:**159, 160, 161, 192; **4:**11, 27, 104, 183, 184, 188; **5:**8, 9, 38, 115, 164

marlin, **2:**1, 147; **3:**163

marmalade, **1:**195; **5:**142

marmelada, **2:**184; **4:**119

Marrakech, **3:**209

marrow, **2:**179; **3:**65

marshland, **2:**95

marzipan, **3:**81, 163, 211; **5:**28

mascarpone, **3:**17; **4:**8, 69

massalé, **4:**167, 168

maté, **1:**120; **4:**92

matoke, **5:**118, 119, 122, 124

matsoni, **1:**64, 65

matza, **3:**14

mawby, **1:**81; **2:**166; **5:**95

Maya, **1:**101, 102; **2:**152, 174; **3:**178, 182

mayonnaise, **1:**33, 35, 37, 51, 60, 61, 83, 91, 96, 97, 98, 99, 110, 192, 225; **2:**34, 50, 104, 129, 167; **3:**87, 165, 166, 185, 192, 198; **4:**10, 152, 182, 215; **5:**7, 112, 113, 146

mbika, **1:**218

mboum, **4:**152

mboung, **1:**25

mbudzi, **5:**207

mealie, **4:**200; **5:**196, 197

mechoui, **3:**169; **5:**99

meditative, **2:**213

medlar, **3:**159

Melanesia, **4:**55, 83

Melanesian, **2:**89, 92; **4:**16, 80; **5:**172

melon, **1:**1, 2, 41, 60, 76, 77, 120, 127, 197, 209; **2:**192, 209; **3:**1, 17,

30, 36, 65, 138, 178, 192, 195, 217; **4:**1, 35, 37, 56, 65, 91, 97, 114, 123, 137, 159, 165, 176, 201, 207; **5:**1, 38, 45, 50, 55, 58, 71, 98, 109, 137, 167, 177

merchants, **4:**165, 168

merguez, **4:**156, 157; **5:**98, 101

merienda, **3:**179; **4:**208, 216

meringue, **1:**48, 53, 68, 81; **5:**28, 152

mesob, **2:**36, 73, 74, 84

mesquite, **4:**33

mestizo, **1:**193; **3:**178

mezze, **1:**7, 72, 74; **2:**21, 142; **3:**68, 92, 93, 94; **4:**145; **5:**39, 105

mice, **1:**160; **5:**196

Micronesia, **3:**185; **4:**58, 59, 60, 61, 62

Micronesian, **4:**58, 60, 80

microwave, **1:**166, 188, 202; **2:**189; **3:**125; **4:**64, 90, 214; **5:**9, 56, 123, 136, 185

milkfish, **4:**97, 98, 99

milk-powder, **2:**194

milkshake, **1:**36, 155, 224; **2:**2, 16, 148; **4:**76; **5:**51, 178

millet, **1:**11, 24, 26, 126, 145, 149, 179, 183, 184, 185, 187, 198, 218, 223; **2:**55, 69, 70, 73, 83, 116, 117, 190; **3:**45, 50, 51, 52, 59, 60, 134, 151, 152, 154, 156, 157, 168, 213; **4:**1, 5, 35, 38, 41, 43, 130, 151, 152, 153, 154, 156, 157, 171, 188, 195, 196; **5:**10, 11, 51, 63, 77, 84, 85, 105, 109, 110, 118, 119, 120, 131, 166, 190, 196, 207, 208

Mineira style, **1:**131, 134

minorities, **1:**22, 30, 35, 41, 60, 81, 90, 131, 135, 140, 154, 165, 186, 191; **2:** 40, 55, 72, 78, 93, 95, 122, 128, 174, 209; **3:**10, 29, 44, 59, 112, 128, 134, 173, 187, 192, 197, 217; **4:**4, 9, 16, 30, 70, 75, 108, 159, 195, 200, 207; **5:**22, 28, 38, 44, 50, 57, 63, 71, 77, 104, 109, 115, 118, 131, 141, 153, 161, 166, 183, 190, 196, 207

mint, **1:**1, 3, 6, 7, 8, 9, 12, 13, 14, 23, 42, 60, 63, 88, 94, 122, 158; **2:**22, 57, 126, 127, 142, 153, 212, 213; **3:**2, 13, 14, 15, 65, 79, 80, 83, 84, 93, 94, 105, 106, 115, 123, 125, 155, 156, 154, 159, 160, 161, 168, 169, 207, 208, 212, 218; **4:**5, 6, 30, 36, 68, 188, 189, 198, 199; **5:**19, 38, 60, 61, 98, 99, 104, 105, 109, 112, 134, 138, 140, 152, 170, 180, 183, 184, 185

mirin, **3:**34, 35, 36; **5:**54

Miskito, **4:**30

miso, **1:**198, 201; **3:**30, 31, 32, 33, 35; **5:**53, 143

missionaries, **2:**93; **3:**56; **4:**55, 58, 136; **5:**93

mitsuba, **3:**30

moambé, **1:**222; **2:**114

mocha, **5:**190, 191, 195

mochi, **4:**64

Mogul (Mughal), **1:**76; **2:**192, 197

mojito, **2:**16

molasses, **1:**81, 171, 175; **2:**207; **3:**2, 103; **4:**13, 47, 50

mole poblano, **3:**182

molokhiya, **2:**56; **5:**13. *See also* flax

monasteries, **1:**202; **5:**77, 80

mongongo nut, **4:**1

monkey, **1:**162; **2:**111, 115; **4:**151

monks, **5:**83

Monrovia, **3:**102

monsoon, **4:**58

Montagnard, **5:**183

Montana, **2:**95

Monterey, **1:**168; **2:**110; **4:**88; **5:**162

moon, **4:**98, 144

Moorish influence, **1:**131, 132; **4:**109, 207; Moors, **2:**15; **3:**211; **4:**209

moose, **4:**44, 47

mopane tree, **1:**129

mopane worm, **1:**127, 128, 129

mora, **1:**212

morbi, **5:**95

morros y cristianos, **2:**15

mortadella cheese, **4:**138

mortar and pestle, **1:**25, 26, 79, 107, 117, 147, 150, 162, 171, 180, 222; **2:**114, 127, 194, 202; **3:**14, 42, 67, 83, 156; **4:**17, 42, 112, 170, 175; **5:**25, 72, 120, 193, 195

Moscow, **4:**123

Mossi, **1:**144, 145

moth, **1:**129

mountain ash, **5:**26. *See also* Szechuan pepper

mourn, **2:**138

mousaka, **1:**7, 42; **2:**20; **4:**118

mozzarella cheese, **3:**17

mpondu, **1:**222

muesli, **2:**31, 129; **3:**110; **5:**34, 116

muffin, **1:**49, 50, 68, 159, 166; **3:**8, 9; **4:**22; **5:**56, 154

Muhammad, **4:**144, 156

Muharram, **1:**71; **3:**70

mulberries, **1:**1, 6, 60, 61, 88; **5:**39

mulled, **2:**129; **4:**183

mullet, **2:**20, 56, 102; **3:**17, 91; **4:**38, 70, 108, 151, 152; **5:**98, 109

multicultural, **2:**89; **3:**173; **3:**60

multinational, **5:**154

pancake (*continued*)
2, 29, 64, 72, 116, 131, 132, 138, 154, 178, 185; pancake-shaped, **1:**6

panch foran, **1:**76

pancit, **4:**98

pandanus, **1:**135, 137; **3:**56, 144, 145, 148, 149, 164, 165; **4:**56, 59, 60, 80, 177, 178, 179, 180; **5:**1, 3, 4, 44, 72

paneer, **2:**193

panela, **1:**212

panfried, **5:**7

pangsit, **2:**201

papadam, **2:**196; **5:**2

papaya, **1:**30, 76, 81, 105, 110, 111, 113, 115, 135, 154, 171, 181, 185, 220, 225, 226, 227; **2:**2, 15, 17, 41, 46, 52, 94, 153, 165, 200; **3:**79, 81, 83, 84, 141, 145, 146, 151, 164, 183, 186, 213, 216, 217; **4:**4, 16, 17, 18, 19, 20, 41, 59, 60, 76, 80, 91, 97, 130, 140, 143, 151, 165, 199; **5:**1, 4, 10, 17, 44, 46, 50, 51, 63, 64, 71, 72, 89, 91, 92, 93, 118, 172, 173, 175, 177, 178, 183, 184, 190, 191, 201, 207, 211

paprika, **1:**12, 13, 16, 54, 56, 67, 69, 73, 74, 75, 101, 102, 120, 121, 124, 141, 142, 156, 172, 173, 174, 175, 193, 194, 223; **2:**1, 2, 3, 7, 8, 13, 27, 28, 33, 65, 74, 79, 95, 137, 138, 176, 179, 183, 194, 195; **3:**92, 108, 123, 169, 203, 209; **4:**12, 42, 77, 89, 93, 160, 161, 162, 163, 182, 183, 185, 186, 208, 210, 212; **5:**4, 38, 41, 73, 79, 80, 82, 100, 107, 112, 145, 157, 192, 204

paradise, **4:**176; **5:**98

paratha, **1:**77, 115; **2:**193; **4:**65

parfait, **5:**159, 188

parmesan, **2:**66, 106; **3:**17, 50; **4:**106; **5:**79, 82

parrillada, **2:**47; **5:**161

parrot, **4:**133, 165

parrotfish, **2:**89; **4:**38, 167, 168

parsnip, **1:**49, 50; **2:**179; **3:**116, 168; **4:**126; **5:**142, 147, 148

partridge, **1:**18

Pashtun, **1:**1; **4:**65

Passover, **3:**14

pasticho, **5:**177

pastrama, **3:**187; **4:**118

patacones, **2:**52; **4:**76

Patagonia, **1:**36

pâté, **3:**81; **5:**184

patis, **3:**80, 82, 83, 84, 219; **4:**97, 99

patisserie, **2:**103; **4:**189

patlijan, **1:**42

patois, **2:**147

pawpaw, **1:**81, 113; **4:**59; **5:**93

peach, **1:**2, 21, 35, 41, 48, 120, 140, 165, 191, 192, 209; **2:**56, 103, 122, 141; **3:**15, 17, 30, 44, 59, 118, 128, 141, 159, 164, 183, 198; **4:**65, 76, 95, 137, 182, 201, 207; **5:**33, 34, 35, 50, 153, 161, 164

pear, **1:**15, 54, 85, 86, 89, 95, 114, 119, 123, 124, 165, 191, 197, 209; **2:**25, 44, 56, 103, 129, 179, 192; **3:**17, 30, 59, 91, 118, 141, 192; **4:**97, 107, 108, 118, 123, 137, 182, 188, 193, 201, 207; **5:**29, 33, 50, 77, 101, 115, 132, 142, 153

peasant, **1:**55; **2:**55; **3:**88, 203; **4:**11, 123, 190, 192

pecan, **2:**177; **3:**14, 182; **4:**92; **5:**97, 153, 158, 159, 160

pecorino, **3:**17

Penang, **3:**139

penne, **3:**17, 19

pepitas, **1:**178, 218

pepperberry, **1:**48

pepperoni, **4:**163

perch, **1:**54, 216, 217, 223; **2:**96, 179; **3:**151; **4:**80, 103

perilla, **5:**183

periwinkles, **4:**40

Persian, **1:**41, 45, 60, 61, 71, 76; **2:**190, 193, 196, 198, 209, 210; **3:**1, 48, 49, 65, 70; **4:**114; **5:**38, 57, 101, 104, 126, 201, 203

persimmon, **3:**10, 59, 60

petai, **1:**135

petal, **1:**66, 125, 141; **2:**127; **4:**119; **5:**98, 101, 104, 108, 167

phak kaat dong, **5:**73

pheasant, **1:**95; **3:**44; **5:**115

Phoenician, **3:**160; **4:**207; **5:**98, 148

phoenix, **1:**209

phosphorus, **2:**73

pickle, **1:**50, 56, 57, 60, 81, 82, 83, 111, 125, 141, 155, 187, 198; **2:**63, 65, 81, 103, 128, 129, 130, 132, 160, 174, 185, 186, 196; **3:**12, 17, 23, 32, 33, 44, 59, 60, 61, 66, 87, 107, 111, 112, 117, 173, 189, 194, 198, 209, 218, 219; **4:**4, 5, 31, 44, 45, 70, 103, 105, 119, 123, 124, 126, 134, 145, 159, 183, 189, 191, 201, 207; **5:**28, 50, 51, 52,

53, 73, 93, 95, 104, 105, 113, 115, 131, 132, 135, 143, 162, 166, 190

pickles, **1:**2, 3, 42, 55, 77, 78, 197; **2:**11, 21, 39, 58, 99, 122, 128, 129, 193; **3:**11, 12, 31, 33, 34, 57, 60, 61, 62, 87, 91, 123, 187, 195, 202; **4:**105, 145, 162, 168, 191, 201; **5:**39, 40, 116, 162, 204

pideh, **1:**41. *See also* pita

pie, **1:**38, 55, 81, 82, 102, 110, 125, 166, 169, 195; **2:**96, 109, 142, 170, 188; **3:**17, 33, 100, 122, 159, 165, 166, 195, 196, 207; **4:**104, 189, 201; **5:**17, 95, 111, 143, 149, 161, 163, 198, 207, 211

pig, **1:**32, 54, 61, 67, 101, 120, 132, 141, 186, 204, 212; **2:**40, 52, 89, 102, 122, 147, 165, 191, 206; **3:**18, 23, 139, 178; **4:**55, 58, 60, 75, 80, 91, 92, 97, 109, 118, 133, 208; **5:**6, 89, 153, 172

pigeon, **1:**41, 67, 69, 85; **2:**46, 56, 60, 147, 161; **3:**53, 54, 134, 207; **4:**75, 133; **5:**6, 7, 8, 65, 94

pike, **2:**96, 179; **4:**103, 118; **5:**131

pike-perch, **3:**44

pilaf (also *pulao, polo, pirão*), **1:**7, 28, 41, 42, 60, 61; **2:**194, 196; **3:**45, 48, 49; **4:**50, 165, 168, 202; **5:**57, 59, 104, 105, 106, 109, 110, 127, 168

pimentos, **2:**34

pine nut, **1:**1, 6, 7, 18, 41, 45, 138; **2:**46, 56, 61, 142; **3:**13, 40, 41, 65, 68; **4:**70, 146, 207, 208; **5:**99, 107, 137, 139

pineapple, **1:**30, 31, 33, 50, 52, 84, 105, 135, 154, 177, 181, 185, 212; **2:**1, 2, 6, 34, 46, 47, 52, 63, 89, 92, 112, 152, 153, 156, 174, 175; **3:**23, 25, 51, 128, 133, 146, 164, 173, 181, 187; **4:**16, 18, 30, 33, 34, 37, 41, 75, 76, 91, 97, 151, 165, 171, 177; **5:**1, 10, 17, 22, 44, 45, 48, 55, 56, 89, 93, 94, 96, 108, 118, 120, 121, 153, 157, 172, 175, 177, 201, 202, 205

pinga, **1:**132

piranha, **1:**132

piri-piri, **1:**22, 147; **2:**71; **3:**215; **4:**109, 200, 201

pirogi, **4:**124

pisang goreng, **2:**201

pistachio, **1:**1, 5, 41, 80; **2:**56, 61, 192, 194, 197, 198, 209, 213; **3:**5; **4:**8, 69, 71, 146; **5:**38, 43, 61, 62, 99, 107, 109

About the Authors

JEANNE JACOB has written on Japanese food with her husband, Michael Ashkenazi.

MICHAEL ASHKENAZI is a food scholar specializing in Japanese cuisine. He is the author, along with his wife, Jeanne Jacob, of *Food Culture in Japan* (Greenwood, 2003).